eden

eden

TIM SMIT

BANTAM
PRESS

For my great-aunt Cecily
1 October 1906 - 20 September 2001

who would have loved
seeing so many square pegs
find themselves a round
hole big enough

In Memoriam

Bill Rickatson, Sir Ralph Riley
and James Wilson

contents

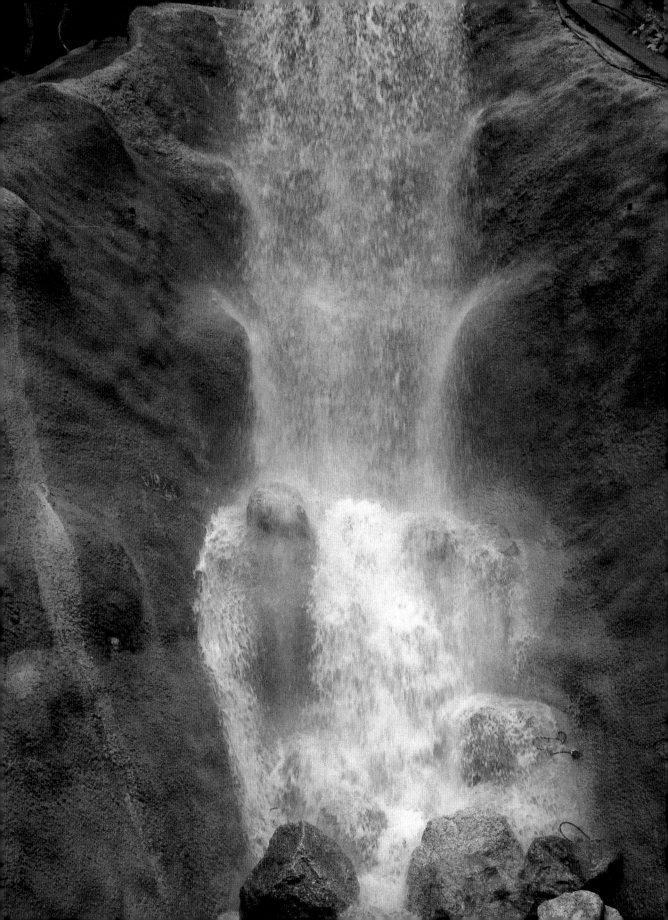

...and the sky monkeys came down from heaven

The mists hung heavy, rising as if from the moist dark earth itself, enveloping the lush tropical vegetation in a ghostly embrace. The rumour of a breeze whispered through the treetops, stirring pulpy leaves and feathery fronds into a languid Mexican wave that rippled gently down into the valley below. The air was thick with the rich perfume that islands make when approached from the sea, bearing the promise of leisured plenty. From the cliff above me a wall of water sheeted down, broke into a thousand spitting eddies on the granite boulders that blocked its path down the hillside, finally easing into a luxuriant palm-fringed pool rimmed by a beach of the purest white sand.

Far below, in another country, a forest clearing revealed gardens of abundance and a glimpse of the rusting corrugated-iron roof of a bamboo house. The shirt stuck to my back and the sweat dripped from my chin. As if by magic a melancholy lament floated down from above, its plangent notes weaving a spell which filled this gigantic space with emotion. High, high above, no larger than an ant, a kilted giant played the Cornish pipes from a basket of steel, reached by the flimsiest of filigree steps strung from the roof. His every breath became a rising celebration of the passion of life. Down below a stillness settled on the throng drawn to this special place. Our numbers grew soundlessly. No cynics here; all doubts put aside, we felt humbled, small, human and fragile in the face of a moment we will remember for ever.

None of the Great and Good, no fancy Dans, no civic dignitaries, no pop-star endorsements, no fireworks, feasts or binges. We had promised ourselves this, a pause for reflection, without performance. A reel of intricate intensity from the piper drew our attention upwards once more. And then we saw them. The sky monkeys.

On ropes they hung, two of them, swaying in the translucent eaves. Behind them, in the early morning sunlight, a kaleidoscopic shadowplay, a stained-glass window of hexagons, the open roof vents like the flower petals of lilies reflected on to cliff walls the colour of gunmetal. Slowly, as the pipes soared, they descended, inch by inch, for what seemed like an eternity. We craned our necks and whispered to each other in excited anticipation. Even the construction crew, who thought they'd seen everything, gave up all pretence of professional detachment. We were one family waiting...for what? Men bearing gifts?

And then they were among us and the tension broke and we roared and we clapped and we dug one another in the ribs. The gift the sky monkeys had brought was a certificate saying that the job was done, and the project manager, his face alive with emotion, solemnly took it and on behalf of the builders said a few words about what it meant to him and his team, and we cheered to the rafters once more. Then he handed the gift to the leader of our team. No one had done more than her to bring about this special moment. Those endless hours, days, weeks, months and years of meetings that lasted long into the night, persuading the boys in suits to take courage in the face of doubt, now seemed to melt away. She spoke for all of us in saying that this wasn't an ending but a new beginning, and that this place was for everyone and that we were all one team, which was why we had succeeded. The tears welled in the project manager's eyes and we whooped once more.

Then from out of the crowd stepped the bishop. We had asked him to say a few words of blessing. He understood instinctively that his particular religion was not the point. He made a joke about his amazement at being the only member of 'the

Chain Gang' present, and said that this was the first time in his life that he'd been the best-dressed person in a crowd. Then the tone changed, everyone fell silent, and there was a great sense of stillness: 'As we stand in this new Eden, made like the first out of chaos, we give thanks for the vision, energy and enthusiasm which have made it one of the wonders of the world. We give you thanks for all those who have contributed to it in any way and we pray that it may be a place of enjoyment and a place of education; a place where we recall our responsibility, the power we have to destroy as well as create and in which we remember our own creatureliness. So as we stand in Eden, a symbol of hope and new possibilities, in the name of God we bless this place and all that's in it and ask that it may be a blessing and a joy to all those who come here. We ask this in the name of Jesus Christ Our Lord.'

I haven't the comfort of being religious, but of one thing I am sure. No one was untouched by that moment. As I looked around our fabulous team I noticed the horticultural crew in a group together – for day after scorching day, night after endless night, they'd been out here in the heat, stretching every sinew to prepare for this moment. They had done what everyone had said was impossible, they had created earth, they had propagated and planted countless thousands of living things. Now they were so tired they were running on empty. And then there was the building crew, who had fought against everything nature could throw at them to move millions of tons of muck, to lay miles of foundations, to forge structures

on an unprecedented scale, pioneering with the delicacy of jewellers the use of materials never before employed in this manner. All of us, in our own way, had turned our Eden into a collective act of redemption. We really had done the best we could; for the moment, we had nothing left to give. There were tears and hugs as we broke into smaller groups to take one final look at our kingdom.

We had built the largest conservatories the world had ever seen. The greatest challenge now was to prove that it was all worthwhile. As I watched the first visitor walk open-mouthed into our great green cathedral, and as small groups became hundreds and then thousands followed on behind, I thought to myself, the truly special thing about Eden is not what you see, although that is awesome enough; it is the spirit that brought so many 'ordinary' people together, to add up to so much more than the sum of their parts. That was the real reason for hope. If we could do this, what could happen if even more were harnessed together? We'd built a magnificent Living Theatre, but the world is really the stage.

The story I'm going to tell is of both a mission and an adventure. It is a personal view of events, and of people I feel intensely proud to have been able to call colleagues and friends. I make no apology for some of the boring bits about how we got from A to B. Only by understanding crushing boredom can one delight in the relief from it! Neither do I make any apology for being optimistic about the future.

I am.

chapter 1

the whole opera

Have you ever stood in a bar like I have and heard yourself holding forth yet again about what you'd really like to do with your life? The pipe dream comes alive for a happy hour or two, but does it fade by morning, leaving that growing sense of self-hatred as you realize you haven't got what it takes to do the interesting or brave thing? If you're a successful barrister, or financier, or teacher, and that's what you always wanted to do, fine, be happy. But suppose what you really wanted was to be a boat-builder or an explorer or a bug collector instead? How many times have you heard friends, even very 'successful' friends, in despair at what they've made of their lives? As my grandmother used to say, 'When you're on your deathbed make sure you can say I'm glad I did, rather than I wish I had.'

Early on in my life I realized that I was fundamentally lazy, and if I was to achieve anything I would have to develop tactics to trick myself into action. The tactic I came up with was lying. I lied all the time. Not in a fantastical way; I didn't claim to be the heir to the Ford fortune or the hundred-metre champion. But anything I really wished had happened, I would pretend it had in order to make it so. For example, when I was eighteen I was much taken with a girl and wanted to impress her. I found myself telling her I was a diver. From the moment the words were out, I had to become one. I immediately booked a two-week course in Plymouth in midwinter and the wish became a reality. It's a great, if stressful, technique, of questionable morality; I like to think of it not as lying but as telling future truths.

John Nelson

I don't know if I am typical, but I have always busked my way through life in this manner. You can get quite a long way on quick wits and taking pleasure in good company. If you're honest with yourself, however, you know that an easy facility with words and a gift for argument are no substitute for real thought and feelings. There comes a quiet moment when you have no audience except the harshest critic of them all: yourself.

Heligan changed me. In restoring the Lost Gardens I learned the meaning of work. I began to understand the processes by which ideas are turned into action. No one has a monopoly on dreams, but only a rare few discover the alchemist's art of making them real. Making things real demands a commitment that goes way beyond what a busker can give; it requires a single-mindedness and determination to succeed that persuade others as much by the force of your conviction as by the idea itself. Bankers and investors always talk from the outset of the need to establish an exit strategy, a way out when things go wrong. This may be why Britain is not the easiest country in the world in which to turn dreams into reality. In my view, if you really believe in something you should allow yourself only one exit strategy – death. It concentrates the mind most wonderfully. If those around you trust you, they will draw comfort from your conviction. If they don't, you deserve to fail.

Two ideas are central to this philosophy: Tinkerbell Theory and Last Man Standing. In *Peter Pan*, Tinkerbell is a fairy who exists only if people believe in her. I know that if enough people can be made to believe in something it will happen. Last Man Standing, on the other hand, is a polite way of saying that you intend to turn being an awkward bugger into an art form. In other words, you won't take no for an answer. The footnote to this is that bankers, lawyers, civil servants, investors or volunteers will have mastered the art of saying 'no' in many different ways long before you have even begun to make your pitch. Assuming that they are professionally competent, what makes people say yes when it's easier to say no is often the difference between an ordinary day at the office and a life-affirming experience that inspires the imagination. We are all human.

In 1987 I decided to change the course of my life. I moved to Cornwall with my wife and young family to get away from London and a profession, the music business, which demanded that I regularly got into aeroplanes – something which I was increasingly finding myself unable to do unless under the influence of alcohol. The intention was to build a recording studio at the farmhouse we had bought where I would compose film and television music, making it unnecessary to go on the road accompanying artists. John Nelson, a local builder, came to renovate our house and we became friends. When I was invited to explore an old estate in the company of its new owner I jumped at the opportunity. This was partly because at the time I was interested in setting up a rare breeds farm and this sounded like the ideal location, and partly out of romantic curiosity.

On 16 February 1990, within minutes of cutting my way into what was later to become known as the Lost Gardens of Heligan, my life changed for ever. My epiphany came on breaking into the largest of the walled gardens, where we discovered a range of vineries. There, under a shroud of bramble, survived a solitary old vine, snaking in and out of the broken panes of glass the length of the

'...this was what I had been waiting for'

house, defiant against the onslaught of decay. Hanging on a nail in the wall were the vine scissors. Further explorations revealed more walled gardens, a vegetable garden, pleasure grounds; eventually, in the valley below the Big House, we were to find the remains of a sub-tropical garden, choked to dank submission by self-seeded ash, sycamore and willow. Something inside me told me that this was what I had been waiting for.

Over the next six years John Nelson and I, along with a team of volunteers who would eventually form the backbone of the Heligan staff, restored the gardens to their original condition. Inspired by finding the names of the garden staff scratched in the lime-plaster walls of the Thunderbox Room (the garden toilet), we decided to tell the story of the ordinary men and women who had worked here, rather than simply the usual tale of lords and ladies. One thing led to another. The writing on the wall was dated August 1914, just before the outbreak of the First World War. When we discovered Heligan's workbooks in the Record Office in Barnstaple I pieced together their working practices and read that dread word: 'enlisted'. The next time I came across the majority of these names was on the war memorials at St Ewe, Gorran and Mevagissey. Later still we traced the surviving

members of those families and were amazed and moved to find that almost all the names on the wall were still represented in the area. This shaped our response to Heligan considerably. It robbed us of the arrogance of a sense of ownership and replaced it with one of stewardship; this was a stage on which communities had played out their lives for generations until the war altered things for ever. Indeed, one of the most remarkable things that happened at Heligan was that once the restoration was all but complete, and planned husbandry rather than crisis management took over, we found that the staff had slotted into exactly the same roles as they would have done under a Victorian model before the Great War; we even employed exactly the same number of gardeners, twenty-two.

There were two powerful influences on what we achieved at Heligan: Peter Thoday and Philip McMillan Browse. Peter was heavily involved in the popular television series *The Victorian Kitchen Garden*, which had turned him into everybody's favourite Victorian garden expert. I had invited him to Heligan shortly after finding the gardens, but he thought I was a crank and wouldn't take me seriously. A year later he finally succumbed, and became hugely excited. The reason for his enthusiasm was that although its productive gardens were completely overgrown

The Jungle at Heligan

and the structures had mostly collapsed under the weight of dozens of encroaching mature trees, Heligan hadn't been knocked about, converted or modernized in any way, rendering it capable of complete restoration without compromise. This would make our wonderful place unique in Britain, where productive gardens, deemed to be of no interest to the largely middle-class garden visitor, had generally been neglected. The finest, at Chatsworth and Tatton Park, had been bulldozed to make way for other commercial activities as recently as the early 1980s.

It was Peter who turned to me at the end of his visit and threw down the gauntlet: did we want to create a greatest hits record, or were we brave enough to perform the whole opera? Were we prepared to restore everything to full function and run it exactly as it would have been in the middle of the nineteenth century?

Philip McMillan Browse had been the director of RHS Wisley and before that of the Saratoga Institute in California. A Scillonian by upbringing, he had recently moved to Cornwall to get back to his roots. He had taken up a part-time job as county horticultural adviser and it was in this context that we first met. I asked him for advice. He came, gave some advice, became hooked by the project and got his hands dirty. We then made an honest man of him by inviting him to become our horticultural director. Philip would undertake the research into old varieties of fruit, vegetables and cut flowers that would have been grown in the productive gardens. In Philip, Peter had a ready ally for performing opera.

One of the first issues we had to deal with was a philosophical one. In 1992 I was invited to a conference hosted by the Historic Houses Association in London. I said

John Nelson, TS and Peter Thoday ponder the restoration of Heligan's pineapple pit

to the audience that if you couldn't get drunk, dream or make love in your garden, you might as well tarmac it. What I meant by this rather in-your-face assertion was that Britain had become fixated on heritage, whereby anything old had to be preserved at all costs without much critical evaluation going into the process. Preserving history in aspic, which is tantamount to a fear of the future, held no appeal. For us the interest lay in restoring the gardens to a working condition and establishing which traditional working practices were relevant today and which had genuinely been improved upon since. The irony of the history-in-aspic mentality is, of course, that any head gardener worth his salt would have needed an enquiring mind and would have wanted to experiment all the time both with technology and with newly introduced crop varieties. How else was progress made? How did the primitive Georgian woodstove-heated glasshouse turn into the Crystal Palace?

The past was being sanitized to fit into some lifestyle-magazine myth of organic growing methods and flower gardens looking like chocolate boxes. In fact the Victorian era was completely wrongly associated with wholesomeness. A cursory overview shows that the Victorians sprayed chemicals on everything; the bucolic image of aristocrats and cap-doffing gardeners conferring about the latest plant introduction from the Far East was all very well, but the life expectancy of the working man was half that of his employer.

To cut a long story short, the Heligan experience threw up all sorts of unexpected complications and delights. While John Nelson and his crew renovated all the structures, Philip and his team recovered the soil fertility and in two to three years had a burgeoning productive garden, including wall fruit and exotics in the glasshouses. Our most public triumph was the restoration of the eighteenth-century manure-heated pineapple pit; after years of experimenting with manure heating methods, a new crop of the original varieties of pineapple grown at Heligan was successfully fruited. Philip had secured the original varieties of vegetables, fruit and flowers from a rich range of sources. The Henry Doubleday Research Association, based at Ryton near Coventry, is dedicated to conserving heritage seed, and was very generous with its large collection. To fill in the gaps we were reliant on dozens of individuals who were fanatical about one or two varieties and kept their collections alive on allotments.

Then there were the super-collectors such as Mrs Maclean from Dundee, who owned the largest collection of potatoes in the world outside Peru. She too gave freely of what she had, as most true gardeners and horticulturists do. Incredibly, she gave Philip some of her very rare Salad Blue variety, a potato whose flesh remains blue after cooking. We bulked it up, and two years later when tragedy hit her collection we were able to repay the compliment. The tradition of generosity and sharing is based on a very sound principle – stewardship of resources. To have all your eggs in one basket, so to speak, poses an extreme risk.

Once the foundations of the collection had been established, we became increasingly interested in sorting out a philosophy for its future which would define our conservation priorities. Saving something just because it is old is sentimental and of questionable scientific or cultural value. Heritage of itself is worthless without a context. It boiled down to a balancing act, with flavour on the one hand and pest control and cropping levels on the other – though we have to admit to growing a number of low-cropping, disease-riddled varieties on the basis of their consummate flavour, such as Royal Sovereign strawberries – alongside issues such as whether to grow certain varieties for the length of their cropping periods or for their keeping qualities.

One of the great challenges facing the heritage industry concerns its need to balance the conservation of the past with an evaluation of the spirit which brought it into being. This is a problem peculiar to gardens, rather than the built environment. Periodicity is all very well when restoring a vegetable garden to a specific period, say, but it misses the point; to grow Victorian peas, which are by and large inedible, as opposed to a modern variety full of flavour would be absurd.

The conservation of old vegetable varieties should not be seen as a quaint rural hobby. When giant corporations supply the Western world with ever-narrower ranges of crops in a quest to control the market, a genetic weakness, such as a susceptibility to pest or disease, can have catastrophic results. The cure for the blight that brought Ireland to its knees in the nineteenth century was eventually achieved by reverting to cross-breeding with older potato varieties found in their country of origin, Peru. Today the world's richest nation, the USA, for all its high technology, depends on wild wheat varieties from Ethiopia to breed vigour into its vulnerable breadbasket. One rust attack, at the wrong time with the wrong prevailing winds, could see the mighty USA in terrible food jeopardy. Greater genetic variety would protect against this possibility. Most scientists would accept this intellectually, but the human condition seems to demand denial until things go wrong. 'Something will turn up,' was Mr Micawber's motto. We wouldn't run our families like that, so why the whole species?

The last fifty years have been an object lesson in the continuous overestimation of what science can achieve. Benefits get the headlines; years later, in the small print, one gets the debit side. It is as true of chemical applications against pest and disease as it is of the focus on a small number of high-yielding varieties freely available to growers in the name of greater productivity. This is not to question the value of scientific advances, without which our current global population would have been totally unsupportable. It is simply to suggest that we should not worship at the altar of science without exercising a correspondingly sensible stewardship over the gene-bank. To return to basics: if we think it important for individuals to grow their own vegetables and fruit, we must bear in mind that most modern, popularly available varieties, being based on industrial crops, have a very short fruiting period, thereby leaving the average domestic grower with a glut. The older, naturally pollinated varieties crop over a far longer period and are ideal for the home grower. What began for us as a discussion about a restoration philosophy for a heritage garden turned into an issue with global ramifications.

Cornwall's mild climate, bathing as it does in the outer fringe of the Gulf Stream, has created an environment that is unique, supporting anything from moorland sub-tundra flora to the sub-tropical valley gardens – Tresco, Trebah, Glendurgan, Trewithen and of course Heligan itself – for which the county has become internationally famous. It is because of the plant hunters that Britain, and especially Cornwall, is so rich in flora. These intrepid men travelled to the furthest reaches of the known world in the quest for exotica to supply the great new botanical institutions such as the Royal Botanic Gardens at Kew. Entrepreneurial nurserymen such as the Veitches made fortunes satisfying the curiosity of the aristocracy, and later of the burgeoning middle classes. Collecting became a status symbol, especially with the introduction of orchids.

Under Philip McMillan Browse's tutelage I was soon looking at the Heligan plants with fresh eyes. *Trachycarpus fortunei* ceased to be just a palm; it had a story, the smell of adventure. Robert Fortune brought it back from the Chusan Islands at

Tresco Abbey
Gardens

the mouth of the Yangtse. He had fought brigands, suffered terrible illness, and finally died shooting duck in a swamp in the middle of nowhere.

Then what of *Drymys winteri*, an unassuming laurel lookalike with daisy cluster flowers? Captain Winter was on Drake's circumnavigation of the globe, his men in a desperate condition from scurvy as they entered the Straits of Magellan at Tierra del Fuego. On the coast they found Indians making a soup from the latex-like sap of a plant. Winter took a gamble and fed his men a disgusting brew described as tasting like rhubarb to the power of ten, but it worked. He had discovered possibly the most vitamin C-rich plant in the world, and brought it back with him.

The list of stories was endless: David Douglas, who had a fir named after him, and died a horrendous death on Hawaii after falling into a hunter's pit already occupied by a wild bull; Archibald Menzies; De Bougainville; Ernest 'Chinese' Wilson; Père Armand David, the French explorer priest; the Cornish Lobb brothers; Frank Kingdom Ward; these were names to conjure with. I suddenly felt in touch with a spirit of adventure I had never previously associated with plants.

Then I came across Joseph Dalton Hooker, bearded, severe and totally obsessed. His father, William, rose from gardener to become director of the Botanic Gardens in Glasgow and went on to become the first proper director of the Royal Botanical Gardens at Kew; his son caught the bug and eventually also ended up as Director of Kew after years exploring the world hunting plants as well as pursuing other scientific interests. He sent back thousands of specimens from his four-year expedition to the Himalaya (1847–51). Many of these, especially his remarkable collection of rhododendrons, ended up in the gardens of Cornwall, where some of them survive to this day. The seed first went to Kew, and was then distributed to friends and supporters to establish where the plants might thrive. Heligan ended up with nineteen varieties of Hooker rhododendrons because the owners, the Tremayne family, were related by marriage to great friends of Hooker, the Lemons of Carclew, near Truro.

Philip was greatly interested in the biographies of the major Victorian scientist-explorers, especially Hooker, Darwin, Lyell and Huxley. We often talked of their intellectual bravery, and tried to imagine the sense of excitement that must have prevailed in that pre-media age when the general public flocked to hear their lectures. Philip wanted to know why I hadn't previously found plants interesting. I had skipped all the sciences at school, and I now seriously regretted wanting not to be seen as a nerd. I began reading more widely, and began to understand. The Victorians were working with an amazing canvas of the unexplored and unexplained, and started from a generalist viewpoint. No -ologies or -isms here; the natural world was seen as an integrated whole. Darwin was interested in all living things, as well as geology; *The Origin of Species* is not only a massive philosophical and scientific landmark of a book, it is also

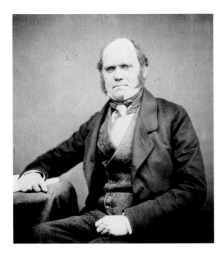

The Victorians: *(l to r)* Darwin, Hooker, Lyell

The great precursor: Burton and Turner's Palm House at Kew, 1844–48

a virtuoso polymathic celebration of observation and description. Most important of all, it is holistic.

By 1994 the productive gardens were largely restored, and Heligan was self-supporting. Interestingly, we were welcoming increasing numbers of school groups, drawn by our rather unusual approach to information. At that time all the signs in the garden were written in a conversational, anecdotal style and in big print. We also hosted many guided tours which we treated like theatre, attempting to convey to others our own excitement at the discoveries we were making, as well as explaining the underlying horticultural principles in a way all could understand. There is a wonderful review reprinted on the back of Richard Dawkins's book *The Selfish Gene*, which says, 'I loved this book, it made me feel so damn clever,' or words to that effect. There someone has captured perfectly the act of revelation that is education at its best. We were all hooked on the pleasure our visitors took in having their interest excited – and reaching, in however rudimentary a way, a new understanding of the world around them. I've been there: monochrome to sepia to colour in easy stages.

The school groups provided the greatest challenge. Most children find plants about as exciting as watching paint dry, but we soon discovered their collective Achilles heel. Building on my own awakened interest in the derring-do of the plant hunters, we discussed ways we knew we could get them to take notice. The Roald Dahl approach worked even better than we dared hope. We told a story about poisons and the variously horrible deaths suffered by the victims. We raised the tone by developing a historical context. The Aztecs, for example, used a plant-based drug to paralyse their live human sacrifices, thus keeping them quiescent long enough to have their hearts ripped out, still pumping, to celebrate the summer solstice. Eye-boggling attention was the result.

The children were now ready to find even the humble potato interesting. Actually the productive gardens were very popular, because almost everything they saw they had eaten in one form or another. The truly amazing discovery was how many children had no idea where such simple things as carrots, cabbage or potatoes came from, let alone pineapples and bananas.

We were pushing at an open door. The stories of the great plant hunters, the productive gardens and the plants that changed the world were irresistible in the right hands. Who can be bored by Captain Bligh and the mutiny on the *Bounty*, which leads to the story of breadfruit and why it was being taken from Tahiti to the Caribbean? Or the Duchess of Cinchon dying from malaria in Chile until a priest cured her with the powdered bark of a tree now named after her, *cinchona*, quinine, thus unleashing the imperial age by making it possible at long last for white men to penetrate the dark fastnesses of the hot continents? Without doubt this is the plant that has done most to shape world history.

Heligan:
the vineries

By influencing the audience we were changing ourselves. Stephen Sondheim, in his excellent musical *Into the Woods*, plays on the differences of perception between adults and children in a reworking of famous fairy stories such as Jack and the Beanstalk and Rapunzel. He points out that what to a child appears totally reasonable is actually morally vacuous. Take Jack, for instance: he climbs a beanstalk and sets about stealing things from a big bloke who has never done him any harm, and eventually kills him. Our stories, our interpretations, were leading us into similar deep water. After all, our heroes at Kew and elsewhere were actually systematically stealing assets from others and reshaping the world for their own ends. For much of the eighteenth and nineteenth centuries the great botanic gardens were little more than the economic development arms of the British or Dutch East India Companies.

The great walled flower garden at Heligan contains a large peach house and a series of vineries that once formed half of a mirrored pair on either side of the central doorway into the garden. The other half was still visible in the form of broken brick foundations, a flaking rendered wall and a few shelf brackets. The only trace of the former occupiers was an enormous fig now growing in the open air. The Tremaynes probably did not realize that figs could grow outside very comfortably in Cornwall, and instead copied London fashion. In the spring of 1994 Philip, John and I discussed at length what we should do with the space. We could restore it as a so-called stove house, a typical Victorian conservatory for hothouse plants. This would have been a historically acceptable addition to our collection of productive houses.

We kept coming back, though, to the writings of an antiquary who had visited Heligan in 1824 and had noted approvingly that he had seen a glasshouse filled with 'strange and aromatic plants'. We were convinced that a glasshouse growing a range of the plants that had changed the world would generate

The Top Lake
at Heligan

great interest as well as being in keeping with the spirit of the place. We spoke of spices, cotton, rice, exotic fruits, rubber, tea and coffee. In little more than an hour we had a list that would not only have more than filled the planned conservatory, it would have filled the whole Northern Garden at Heligan. Obviously we would have to go back to the drawing board.

Suddenly we remembered an expedition that John and I had made down the old Long Drive, formerly the main entrance to the estate, in search of Dart's Well, which no one had seen for more than seventy years. We found it buried under overgrowth and fallen trees. As we sat having a quiet smoke, happy with our new discovery, we looked down through the trees and became aware of a large stone quarry – called, we found out later, the Dairy Quarry. It had a flat bottom and a

terraced northern face, and at the time we had talked excitedly about its potential as a modern Mediterranean garden, with ornate water features and exotic terracing, with a glass roof over one end to contain the fruits of the region. This would be something completely new for Heligan, yet something that the Tremaynes might have been as excited about as I was. Nonetheless, the idea had taken root in my imagination, where it would stay until we could find a pocket deep enough.

chapter 2

the big fat idea

Cornwall is littered with gardens that were once
famous but are now, through neglect, development
or lack of resources, on the brink of being lost.
Enys, Tremough, Penjerrick and Carclew, for
example, were all repositories for the spoils of
the plant collectors, each one a monument to
the passions of generations of plant-loving owners.
For the last thirty years the heritage agencies have
promoted policies of restoration and conservation,
with a view to protecting the historic designed
landscapes and built environment, and they
deserve much credit for saving many undoubted
treasures for the nation. It is thanks to them that
we are familiar with the works of Lancelot
'Capability' Brown, Humphrey Repton and the
others who have shaped the British landscape.

The hurricanes of 1987 and 1990 drew attention to these historic landscapes not only as works of art, but also as the repositories for a valuable gene-bank. The work of the heritage and the environmental conservationist had until then been seen as completely separate. Now their interests merged, generating an opportunity for plant conservation initiatives which, in turn, provided a new context in which the heritage agencies could operate, giving them, if you like, a future as well as a historic remit.

To the rash of restoration plans drawn up to repair the damage to the historic landscapes were appended surveys of the existing trees, shrubs and flowers, and notes on the original plantings gleaned from the archives. While many conservationists became aware that these plant collections were perhaps being looked at in too narrow a way, some, such as Dr Chris Page from the Royal Botanic Gardens at Edinburgh, decided to do something about it. He drew people's attention to the

Hooker in the rhododendron forests

plight of the temperate rainforests of South America, especially Chile, where indiscriminate clearance by Far Eastern paper companies was resulting in the loss of millions of hectares of forest, at a rate so great that the gene-bank itself was under threat. He and his colleagues felt that promoting replanting schemes in the countries concerned was not enough; it was essential to implement conservation programmes in similar climates so as to create a wider gene-bank for the future. It is ironic that Britain, the pioneer of the exploitative plant-hunting tradition, now harbours a larger gene-bank of original species than the country of origin. Cornwall, with its mild climate, was a natural home for part of the project, and many of the great gardens have joined the scheme.

The gardens of Cornwall contain the widest range of Himalayan species rhododendrons outside their countries of origin. The rhododendron forests of the mountain kingdoms of Nepal, Sikkim and parts of Bhutan, where Hooker made his great plant-hunting expeditions a hundred and fifty years ago, now suffer from severe erosion caused by agricultural clearance and fuel cropping. Philip had started to take a keen interest in the Cornish rhododendrons, with a view to creating a master collection for propagation and subsequent distribution to other gardens and ultimately for reintroduction, where appropriate, to the wild. We had discussed an innovative commercial scheme where the fruits of the propagation would be sold at a premium, with the profits going into the reintroduction programme. The question now arose of where to do it.

Mark Stocker

By the spring of 1994 our big fat idea didn't yet have a shape or name, but it had qualities and a sense of quantity – big. Having realized that a conservatory in Heligan's Flower Garden was out of the question, we kept returning to building something in Dairy Quarry. In May of that year Philip and I drove up to Peter Thoday's home near Bath to discuss the restoration of the hothouse in the Flower Garden at Heligan, the rhododendron scheme, the plants that had changed the world and something else which would eventually dominate the next seven years of our lives. First I must step back for a moment.

Some people crop up at important points in your life. Mark Stocker was one of these. Our children had become friends at the local school in Gorran, and over several years we had ourselves become good friends. It was Mark who had effected my introduction to Peter Thoday at the start of the Heligan restoration, for example. Mark subsequently came to work with me at Heligan, managing our events programme. We would often retire to the pub at the end of the day and discuss one of his pet subjects, the future prosperity of Cornwall. Although he had worked 'away' most of his life, his roots were Cornish and he was profoundly depressed at what he perceived to be the lack of impetus for regeneration in Cornwall.

We had seen the phenomenal speed with which our local fishing village of Mevagissey had picked up economically through the success that Heligan was now enjoying; new restaurants, art galleries, shops and pub refits were drawing our visitors to its bustling, narrow streets. The same was happening at the Tate of the West, where an ambitiously designed outstation of the London Tate was tempting hundreds of thousands of visitors to rediscover the unique qualities of St Ives that had so inspired the artistic tradition that bears its name. I mentioned to Mark that I believed something, I knew not what, could be done in the clay district around St Austell, and I tossed around some of the ideas that Philip and I had been mulling over.

At Heligan I had worked with a number of the large state funders, most notably the Countryside Commission, who had granted us in the region of £400,000 towards the restoration programme, and the Rural Development Commission who had awarded us £130,000 towards the restoration of the glasshouses and working buildings in the walled gardens. It was Mark who brought up the subject of the great garden festivals. He had been working in Liverpool in the early 1980s when Michael Heseltine, then Minister for the Environment, initiated a scheme to create a massive garden festival as a catalyst for regeneration. The year-long event's success in attracting millions of visitors encouraged festivals at other economically and environmentally depressed sites such as Gateshead, Glasgow, Stoke and in the former coal-mining heartland of Ebbw Vale.

The scale of investment was impressive; Ebbw Vale had cost £70 million. Much of this was channelled into infrastructure, landscaping the coal tips, putting in roads and offices, creating exhibition areas that could be put to other economic uses after the festival was over. Mark pointed out that the St Austell area was surely as deprived as any of the other sites, so why not hold one here? I agreed; of all the places that could hold such a festival Cornwall, with its famous garden history, should surely stand a chance. My one reservation centred on the fact that the festivals lasted for only a year. I could understand that in the urban locations this might have been appropriate as a pretext for turning brownfield sites into development land. It didn't seem to be the right answer for Cornwall, where the eventual user might wish to build on the horticultural or agricultural tradition of this largely rural region. However, a seed was sown…

It was with this thought uppermost in our minds that Philip and I arrived at Peter Thoday's house. Peter is a remarkable man who doesn't suffer fools gladly. His temper is legendary, but more than matched by his passion and commitment to his beloved horticulture, a craft he has practised for fifty years. If he has a greater passion, outside his family, it is for his students, for whom he is mentor, mother hen, big stick and, ultimately, friend. His generosity is boundless, and his love of good conversation and argument has seen the home he shares with his wife Ann become a hub of the literate horticultural community, so many of his students having gone on to successful careers in the field. We would come to rely heavily on this pool of talent over the next few years.

Peter had worked all over the world on agricultural and horticultural projects before ending up at the Department of Horticulture at the University of Bath. From here he went solo to act as the consultant for *The Victorian Kitchen Garden* and *The Victorian Flower Garden*, two documentary series for the BBC, and to carry on his own horticultural consultancy. I hope he will forgive me if I describe him as having the facial appearance of a deeply weathered Ottoman, with a fine moustache and glasses that perch on the end of his nose. He is invariably dressed in comfortable clothes, wears slippers and has a taste for good whisky. We became firm friends.

Philip couldn't be more different; he is always immaculately dressed, in a Scott Fitzgerald kind of way. A fine rugby player in his youth, he pursued the sport to a ridiculous age. The consequent attrition to his joints causes him a discomfort that we can only imagine, because he would never dream of discussing it. He is meticulous to a fault and passionate about plants, but, on his own admission, almost devoid of interest in how they are displayed. One day, on our way back from visiting friends restoring Hestercombe Gardens in Somerset, I asked him whether he'd prefer to visit another famous garden or try out a pub that had a rather good reputation for real ale. No contest. 'I've seen all the plants, they'll just be in a different order,' was his reply.

Peter Thoday

The phrase 'You can't tell a book by its cover' could have been coined for Philip. On the one hand he is every inch the patrician, slightly aloof, not to say secretive, but on the other he is a tireless activist against low pay and exploitation of any kind – something that usually caused friction at the venerable institutions he had led in his previous career. In short, Philip appeared vain but was the opposite. What are you to do with a man who 'forgets' to put his postgraduate achievements on his CV and omits to mention that he's written the standard work on propagation in use throughout the world? He appears conservative but is something of a humanitarian radical, loathing privilege without merit while retaining a sense of duty born of responsibility – something he would never shirk, even at the hardest of times. He seemed aloof but was, in fact, passionately committed. Time after time I have seen him offer to sacrifice his own self-interest in favour of someone worse off, and as the project stuttered through its early incarnations he would often say to me that he had something put aside if it would help. His trust in the young was terrifying, and his motto – 'You can only achieve the impossible by

asking the young, because they don't know it can't be done' – should be inscribed on our coat of arms if we ever get one. He is a complete fifth columnist when it comes to organizational normality; he could see, and taught me to see, that it was the carrying of departmental baggage from the past into the present that was atrophying the institutions now responsible for change.

Like Peter he can talk splendidly about being a team player, but ultimately, like Peter, he is a twenty-four-carat maverick who does things his own way. Fortunately for all concerned, Peter and Philip's combined 130 years added up to wisdom rather than age. What they shared was an old-fashioned but crucial virtue, respect: for each other, for their colleagues and for the profession they practised. I think the reason they became such a powerful combination, with their constant testing of attitudes and positions, was that they had arrived at the same place from opposite extremes. Philip had led institutions and could see their flaws and wished to redress them. Peter had begun on the practical side of horticulture and had entered academia later, carrying with him a deep respect for his peers and making

Heligan: the
Flower Garden
in high summer

'...a 24-carat
maverick': Philip
McMillan Browse

him perhaps a little more forgiving of their ways.

One last thing they shared – both thought they were moving gently into semi-retirement. Both were horribly mistaken. They didn't know it then, but they would fly thousands of miles and talk to thousands of people over the next three years, drawing on every contact and pulling every favour their years in the business deserved. Pretending it didn't matter much and faking a professional detachment, they were back to their fighting weights in no time at all.

In the early hours of a May morning in 1994, the best part of a bottle of whisky to the good, we had a concept that, though rough around the edges, excited us. There would be five glasshouses, or giant poly-tunnels, linked together for a walkthrough experience. Four would focus on a particular climate region of the world and the fifth would contain a composite of the world's productive domesticated plants. As I recall we suggested rainforest, sub-tropical rainforest, Mediterranean, and a combination of savannah and desert. At the time we were focused on celebrating the floristic riches and the productivity of the planet, with a nod towards conservation – in essence a large-scale theme park fit for a garden festival that intended to make a case for permanence. As we will see, this would change radically.

On the drive home Philip was already thinking of the practicalities. He was excited, but something was gnawing at him. It was not the concept as a whole or its scale, it was the logic of the exhibitions and the separation between wild flora and the productive crops. He wouldn't put his finger on it till later, but it would revolutionize the idea.

Throughout the summer we toyed with the plan. Mark had kicked off the process of finding out about the garden festivals and how they had financed themselves. Large amounts of bumph arrived in the post, and we had spoken to English Partnerships, the government's regeneration quango, and had been politely rebuffed. There would be no further garden festivals, there had been an agreed programme which had come to an end. Wait and see what we've got planned, we said to ourselves. It was dawning on us, however, that the scale of the project we were imagining was completely out of our league. We had no idea how much it might cost, whether it was in fact buildable, manageable or fundable, or indeed whether we could even obtain the land we would need and the support from the council and government that would be essential. We were complete amateurs, out of our depth and fuelled only by the belief that the 'can do' culture of Heligan would somehow find a way through.

We were going to have to get real. In early September Mark talked to the organizers of the Ebbw Vale Garden Festival, who were in the process of winding down their operation. They were helpful and encouraging, and offered to talk us through the process, highlighting the problems that they had experienced on the way. We agreed to go and see them in October.

'...a human tornado': Jo Readman in a rare moment of repose

Meanwhile, Heligan was a hive of activity. The press were being generous in their coverage and West Country Television was completing a documentary about our work for a Christmas showing. In the middle of this, Channel 4 asked us whether we would agree to our new pineapple plants featuring in a magazine series to be called *Fruity Stories*. A human tornado turned up at Heligan in the shape of the series producer, Dr Jo Readman. Her colourful clothes and the long coal-black hair cascading to the small of her back might have led you to believe that she was something of a hippy, but this would have been a big mistake. The energy just crackled off her. I had never met anyone so animated, passionate and knowledgeable about her subject. She had the best scientific credentials, but her skill lay in conveying what she knew to the widest possible audience; her life seemed to be a quest for the best medium through which to do it. In between explaining the principles of photosynthesis, how to motivate dysfunctional teenagers, the thrill of computers and the joys of swimming in the sea in winter, she persuaded us to participate in her filming. Not that we needed much persuading.

I mentioned the special project we were brewing, and the cork exploded out of her bottle. She blew me away with her excitement. She was so convinced she offered to give up the TV life the moment the project began to look remotely possible, move to Cornwall and do whatever was needed to help. In the meantime, if there was anything she could do I should just ask. As an after-thought, she mentioned that an acquaintance of hers, Ivor Stokes, had just taken over the running of the most modern glasshouse in the world, Plantasia in Swansea. It was unthinkable that we should be going to Ebbw Vale without also getting the lowdown on glasshouse technology from Ivor. I mutely concurred. As we talked, I realized that someone had walked into my life who was destined to turn it upside down.

Abergavenny on a dark autumn evening is not for the faint-hearted. Not much open, but not much closed either. Mark and I had an Indian meal in a high street that otherwise made no concession to the last fifty years. How was this possible with a garden festival seven miles up the road? It was 10 October. We were staying at the only hotel that seemed to be open on the way to Ebbw Vale, all sunburst glass doors and swirly carpet, cold comfort service, and a tea-maker in the bedroom that must have been the reason for the stars on the roadside sign. The following morning we went to the festival site. An immense amount of work had gone on, sculpting and replanting slag heaps, removing mining infrastructure and creating space for buildings. Obviously most of the temporary exhibits had been removed save for the willow and earth sculptures, glasshouse and office accommodation, but nonetheless we were struck by the complete absence of any aesthetic or cultural vision. Here was development completely uninfluenced by any philosophy save functionality. It reeked of committees untainted by inspiration. It felt like a job of work had been done, no more, as if the process itself was assumed to be enough to create the regenerative impetus they so craved. We felt rather mean when we met such a warm welcome from the organizers, who couldn't have been more generous with their time or advice.

We were talked through the project management issues they had dealt with and the contract difficulties they had faced; we were treated to charts of organizational structures, reporting lines and development programmes until we could take no more. Then, over coffee, they spoke frankly of the shortcomings. The most glaring example was the lack of integration, or even coordination, between all the bodies involved in the project. There were County Council, District Council, Welsh

'Plantasia was a different kettle of fish…'

Development Agency and English Partnership interests to be served. Full marks, they had opened on time, but…the railway line stopped a mile and a half short of the site, there were no hotels close by and none had been factored in. Very few of the sites intended for future occupation had been presold.

Worst of all, in the view of our hosts, was the procurement mechanism, which had been a shambles. With the closure of much of the mining industry in South Wales many of those who had been made redundant had set up in business on their own, mostly one-man-and-his-dog operations. The whole reason for a project such as this is to stimulate the local market, but it had been planned in such a way that the lead times for supplying anything from souvenirs in the shop to uniforms for the staff were so short that local companies did not have the time to gear up. A huge amount of stuff was therefore procured outside Wales, causing much local anger and resentment. We left, impressed by the people we met, depressed that so much effort could have created so little of lasting value for the community it was meant to serve.

Plantasia was a different kettle of fish. Built in the middle of a new shopping mall in Swansea city centre, as part of the planning gain negotiated with its developers, it was an impressive glass pyramid, not dissimilar to the I. M. Pei building at the Louvre in Paris. Ivor Stokes, the director, was a marvellous host and talked us through his triumphs and disasters. We spoke of disabled access, the problems for phobics of having birds in confined spaces, of butterflies with pernicious caterpillars, and architects who don't understand the needs of plants. He told us that within six weeks of opening he had insisted on changing the computer-operated window-openers, watering systems and sunblinds back to manual operation, because if the systems broke down you could bake or freeze before they could be overridden. Nonetheless it was a fine building with a real sense of theatre, particularly in its impressive sweeping walkway that meandered under a waterfall. Ivor gave us an idea of costs, a list of contacts to chase up and an invitation to call him at any time, and we left Wales a lot happier than we were when we entered it.

One thought occurred: if an industrial wasteland at Ebbw Vale could be reclaimed, admittedly at vast expense, to make a garden, just think what we could do in Cornwall, with its more congenial climate, if we got serious about it!

if you're not on the edge, you're taking up too much space

The wheels of my beaten-up Volvo estate bit into the gravel, kicking up a wall of dust behind. Another dead-end mission, another addition to my collection of China Clay Pits I Have Seen. This was the works entrance to Bodelva, a relatively small pit nearing the end of its economic life. It specialized in extracting clay for the upmarket end of the paper industry. I drove past the forbidding Soviet-style concrete works buildings, with their grey asbestos roofs and cracked and grimy windows, and pulled up outside a temporary cabin that had long since become permanent.

Battered and dust-covered, it kept the wind and rain out but had nothing else to recommend it, unless you like chewed lino floors, the smell of instant coffee, a few cheap desks covered in maps, protective clothing hanging from pegs, and the obligatory pin-up calendar. This was prospector territory, with frontier comforts. Reception received me and gave me a hard hat in return for a signature waiving their responsibility in the event of any incompetence on my part.

I hadn't paid any attention to the landscape on entering, so low were my expectations. In fact when my friend Bill Rickatson, managing director of Lord Falmouth's Goonvean and Restowrack China Clay Company, had called I had agreed to take a look simply out of courtesy. When someone's trying to help you it's rude to point out that they haven't understood the situation. Bodelva was in the south-east of the china clay district, near the village of St Blazey, about as far away from the crucial main arterial road through Cornwall as it is possible to get. So, muted optimism being the order of the day, I strode out across the yard to take a look.

Wow!

I felt something shift inside me as I crossed the yard. To the south, a mile distant, the ocean glistened in the sun. The Gribben Head to the east and Black Head to the west framed St Austell Bay in a perfect horseshoe. In the foreground was a magnificent sweep of wooded parkland and farmland that formed the Carlyon Estate at Tregrehan. I turned to the north and saw in the far distance the spoil heaps, the so-called Cornish Alps, but again the foreground appeared to be

wooded country. The rim of the pit was dense with self-sown trees and scrub, and the air was thick with the coconut aroma drifting in from an impenetrable wall of flowering gorse on its northern edge. Here and there I could make out copses of mature Atlantic woodland, with their signature oaks, sycamore and ash. I approached the edge with mounting excitement.

It was the strangest thing. The instant my eyes fell on Bodelva Pit I knew it was the one, exactly as it was meant to be. I felt as if I had been there before. Every lump, scar, crevice and cliff face felt familiar. It was a huge, deep, multi-coloured oval, decreasing in depth at its southern end, where one of those extraordinary milky emerald lakes so much a feature of the clay area glinted in the alien landscape. Minerals of many kinds bled into the landscape as if from a prehistoric wound. Burnt sienna, livid greens, reds, greys and of course every shade and texture of white made up a primal palette. The sheer faces at the northern end plunged two hundred feet to the base, where men small as ants worked their monitors, water cannon with enormous power that won the clay from the rocks. A river of white formed a flood plain behind them. Occasionally a tiny truck would come into view carrying spoil; it was a shock to realize, when they reached the top of the pit, that they could carry seventy tons and each wheel was the size of a man.

'I approached the edge with mounting excitement'

Overcome with relief that the quest was finally over, I sat down on a boulder to soak up the atmosphere. A pair of buzzards wheeled effortlessly upwards on the

thermals from the pit bottom. Their languid progress was measured in shadows against the almost barren backcloth of the granite cliffs. Here and there lonely scrub trees nestled in the crevices, and for a moment you could have believed you were in the High Sierras. I screwed up my eyes to keep the birds in sight as long as possible, until the glare forced them closed. The red glow behind my eyelids pulsed into a kaleidoscopic pattern that I would remember with a smile many years later. Maybe this was what was meant by 'in the mind's eye'? I fished around in my breast pocket for a cigar and lit it ostentatiously, drawing the sour smoke into my salty mouth. If you could describe explorer as a flavour, this would be it. Here, in the company of buzzards, on my rock in the middle of nowhere, with the sun beating down on my threadbare scalp and a mouth that was beginning to taste like the bottom of a budgie's cage, I knew we'd found our Eden.

Cornwall's Clay Country first took hold of my imagination as long ago as 1987, when I travelled through it on my way to dive on the famous Runnel Stone near Lamorna Cove. Bodmin Moor introduces a region of mists, of heather-covered heathlands, granite outcrops and pea-soup lakes; an essay in greens, purples, browns and cold slate greys. The monotony of this desolate yet beautiful place is broken only by the occasional isolated farmstead, an oasis of normality in a landscape otherwise dominated by a big sky that seems to weigh heavy on the land. The wizened little trees, bowed in mute surrender to the unforgiving winds, provide a warning that elemental forces are at work and we are as nothing in their presence.

There is a granite backbone that runs from Dartmoor in the east to Land's End in the far west. Granite decomposes into very fine particles of china clay alongside hard gritty sands called mica and quartz. In simple terms china clay is extracted by blasting water at the decomposing granite and putting the sands and clay into solution. The sands, being heavier, sink, leaving the clay to be collected at the end of the process.

From high up on the moors a distant kingdom beckons, a Brothers Grimm land of castles and mountains. On getting closer you find that romance gives way to a more uneasy response. There is no fanfare at the spot where one enters the China Clay capital of the world. Is this typical British understatement, or a tacit recognition that the price one pays for such distinction is high?

Mid-Cornwall is dominated by the clay industry. It permeates almost all aspects of economic and cultural life, not to mention the physical landscape. Although the last twenty-five years have seen the labour force shrink from nearly 18,000 to some 3,500, the output has remained fairly constant at around 2 million tons per year. Its main market has become the paper industry, where it is added to wood pulp to increase the bulk of white paper. At the top end the finest clays are used as gloss coatings for fine paper. It is also used in the rubber, paint and plastics industry.

'Bodelva, a relatively small pit nearing the end of its economic life'

The original 'White Goldrush' which began all this was the search for the secret of fine porcelain. The art of making porcelain was mastered by the Chinese more than a thousand years ago and their wares were highly prized throughout Europe, yet despite all efforts it wasn't until around 1710 that their secret was discovered, in Meissen, Saxony. The Meissen porcelain factories soon dominated this lucrative market. In the mid-eighteenth century William Cookworthy, a chemist from Plymouth, discovered that Cornish clay was excellent for making hard white porcelain. After a slow start, dozens of companies opened hundreds of small pits in the quest for white gold.

Wherever you go in the Clay Country you are confronted by its past. The fact that the industry began in the middle of the eighteenth century means that there are many areas that have returned to the wilderness – impressive evidence of nature's capacity for regeneration. You have only to venture into the undergrowth to stumble upon the remains of buildings, tanks, driers and, more worryingly, shafts. From horse-powered water pumps to steam-powered beam engines, from men with shovels to giant bulldozers and water cannon, the clay industry provides a microcosm of the Industrial Revolution and the innovative power of capital. Unusually, because of the unique geology of Cornwall, the entire evolutionary process is captured in one place, while the casual disregard for land as a resource in a time of plenty has meant that the technologies, although rendered obsolete by each succeeding development, were rarely removed but simply left to rot. So plentiful are the archaeological remains that perhaps the most surprising feature is that humans hadn't got round to vandalizing them before they sank beneath the encroaching greenery.

The history lesson begins with primitive settling pans, shallow depressions in the open landscape linked by what a layman might call sluice gates. These were located alongside the pits, and here the heavy sands were separated out from the clay. The process became more sophisticated with the construction of stone-built separators that distinguished the light mica sands from the clay, thereby attaining a higher degree of purity. Everywhere, even in the most overgrown areas, you find beautifully built chimneys poking up into the sky. When you cut your way through to what lies below it is usually the same: the chimney at one end of a long building with a recessed floor running the length of it. These are clay driers, where the separated clay, once finally settled and drained of water, turned to the consistency of custard, after which it was spread on to a long heated drying floor and cut into squares. After drying the clay was stacked in biscuits for storage.

The naming of the great pits remains something of a mystery to me. Most of them bear names that one could imagine being handed down from a Wesleyan pulpit, full of blood and thunder: Melbur, Goonvean, Goonbarrow, Greensplatt, Blackpool and so on, not to mention the great Baal – it's good to know that

Beelzebub himself gets a name check. When we set out on our quest to find the perfect site we were aware of omens and portents; a primitive superstition told us that we would recognize what we were looking for when we saw it.

The Clay Country is dotted with little communities that sprang up alongside the giant pits to accommodate the workers of all classes who were engaged in the industry. With few exceptions, every community has developed in the same way – a ribbon development of little semi-detached workers' cottages and shops making up Fore Street, and on the outskirts the larger houses and gardens of the mine captains who managed the business of extraction. There is usually a Methodist chapel, a vicarage, a sports and social club and a pub or two. Sons followed fathers into the clay and the industry provided for all in a paternalistic way. The wages were good and the certainty of employment conspired against the evolution of a culture that might prize education as a means of escaping from drudgery.

'You have only to venture into the undergrowth...'

Over the last hundred years, mergers and acquisitions have left just two companies operating in Cornwall: Imerys, the former English China Clays (the world leader), and Goonvean, owned by the Falmouth Estate. The industry was until recently a paternalistic colossus able to set its own agenda and run its affairs without interference from the state. It so dominated the economic landscape that it was able to build spoil heaps and open mines almost at will. It had long-established mineral rights over most of the land at the centre of mid-Cornwall. As an industry china clay is exceptionally intrusive in the management of its waste products. For every ton of clay extracted from the ground there are up to seventeen tons of waste sand that have to be disposed of. Hence the mountains. In areas where there are constraints on the land available for dumping, the technology has been introduced to grade the spoil into its constituent parts – fine sand, coarse sand, small gravel, hardcore and so on.

The larger, unconstrained pits, however, found it more economic to keep dumping, creating ever-larger mountains of waste that sterilized increasing amounts of what could have been productive land. The spoil heaps betray no easily identifiable pattern in the landscape. This is not to say they are random; a suspicion lingers that there may be method in the apparent madness, that someone was deliberately setting out to create Ugly and Brutal in such a way that eventually an inner beauty might reveal itself. There are two clearly distinct types of heap: the jagged, sheer-sided pyramids, like mountains drawn by Chinese calligraphers; and the giant crusty warts, which are generally bigger but squat, compressed, their sides cut into huge steps. The indelible impression is of a land of ogres and trolls, each with their own distinctive fortress.

(overleaf) Pyramids and pea-soup lakes: the clay country

Over the last twenty years opinion has hardened against the mineral giants, partly abetted by the activism of incomers who have no stake in the future of the industry. The word 'moonscape' is often used to convey the impression of a sterile, alien environment. (Indeed, episodes of *Doctor Who* were shot here.) What the term misses in the Cornish context is that this landscape is completely unnatural – it is man-made. No force of nature was at work here. These mountains and valleys are monuments both to the awesome power of industry and to the arrogance of capitalism. One is struck by the staggering carelessness of the rape, as if the land existed only for the taking, with no consequent duty of care to soften the pain. It has been left to a new generation to heal the terrible scarring created by the old. Suddenly the china clay companies had to justify their actions and adopt more sustainable practices, their behaviour closely monitored by the public agencies charged with policing environmental policy. Land sterilization was frowned upon, and the industry was encouraged to use inactive pits as waste dumps. Any sale of land by them was also deemed to be an acknowledgement that their current dumping arrangements were adequate, thus further compromising their ability to obtain new dumping licences from the planning authorities.

'...the word "moonscape" is often used...'

One of the problems the industry faces is that pits can become uneconomic to work while not yet being worked out. Clay deposits are usually shaped like pimples, increasing in diameter, and therefore cost of extraction, the deeper one goes. It has been a tradition to allow these pits to remain fallow until technology or the market advances to a point where they can be returned to economic fruitfulness. They would usually be filled with water in the interim so that they formed a water source for the cannon in active pits. It has to be recognized too that the clay industry is heavily constrained by planning conditions which require the restoration of worked-out pits. The cost of restoration if such conditions were enforced would probably bankrupt the industry, so for any site actually to be classified as derelict is almost unheard of.

When I returned to Cornwall to live by the sea on a headland south of St Austell, the main town of the Clay Country, the clay mountains formed my northern horizon, a constant backcloth to my life. By day you could almost believe they'd always been there, but as darkness fell the arc lights cast an orange glow around St Austell and you remembered that, like rust, the clay never sleeps. Years of driving through them, climbing on them and making friends among those who made their living in and from them have done nothing to resolve the ambivalence of my response to them.

One day, in a moment of horrible revelation, I realized the underlying cause of my unease. I don't know what brought it to the surface, and I don't think I had consciously thought about it for more than thirty years. I was young and living in Zoetermeer, a village outside The Hague in Holland. I was playing fire engines. I sprayed water at my mother's best table lamp and was making the noise of a siren, as all little boys do. Something happened and the lamp was toppling off the table and I remember grabbing it and suddenly the most enormous uncontrollable shaking had taken over my body. I felt possessed. There was screaming and my mother – thank God she understood electricity – didn't grab hold of me, but instead pulled the plug. I fell to the floor and my mother lifted me on to the sofa and for the first time looked at my right hand. It was burned to the bone at the palm, thumb and the next two fingers, deep craters of black and red with burnt bone shiny in the holes. The surgeon said amputate, my mother fought, and nineteen anaesthetic-free operations later I had a rebuilt hand which for the next eighteen months I had to exercise by moulding plasticine in my fist. The benefits were that I had nineteen military Dinky Toys, one for each operation where I beat the tears. I also had a hand that was unbelievably supple and mobile, to the point that I was later able to make my living as a piano player. I had very different prints on each finger, which could have been useful had I wished to pursue a criminal career. It also explains my feelings about the Clay Country. Jagged pyramid peak, crusty wart and pea-soup lake combined with mineral bleeds conjure up something very disturbing in my mind: my burnt hand.

Despite this, I was to visit just about every pit and heap in the clay district between 1994 and 1996, when we found Bodelva. It became a way of life, crawling through undergrowth, entering dangerous buildings, peering into the impenetrable depths of pea-soup lakes and sliding down scree slopes. We even went up in helicopters just to make sure we hadn't missed anything. I was aware of the great generosity of spirit of our friends in the clay industry, who wanted to make a contribution to what we were trying to do and all of whom, without exception, felt a deep responsibility not only to the future of the area but to the notion of making amends for some of the excesses of previous generations. It was an extraordinary privilege to be allowed such free access to their subterranean yet vertiginous world. There was every reason for them not to help, not to go that extra mile, yet they gave their time and their expertise freely and, when it mattered most, dared to make the difficult decisions without which Eden would never have been born.

Originally the quest began with a few simple criteria. For reasons of access it was essential that we should concentrate our search close to the main arterial road through Cornwall, the A30, and preferably near the dual carriageway rather than further west where there was already heavy congestion during the holiday season. This immediately drew our attention to an axis from Roche and Bugle in the north to St Austell in the south. The main focus would become Bugle, a typical clay village with the misfortune to lie on the main road south from the A30. We had to discount all the great pits that were still fully economic. This narrowed the field to spoil heaps and fallow pits for which an argument could be made that they were a special case, thus avoiding establishing a precedent. Towering over Bugle is the giant crusty wart of Goonbarrow, a monster of a clay tip, cut into seven terraces to secure it from sliding into the village. (The pyramid peaks all predate the Aberfan disaster in Wales, where a slag heap slipped and buried a school, killing many children. The crusty warts were the industry's response to the recommendations that came from the inquiry into the causes of the tragedy.)

One evening in the late summer of 1994 I was driving back from the east along the A30 admiring an impressionistic sunset when out of the corner of my eye I caught a glimpse of Goonbarrow. It had turned the colour of Ayers Rock, its brooding presence made even larger by the shadow play on its terraces. For a moment I was put in mind of the Aztec ziggurats of Central America; with my imagination running free, I had soon synthesized an image of tropical rainforests, extraordinary architecture, and the lost worlds so beloved of Arthur Conan Doyle and Edgar Rice Burroughs: a civilization that time forgot, hidden in the crater of an extinct volcano… The theatricality of the image was so powerful that it would leave me dissatisfied with everything we looked at until the right place revealed itself to us.

Goonbarrow is in full operation, and from its table mountaintop you can look down into an enormous hole, so large in fact that it is hard to determine where hole stops and heap begins. In the pit there is huge activity, with monitors, trucks, dumpers and giant swing shovels all working in concert twenty-four hours a day. Every few minutes the air is filled with the whine of a straining engine as another lorry meanders to the top of the mountain to dump its load of heavy sands. Scattered like dinosaur bones, giant boulders litter the ascent. The overall impression is of absolute sterility, save for a patina of green on the lower slopes where grass has been sprayed to bind the sediment together and save the village below from dust storms when the weather turns. The working pit was not available, but the monstrous mountain was. And if not this, then the next best thing would be to cantilever off the side of this crusty wart, with its south-west-facing slope leading down to flat farmland which was also available to us. Not ideal, but still a spectacular site with some very interesting neighbours. Our first bid to the Millennium Commission would be for the flatland below Goonbarrow, before we opted for the drama of the crusty wart itself.

As months followed weeks in the pursuit of the Goonbarrow site I became increasingly depressed. We were trying to put a brave face on it, but when the biting winds began to blow you could feel the grit on your face as the dust was carried across the landscape. What would happen when the big easterlies struck up in the winter? We would spend our lives cleaning windows, and when we could see out of them we'd be looking at the back end of a spoil heap. Then there was the fog. Remarkable as it may seem, for an average of more than two hundred days of the year nearby Roche suffers from fog or mist in the early mornings. Sometimes it doesn't lift until nearly noon.

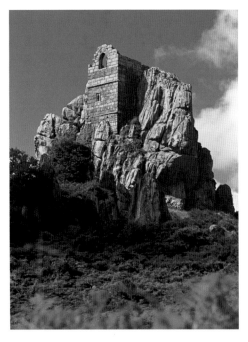

Roche Rock: the Hermit's Retreat

One day I climbed the rickety iron ladder leading into the Hermit's Retreat at Roche Rock. This is a tiny granite building with Gothic windows perched on top of a granite bluff looking out across heath and farmland towards Goonbarrow. From the first floor of the hermitage you can climb out on to the rock and feast on a panoramic view that takes in almost the whole of the northern clay district. Looking out, I knew the Goonbarrow option was wrong, though I was quite impressed by the hermit. It would have been hard to choose a more exposed location for spiritual contemplation.

Clive Gronnow, Roger Preston and Max Pemberton of ECC pored over maps with us, looking for anything that might be suitable. Finally Clive and Roger invited us to see Rose Mellyn, below Goonbarrow. It had ceased operations many years ago and could now be reached only through a number of locked gates, after which you had to walk through a boggy field in which the biggest horseflies I have ever seen were on manoeuvres. Although it is less than half a mile from Goonbarrow, once you were inside you would never have known. It was beautiful.

Thank you, Bill

The horseshoe-shaped pit was filled with water and fringed with lush vegetation, broken here and there by granite cliff faces. A rich variety of waterfowl scuttled around in the rushes. The only twentieth-century intrusion was the run of electric pylons on the skyline. I felt this might be the place, and for weeks we tried to come to terms.

The sticking point was that Goonbarrow pit, unusually, had no water on site, so they had run large pipes down to Rose Mellyn, from where pumps sent a steady supply up the mountain and down the other side. It was a bitter disappointment when we finally realized that we and the pit wouldn't be able to operate side by side. Imagine the situation: many people and agencies are getting excited about the project in which you are involved, and even the County Council are telephoning with suggestions, yet you yourself are feeling desperate because you know it isn't right. You have exhausted all the sites that could possibly be suitable. Although I continued searching and following up leads, my heart just wasn't in it.

Some while back, on top of Goonbarrow with Max Pemberton, I had spotted Wheal Prosper, which belonged to the Goonvean and Restowrack China Clay Company. It was perfect. It had a clearly defined territory, or lip, to its crater and it was just the right size to capture the imagination. Everyone laughed when I said that was what I wanted. It was not that they disagreed, it was simply that it was impossible. I knew that I wouldn't rest until we had something that lived up to the dream. For the time being though, we'd have to be patient.

I had been to see Bill Rickatson of Goonvean several times during my quest. He had tried hard and we had come up with nothing, but Bill was a kindly man who instinctively understood that this wasn't all about business, it was about chasing a dream. He had a twinkle in his eye and a deep knowledge of his industry, but he also believed in the sort of things we were proposing to do. I will never forget that fateful call. I was in the office at Heligan and in near despair when Bill called. Was there anything he could think of that we hadn't turned over numerous times already? Well, he said, as it happens there is one possibility. Goonvean is purchasing two pits from Redland Aggregates any moment now. The easternmost pit, Bodelva, we are taking as part of a job lot; we actually want Greensplatt. Bodelva is nearing the end of its life. I know how much you admired Wheal Prosper – you might just find this suitable. Call me back if you're interested in paying a visit and maybe you can come up and have some tea afterwards. I thanked him, put the phone down, scoured the map, groaned, lost hope, decided to go anyway out of courtesy and the rest, as they say, is history. Thank you, Bill.

chapter 4

clubbing

Life can throw together some pretty strange bedfellows. Jonathan Ball bounced into my life the day after my birthday. We had felt for some time that although the project was taking shape intellectually, our weakness in large-project management and architecture meant that we had few anchor points in reality. Mark had gone to a regional tourism conference at St Mellion some months previously, and had met an architect who had impressed him with his commitment to regeneration in Cornwall. Mark had heard that he enjoyed a good reputation both inside and outside the county, and suggested that I call him. He would be bound to be able to point us in the right direction on technical matters. His name was Jonathan Ball, and he was the head of the Bude-based architectural practice that bore his name.

He had been awarded an MBE for services to architecture, had served on the council of the RIBA and had recently been its vice-president. I called. He was there, he was excited, and he would drop everything and come for a chat. It was 26 September 1994.

Our first meeting was memorable. Jonathan and I spent many hours at a picnic table in front of the Heligan café, and at the end of it I felt as if I'd known him for years. He was remarkable in his indomitable enthusiasm. Well-trimmed beard, blazer, slacks, bow tie, brogues and bright sparkly eyes behind spectacles all gave the impression of a naval officer on shore leave. He could tell a shaggy dog story like no man I've ever met, savouring every nuance of the tale with a chuckle ending in a complete paroxysm of infectious laughter as the punchline was delivered – a real gift. He was excellent company at social occasions. He drove a red Jaguar sports car with leather seats, not so much out of a desire to be flash but because of a bad experience in the past when a client hadn't thought him serious enough in a runabout.

He wore his Cornishness with a benevolent fanaticism that sat slightly uneasily with his metropolitan tastes, and would never miss an opportunity of telling anyone who would listen that sunny Bude, his home town, was the centre of the universe. This carried over into a warm affection for anything Celtic, especially Ireland, a country which he often visited. He made a point of saying that he could have worked anywhere, but wanted to live in Cornwall. He was a leading light in the RNLI and in the Surf Lifesavers, and a keen conductor of the local choir, which was a front for good-natured high jinks, Guinness drinking and awaydays with the lads. The Isles of Scilly were his spiritual home, and he doggedly held on to a routine of a three-week summer sojourn on St Mary's, where he would keep open house for family and friends and indulge his love of walking.

Jonathan had for some time been thinking about various schemes for regenerating Cornwall, and had been ahead of his time in promoting the idea of farm villages, permanent farmers' markets. He immediately recognized the potential for the sort of project we had been developing, and felt he could make a major contribution on a number of levels. Having lived and worked in Cornwall all his life, he had built up a network of friends and contacts throughout the region who could be useful in creating the political climate of support. He alluded to his years on the parliamentary liaison committee of the RIBA, and hinted at influence in Westminster circles. Best of all, he was connected to the world of architecture at a national level. With his architectural practice and influence and my track record at Heligan it was worth a punt, he said. He impressed me greatly with his selflessness when he told me that a venture such as this needed a big-name architect to give it credibility; his own practice was better suited to developing a brief and maybe picking up a few scraps on the periphery. We shook hands and agreed to work together.

I never had any doubt that the project would eventually be successful, nor that it would soon become all-consuming, leaving me no time to nurture my beloved Heligan through the next stage of its evolution. I would need someone very special to whom I could entrust my baby. As if by magic, he turned up shortly after this fateful meeting. He was Peter Stafford, polymath, cynic, former British Wildlife Photographer of the Year (the first person to film moles underground), and a self-made man with a string of business successes behind him, the proceeds of which he poured into a private bird reserve in Devon. He was a complex character; a man who didn't need to work, but one possessed of a restlessness akin to a constant mid-life crisis. An hour or two in his company would reveal a passion for the songs of Tom Lehrer and Flanders and Swann and the monologues of Alan Bennett. He claims not to like company or parties, but, when called upon, is able to make very witty speeches and perform in the village pantomime, which he does every year – sometimes even writing it. At times he turns into a latter-day Don Quixote, tilting at local injustices. The more improbable the odds, the more he enjoys it – and the more you sneakily sympathize with his opponents, who will have underestimated him at their peril. He deals with problems in 'bite-sized chunks' and by 'turning off dripping taps', and is the best manager I have ever met.

Peter Stafford points the way forward

I am fortunate in my friends. Peter came to Heligan for six months, and at the time of writing he remains there, having turned it into the place I dreamed of but could never have made myself. Along the way, he would also act as my confidant as Eden turned into an organizational monster, encouraging me to take risks I might have lacked the courage to take on my own.

Although Jonathan and I had both been to public school, the similarity ended there. I had loathed my schooldays, and spent them terrified that they might turn out to have been the best days of my life; for Jonathan I got the impression they truly were. I had been forced to go to a boarding school because of my father's foreign postings in the airline business, and his company paid. I was Dutch enough to find the whole notion of privilege distasteful, and I disliked the alliances that had to be forged to get you through unscathed. I also had a character trait that made my schooldays tricky: I found it impossible to accept an order. I would take any amount of punishment from masters or prefects, but I could not do as I was told, only what I was asked. I went further to the bad by developing an early addiction to rock music, Number 6 cigarettes and shoplifting the odd top-shelf magazine. I was eventually expelled after undertaking a particularly daring and insanely stupid expedition to Ireland.

I suppose I had a bit of an attitude problem. I'm not a rebel. To my everlasting regret I never had the body for a tight white T-shirt and a leather jacket, nor the intelligence or cool to make social comment with a sneer. School gave me one thing, however, that was to influence my life in every aspect: we went co-ed in my first sixth-form year, and I discovered that I liked the company of women.

Jonathan and I would banter constantly about our opposite views of the world. He had, as one of the country's bright young up-and-coming professionals, been invited to join a select gentlemen's club, a real honour for which ordinarily one would have to wait years. Protocol apparently forbids me mentioning it by name, but it's a fantastic place in the heart of London with wonderful pillars and a gold figurehead launching out from its portico. It boasts one of the finest private libraries in the world, and employs a phalanx of librarians that would make the average civic library green with envy. Every member donates something special to the institution: Elgar, for example, donated one of his sumptuous scores. Jonathan arranged one night for me to see the first edition of James Bateman's *Orchidaceae of Mexico and Guatemala*. Bateman was the man behind Biddulph Grange and a great sponsor of plant hunters; his exquisite book, the largest illustrated botanical work ever published – it weighs thirty-eight pounds – is regarded by aficionados as the bee's knees. The club has an exceedingly good cellar and kitchen at reasonable prices, and chaps can go there to read, socialize and generally mix with other exceptionally talented and able chaps. It has also got the best toilets I've ever seen, where you can have a pee secure in the knowledge that there's a big splashback guard to stop you wetting your gaiters should you happen to be a bishop.

A Bateman orchid

There is a superb reading room about a mile long, lined with books, long desks and suites of leather chairs and sofas clustered around multiple fireplaces. Here one can lounge over coffee, high tea or G&T depending on the hour. Most glorious of all is the fact that once you are inside no non-member can directly contact you except by interfacing with doormen of such discretion as to make Kosygin look like a loudmouth. There are fine rooms that can be hired for entertaining, and bedrooms to sleep in – on your own. In fact, it is a wonderful home-from-home unless you happen to be a woman, in which case you are consigned to the basement restaurant during normal hours. There's a special dispensation that allows you in at some other time, but I can't remember when. There are a number of other club rules. You mustn't do business there, and just in case you're tempted you must leave your briefcase in reception. Anything you hear inside this oasis is governed by a variation of the Chatham House Rule: not only is what you have heard in confidence, but you must not profit from the knowledge.

It's a great bolt-hole, not to mention alibi. Jonathan loved all the hobnobbing, the hail-fellow-well-met bonhomie, the thrill of mixing with the insiders who really run the country, don't you know. Early on he generously suggested that I might like to consider being put forward for membership, but after a rather unfortunate and loud misunderstanding with a doorman during which I let forth a stream of language apparently more suited to a barrow-boy, it was never mentioned again.

I may poke gentle fun at such a place, but it would be hypocritical of me to deny that it is the most wonderful resource for its members. Indeed it has an esteemed tradition of encouraging academic excellence in many departments. It also has two opposite effects according to your point of view: it either makes you humble in the knowledge that some of the brightest and best men in the country can be counted among its members, or it makes you pompous in the assumption that you are one of them.

Jonathan classified people according to a system of his own, ranging from 'a bit of a lance-corporal' at one end, used to denote someone with pretensions above his station, to 'the Great and the Good' at the other. Sub-categories of the Great and the Good included 'serious grown-ups', 'players', 'big hitters' and so on. We would solemnly decide 'who should bat for us', having first established that we were 'singing from the same hymn sheet'; while being mindful that 'the good is the enemy of the great', 'we should walk through the fire together', though always bearing in mind that 'gentlemen don't indulge in fine accounting'.

I digress. Jonathan immediately swung into action, writing to people he thought might be helpful in creating a constituency of support for the project. Beginning in Cornwall, he then spread his net wider to encompass some of his London connections. He also cranked up the socializing, with a series of lunches held in his offices in Bude. Not only do they enjoy an incredible view, but they also happen to be next door to a rather good restaurant that would serve the food along adjoining balconies. Jonathan and his wife Vicky were excellent hosts; Jonathan was particularly skilled at managing the conversation so that everyone felt they had something to contribute. I can no longer remember who all the guests were, but they ranged from MPs, councillors and civil servants from various important local funding agencies to a smattering of very interesting individuals who had come to live in the area but who had a wide range of interests or influence outside it. One who particularly comes to mind is Henry Boettinger, an incredibly erudite American émigré who had retired to Cornwall with his wife, and had pulled off the impressive feat of becoming Mastermind of Masterminds on television.

In the rather more formal atmosphere of London there is an art to persuading those you wish to influence to come to your 'do'. The guest lists at Jonathan's club dinners were always illustrious; his table placings, and the manner in which conversation was elegantly steered towards the areas in which we were interested, were masterful. There is no doubt in my mind that what at first glance may have looked like elitist junketing was hugely influential in creating a climate of support that would serve us well later.

In hindsight, what is so remarkable was how much we didn't know or understand. We knew that we had the bones of a good idea. We had no idea of cost, no operational business plan, no money and no site. Other than that everything was perfect. Heligan's success fuelled our optimism, and we were completely unfazed by the depth of our ignorance. Had we known what was coming we would probably have retired to a monastery. The fact that the process was one of slow revelation meant that we were able to absorb the pain as we went along.

While we would hit on the Goonbarrow crusty wart by mid-1995, the land we initially identified was next to Roche Rock and belonged to Goonvean. Even though it wasn't ideal we stuck to it in the absence of anything else. Then we had to look around and consider where to go for funding. We were well aware that we couldn't go to the big agencies immediately; our plan was so rudimentary that we would have been laughed out of the door. We needed to do a feasibility study.

During the restoration of Heligan I had come to know most of the councillors and officers in my local borough of Restormel. At the start the relationship had been tricky, because there was a rumour doing the rounds, based on my music business background, that I had become involved in order to develop a site for festivals. This was soon followed by ever-more-fanciful rumours about wildlife parks, and led to protests about the dangers of escaped crocodiles in the sewers of Mevagissey. We were refused planning permission the first time after a very fractious public meeting at St Ewe village hall, where all the protestors had gathered to put the councillors under enormous pressure to believe the rumours. If we got 40,000 rowdy visitors there would be gridlock, but, of course, explained one gentleman, waving his walking stick around in a froth of indignation, this was all a front. We wouldn't attract the visitors, which would enable us to claim the place was uneconomic and therefore apply for change of use and turn it into a festival site. Oh, and what about the vermin that would undoubtedly invade the Big House as a result of the restoration? We were trounced, and only a dogged rearguard action which involved knocking on every single door in the parish and explaining what we were up to enabled us to turn things round next time.

It was during this period that I came to know George Down, my local Gorran parish councillor, and also the chairman of the Borough Planning Committee. The proprietor of a milk delivery company, he had a deep sense of civic responsibility. To some he could appear pompous, with his personalized number plate and membership of a startling array of committees at local and county level. He was a stickler for protocol, a source of much amusement for those with a less reverential attitude to title; he insisted on being called Mr Chairman and addressed fellow councillors with the gravitas of a music-hall master of ceremonies. He had a gift for making enemies, but in truth he often rubbed people up the wrong way simply because of his impatience to get things done. He had a reputation for being a great champion of projects which sought his advice in advance, and a stern critic of those which attempted to plough their own furrow without recourse to it; like many before and after him he enjoyed the vanity of patronage, of people showing respect, for there had to be some perks in return for the long hours of thankless duty which are the lot of a councillor. He may have been prickly, but to his eternal credit it was he who was to steer the biggest construction project in Cornwall's history – one which fell completely outside the County Structure Plan, to boot – through the planning process with great skill, propriety and not a little humour.

We learned three things from the Heligan experience. The first was not to let rumours get out of hand because we thought they were so fanciful that no one could possibly believe them. The second was to trust in the democratic process and not simply pay lip-service to it. This is hard work, requiring endless talking and number-less meetings, but there is no short cut to creating a constituency of support.

Cornwall is a very strange place. Outsiders often think it small-minded and negative about anything new. While this is partly true, it misses the point that Cornish culture is democratic; there is a massive resistance to being bounced into putting up with *faits accomplis*, and to deals done in smoke-filled rooms. Respect is the key. Show it by taking the proper amount of time to give communities a sense of ownership and understanding of what is being proposed, and it will be repaid. A single public meeting where people are told what you are planning to do is like showing a red rag to a bull.

The third was the crucial importance of courtesy. We agreed that under no circumstances would we lose our tempers and be rude, no matter what the provocation. The result was that two years after planning permission had been granted, with 100,000 visitors a year already coming down our narrow lanes with no sign of gridlock and the local village booming, one by one the former protesters took the opportunity of generously making their peace with us.

Once the dust had settled and the national and international press started to write good things about Heligan and the local area, support grew and we would often host visiting dignitaries on behalf of the borough. A real sense of partnership was developing. David Brown, the borough chief executive at the time, was very supportive, as were the councillors at Planning and Economic Development. The officer in charge of Economic Development, Angie Rowe, must be the least likely local government officer around. Glamorous, with a wicked sense of humour and the weary-lidded worldliness of a foreign correspondent, she walked the corridors of Restormel ignoring pleas to build yet more one-man-and-his-dog industrial units and trying to create a climate for big thinking – as she saw it, the only way out of the terminal decline into which the area was heading. She had an ambitious vision, and more importantly she had the nerve to put her job on the line in its pursuit. At the time she was under great pressure, because the councillors were anxious to see more money spent on attracting small-scale local inward investment; they felt that she was wasting her time dreaming of attracting large-scale regeneration programmes. She stuck to her guns, however, and produced a superb piece of work to try to attract the putative University of Cornwall to Newquay. They didn't come, despite the fact – or perhaps because of it – that students would have loved the surfing and the nightlife. Instead they plumped for the middle of nowhere west of Penzance and the university, at least in its first incarnation, was stillborn. But Angie had put down a marker.

When we spoke to her about the project she immediately saw the synergy between leisure, gardens and education, and without hesitation agreed to put her wholehearted support behind us. She was, and remains to this day, a tireless champion. It was she who suggested that we make an application to the Economic Development Committee to raise some seedcorn funding to help with the feasibility study. A date was set and the late Cedric Burdon, its chairman, agreed to promote our cause. I'll never forget the evening of our presentation, held in the council chamber in St Austell. Jonathan and I waited in an ante-room, discussing the merits of the pasties on offer with the councillors, and then were called in to make our presentation. We were nervous but passionate; our case was little more than a plea to 'Trust us, we're doctors', so to speak. Heligan had given them confidence that madness wasn't necessarily bad for the health, but we had no right to expect their support. When it came it was very moving. They were prepared to take a punt and offer us £25,000 towards the study. Not a lot of money to a metropolis, but a small fortune in Cornwall.

I cannot say it often enough: without their support the project would not have happened. If your local community won't back you, everyone else has an exit. This single act of faith was the catalyst that persuaded all the other development agencies in the region to put their hands in their pockets. More than that, though, it seemed to create an almost palpable feeling of destiny in many people, a sense that if ever there was a time to take a risk, this was it. With each succeeding gesture of support, that conviction was reinforced. Sums of between £5,000 and £15,000 went into our fund with no strings attached save to give the project its best chance of success. Behind all the acronyms charged with the regeneration of the South West were flesh-and-blood people who were angry at the region's disadvantage and lack of political muscle. More to the point, they had come to see the project as a symbol, something to show the rest of the world that we weren't hicks from the sticks with straw between our teeth waiting for crumbs to fall from the high table.

Jonathan and I made dozens of presentations throughout 1995, lunching till we dropped and drinking for Britain, creating a background of support. We had a site, now we needed a design. (It had struck us that while some can imagine in three dimensions, others need a drawing to create a reality.) In an effort to catch the atmosphere and scale of our ambitions, Jonathan mobilized his practice to visualize what the great conservatories might look like. In early 1995 they came up with a very striking image that we immediately entitled 'the Cobra Heads', a science-fiction confection that conveyed perfectly the radical change we intended to make from traditional conservatories. Although the design was to go no further, its blend of sleek lines and slightly threatening sensuality succeeded in capturing the imagination. For the moment this would satisfy curiosity, but it wouldn't be long before hard questions would be asked about cost and feasibility.

During the gestation period we came to realize that when the government said they had drawn a line under garden festivals, they meant it. This was partly down to the massive organizational effort involved, and partly because there were clear signs emerging that they were not the quick fix everyone had hoped they would be. All that work for a one-year exhibition was increasingly being seen as a waste of effort and resources, and frustrated local communities were beginning to wonder whether the money might not have been better spent on something permanent in the infrastructure. In hindsight it is a pity that government did not take this on board when they tried it again with the Millennium Dome. The writing was already on the wall if only they had looked.

In February 1994 Peter Brooke, the heritage minister, launched the Millennium Fund. This formed part of the public-benefit provision under which the lottery had been set up. The Act of Parliament stipulated that a portion of all the revenue generated by the lottery should be divided between sport, charities, heritage, the arts and the Millennium Fund. The parameters of the fund were not, and still are not, entirely clear to everyone; but the idea was that it should encourage individual, local, regional and national projects to mark the Millennium that would otherwise never have been funded. As Peter Brooke said at its launch, it was meant as a challenge to make Britons 'lift their eyes to the hills' – to make a statement about where the nation was heading at this pivotal moment. It was hoped that each of the five sectors would have a total of around £1.5 billion to spend.

The Millennium Commission was charged with choosing twelve Landmark Projects with a maximum MC contribution of £50 million per project or 50 per cent of total costs, whichever was the lower. This appeared generous, but the stipulation that each project had to find half its costs from elsewhere would have serious consequences, as a feverish competition to find the matched funding would leave managements concentrating solely on fund-raising rather than developing their plans. It is no wonder that so many were to get into difficulties. The idea was sold on the basis that management teams that could raise the funds would have proved themselves worthy of the title. In truth many cut back on their original ambitions as they realized that they couldn't compete. My personal view is that government was completely in thrall to business, and persuaded itself that achieving sponsorship was the ultimate acid test of merit; it is as though an exhibition could only be called art if a Big Six accountancy practice put its name to it. Quite how we have managed to create a culture that links the imprimatur of men in suits to quality is probably the subject of another book.

It was also stipulated that these funds should not be used to replace funds that rightfully should have been provided by government in the normal course of exercising its responsibilities. It was not government money. This was to become the subject of constant misunderstanding over the years, as communities raged at what they saw as misconceived glamour projects or, worse, follies built in areas with poor provision of essential services. It is hard to argue with someone who feels that the money could have been better used in constructing another hospital, although it is often forgotten that hospitals come with attendant running costs and all the lottery projects were supposed to become self-financing so as not to put a burden on succeeding generations. This was an unrealistic expectation, but those were the rules.

Jonathan and I decided that the Millennium Fund was an ideal target. What could be more millennial than a project dedicated to the portrayal of human dependence on plants? We wrote off, received the forms and studied what we had to do. A project outline was required, together with a programme, a costing and an operational business plan. The first stage was to log an application that could then be worked up. For the time being we decided to call the project the Millennium Project Cornwall, or something like that – we chopped and changed a little as we went. I can't remember how it happened, but the local press caught hold of the idea and interviewed us under the headline 'Kew West' with a photo of Jonathan and me atop the hermitage at Roche Rock.

Just before the first dinner at his club Jonathan introduced me to a friend of his, Ronnie Murning, one of the principals of a London architectural practice of which Jonathan himself was a sleeping partner. They had been friends for many years, and Jonathan felt that Ronnie's particular skills would be appropriate to our needs.

I think the restaurant was Le Pont de la Tour alongside Tower Bridge. All cool lines and sharp clothes. Ronnie struck a chord immediately, with his battered, lived-in face and – with apologies to Raymond Chandler – 'a suit that fitted him like a racehorse fits the stalls'. Everything about him was broad: his shoulders, his infectious naughty-boy smile and his Glaswegian accent. You needed an interpreter. If Jonathan's laugh was explosive, Ronnie's was a screaming car-crash of a laugh, continuous so that it was impossible to understand a word he said; one grinned along so as not to be rude. He was widely interested in the arts and very well read, aggressive and affectionate in turn, fiercely cynical yet strangely other-worldly, a slightly bashful ladies' man who lived alone with his budgies Celtic and Rangers, his smart suits and his impossibly expensive stereo. He had worked with Sir Terence Conran, a character as explosive as himself, and he had also done a lot of design work for the Body Shop. He seemed to have fallen in and out with them all, while maintaining an admirable independence. Ronnie was a connoisseur of gossip, which he would exchange with unabashed relish, although as

'Ronnie's was a screaming car-crash of a laugh'

the years unfolded I realized it was not a harmless mischief, but the working of a tongue so sharp it's a wonder his lips weren't bleeding. Infuriatingly brilliant and committed, uncompromising, opinionated, arrogant, tough and proud as he was, I spent years trying to decide whether to hug him or strangle him. Fortunately for the project I could never quite make up my mind.

Anyway, Jonathan had primed Ronnie and we all agreed that it would be great if he joined the team. Jonathan would work with Ronnie and propose a suitable design team for the project. Ronnie was to work for nothing for the next year and so, unknown to them, were the selected design team. Jonathan came back with two international architects for consideration: Nicholas Grimshaw and Partners, who had recently completed the Waterloo International Rail Terminal, and Renzo Piano, the Italian who had just completed the Osaka Airport project. Both were extremely well known for their work with transparent materials, and both had the sort of reputations that would make sophisticated audiences take notice of us. Before we had a chance to meet either of them we began to realize that it might go down better if we were to work with British architects. Jonathan would make the introductions to Grimshaw's.

During the course of developing the scheme for the Millennium Commission, it became apparent that problems with some of the first projects they were considering were toughening their stance on applications almost by the day. The worst problem, and one that was to create enormous bad feeling, was that the MC would advance no funds to cover setting-up costs. This placed a huge burden of risk on the shoulders of any organization; in the event that an application was unsuccessful, all the investment would have to be written off. Our project was, I believe, the only one that was promoted by individuals and not the public sector, and the consequence of failure would, after a while, become unthinkable. There was no money available save our own and the funds granted us by our local supporters. The funds would have to be found by rolling up our time and that of our future collaborators as an accepted risk to be redeemed at a later date against a successful outcome.

At some point we realized that the MC would also only accept an application in the name of a Trust rather than individuals. At the risk of sounding churlish, this constraint would normally have made private individuals run for cover and leave the field open for public-sector projects only – hardly a recipe for generating eye-lifting ideas. We didn't have a Trust. One of my good friends, Toby Stroh, was not only my lawyer, but also a Trustee of the Heligan Educational Trust. Throughout his life he had taken holidays in Cornwall at a house just over the hill from where I live. His legal firm had acted for me since the start of my music career, so when the Heligan project had started I had asked them whether they would work at risk until we were certain that it would go ahead. They had and it did.

I called Toby and asked him whether he would act for the Millennium Project Cornwall in the same way. Without hesitation he agreed, provided that if sums were made available to us we would try to pass some on. Things moved at a snail's pace, though this was not the fault of Toby or his colleague Richard Monkcom. We applied in early 1995, but the Charity Commission's offices in London were found to contain large amounts of asbestos, and they were forced to move out. This gave a ready-made excuse for huge time lapses in setting up a charity, and it would take us more than a year before we existed in more than ambition.

Trusts need Trustees. We established fairly wide environmental and educational aims and objectives for the Trust, and Jonathan cast around his connections for Trustees of weight who would send the right signals to the MC. We jointly knew Sir Richard Carew Pole, scion of an ancient Cornish family, who lived at Antony House at Torpoint. A very tall man with the sort of clear eyes you can't lie to and a complete disregard for sartorial elegance, except under duress – there were always ink stains on his jacket linings – he had a wonderful instinct for the right thing to do, an easy if slightly diffident charm and a total commitment to the well-being of his beloved Cornwall. He was known for his impatience with politics if it was at the expense of action. In *Who's Who* he lists his hobby as daydreaming. It would be a mistake to assume he had much time for his hobby. Richard was already a Trustee of the Tate and had been instrumental in creating the Tate of the West at St Ives, which had so transformed the town. He was also a commissioner at the Countryside Commission and of the Heritage Memorial Fund, in which capacity our paths had crossed. If there is anyone who has done more to raise the profile of his county than Richard I have yet to meet him. Jonathan knew him through his work for the Surf Lifesavers.

Jonathan then approached Sir Alan Donald, who had been the British ambassador to China among many other distinctions, and to whom he was related by marriage. Alan was a brilliant choice. A man of great integrity, he had a wonderful balance of humour and practical common sense, and it was easy to understand why Lord Carrington had so often asked him to be present at tricky international gatherings when he was Foreign Secretary. Many was the time in those early years when Alan would relax a strained meeting with a wry observation.

Lastly, Jonathan approached Sir Alcon Copisarow, whom he knew from his club. He had, among many other corporate achievements, been the first non-American to head McKinseys, probably the best-known management consultants in the world. He was a man who appeared to see the world as a multi-layered, complex game, for whom intricate schemes, tactics and strategies were second nature, and who carried an air of slightly pained disbelief that the rest of us hadn't spotted this. Alcon told me a story one day, in answer to my question about why management consultants get paid so much. He had been engaged to engineer the merger of two American defence giants and had secured the support of all parties save that of the two chief executives, both of whom had aspirations to lead the new merged company. He invited them to dinner on consecutive nights. To the first he said, you of course are the right man for the top job; if the companies merge there will be a honeymoon period on the stock exchange, but after a while the complexities of the merger will take their toll. I wouldn't want you to go out on a low point after such a distinguished career. Why don't you become the boss for the first eighteen months to nurse the deal through, but announce at the outset your intention to hand over to your successor after that period? If I could secure the agreement of your competitor, would you accept this? Flattered, he agreed. The following night he took the second man to dinner and said, you of course are the right man for the top job, but you have a distinguished career behind you and I feel that there will be teething troubles and the first eighteen months will be difficult; far better that you take over later and come to be seen as the knight in shining armour who consolidated the company's position. Flattered, the rival concurred. Problem solved. I have no idea what actually happened, but when Alcon, obviously forgetting he'd told me this story, tried the strategy on me I couldn't resist a smile.

Sir Alcon would be elected chairman of the putative Trust, and over the next few months, again through Jonathan, two further Trustees would come on board, both club connections. The first was Ian Hay Davison, one of the City's leading businessmen, a no-nonsense action man who, in the little time he served on the Trust, made a valuable contribution to its dynamics. We were unfortunate to lose him when he accepted the chairmanship of Sadler's Wells, but he maintained warm links with our project and allowed us the continued use of his London office for Trust meetings. The second was Sir Ralph Riley, one of the country's leading agronomists and the former boss of Rothamstead Agricultural Research Station. He lived in Cambridge, but his involvement with the Food and Agriculture Organisation (FAO) and the Rockefeller Foundation meant that he was more difficult to get hold of than the Pope. He had an intuitive understanding of the project's potential and introduced us to many of the organizations with whom he was involved. He also made us consider issues that up until that time had been peripheral to the main thrust of the project's ambitions: poverty, population growth and food scarcity. He was closely involved with the Rockefeller Foundation's 20/20 Vision project, which focused on the need to improve yields and distribution, while protecting diversity, in order to cater for an expected global population of around eight billion people by the year 2020. It was Ralph who, by inviting me to the Rank Prize Fund's Conference on Food Security in Bournemouth in October 1997, was to shape much of my future thinking on the effective role our project could play in the debate. Sadly Ralph was to die before Eden was completed. We owe him a great deal.

Nicholas Grimshaw contemplates working on the eighth wonder of the world for nothing

Even before all this, just in time to give our submission a healthy dose of credibility, Nicholas Grimshaw's team confirmed that they were up for the idea of working on the eighth wonder of the world for nothing, and the rest of the design team who had worked on Waterloo International joined in: Davis Langdon and Everest (quantity surveyors), Ove Arup and Partners (environmental engineers) and Anthony Hunt Associates (engineers). Ronnie Murning would coordinate the work on behalf of the project. This was as impressive a list as you could hope for. This would surely give the MC confidence: we *must* be in with a chance!

Jonathan and Vicky came down to Heligan, where we spent an entire afternoon photocopying, collating and packaging up bid documents. Knowing that the MC could award a maximum of £50 million, we were building our proposal based on a cost of just over £150 million for a range of glasshouses to be built on the flat land next to Goonbarrow – remember that Bodelva still lay in the future. We were making the same mistake as all the other projects, seeking a maximum contribution from the MC while not being sure where the matched funding would come from. So, on 28 April 1995, we sent out our message of hope: an outline of the

project and its ambitions, details of our newly acquired professional team, Jonathan's Cobra-Head designs, a letter from the lawyers confirming our application to set up a Trust, a bound folio of letters of support from the West Country which Jonathan had secured, a beautifully written preface called 'The Springs of Inspiration' from Jonathan's friend Henry Boettinger the Mastermind, and a costing you could drive a horse and cart through. (In fairness to ourselves it is impossible to cost something innovative with any accuracy until you have proper drawings, and those would be a long way down the line. We were hoping for support in principle, which would in turn, we hoped, encourage further money from various sources that would enable us to do the necessary work to establish accurate design and cost.) The documents winged their way to London to lie on a table awaiting decision day in the late summer of 1995. We couldn't afford to wait around, so made plans to meet up with the design team as soon as possible to get the real work under way.

In a few short weeks we were to realize quite how far off the pace we were in terms of having a real project capable of delivery. The next few months saw us making giant strides away from fairyland; we were growing in confidence with every passing week. Jonathan and I were coming back from London after a meeting with the design team when we received a phone call on the train. Our bid had been turned down. The MC had three categories: A, which meant you were being considered; B, which meant you were being rejected for now, but encouraged to resubmit; and C, which meant you were out, dead, history, either for not being distinctive enough or for being implausible. We were category C. We both felt sick and numb. The press knew a decision was imminent. How could we face them after so much work? What were we going to say to the design team, whom we'd convinced that we'd be successful? As we drove out of Exeter Station at the start of a long haul through the dark back to St Austell, I called Jonathan on the mobile. Pull over at the next petrol station, I said.

We talked, our breath fogging in the cold night air. It's not over, Jonathan, I said; we're going to bluff it out. We're going to tell everyone that we have caught their imagination and have been asked to work it up some more. And what's more, we're not going to take no for an answer. Jonathan looked at me in disbelief and we returned to our cars. The following day we gave everyone the good news and it was back to work as usual. No one ever questioned us. I would like to take this opportunity to apologize for my bad behaviour.

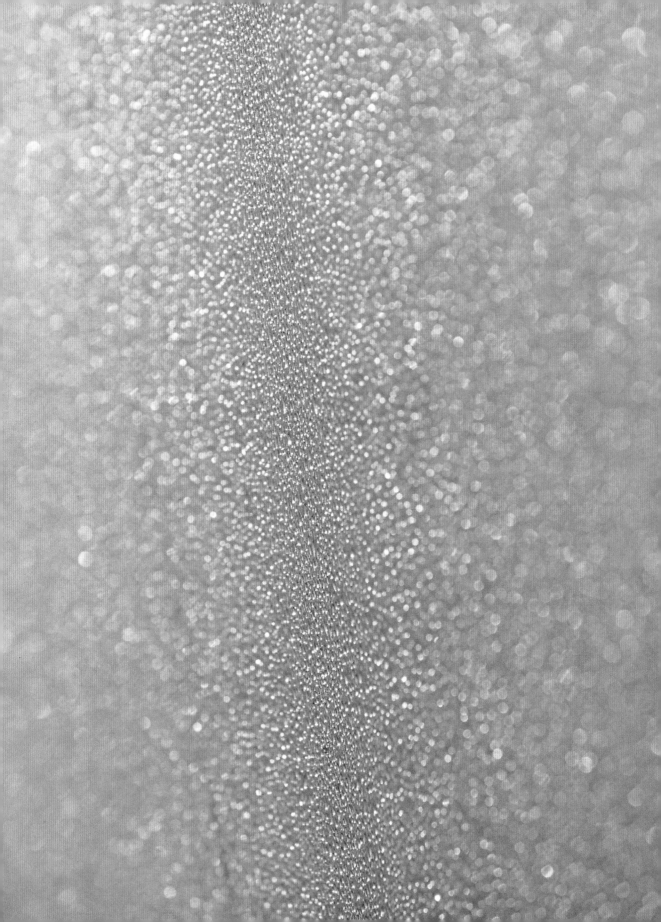

chapter 5

take your partners, please

So, it was game on and every game needs a name.
Thinking up names is a pain. They all sound
wrong until resistance is worn down through
constant use – look at the Beatles. The Millennium
Project Cornwall doesn't quicken the pulse, does it?
In early 1995 Jonathan, Ronnie and I were trying
out names. We knew the Millennium Project
Cornwall was a stinker. The Hanging Gardens of
Cornwall, Paradise Gardens, the Green Cathedrals
and the Paradise Conservatories were among
dozens thrown into the ring to a deafening silence.
I like the word Project. It's got dynamism,
direction and a sense of evolution about it.

TS, Paul Travers: the rock 'n' roll years

In my music-business days, I had hits with the Midnight Blue Project with Louise Tucker. When I began at Heligan we called it the Heligan Manor Gardens Project until I fell in love with the romantic resonance of the Lost Gardens of Heligan a year into the restoration. So, Project it would be. We came up with the name Eden somewhat tentatively because of the religious connotations, but it made sense as a symbol of Mankind in harmony with bounteous Nature. I also enjoyed the conceit that we had been thrown out of Paradise for eating from the Tree of Knowledge; perhaps only now, through the gathering of greater knowledge, could we return. Philip and Peter liked it; Jonathan was worried in case the word might get a negative response in other cultures and would research it. I just kept using it, and after a while it felt natural.

In August 1995 I was joined on the project by one of my very best friends, Paul Travers. Paul and I had known each other since as a sixteen-year-old he had become a sound engineer at the studio where I worked. He would eventually work with me full time until he went on to bigger things. Paul is a golden boy. Whatever he does it's got style. No style – no Paul. He's excitable, funny, gentle and generous with not an enemy in the world, and, like me, lives totally on his instincts.

When I moved to Cornwall in 1987 he and his wife Claire were frequent visitors. Paul would sometimes phone from London and say, what are you doing? Fancy a pint? And he'd just pile down the motorway to arrive before closing time at the Llawnroc pub in Gorran Haven, then we'd go back to the house, talk and play extremely bad snooker into the early hours. Then he'd be off again. As Eden started to take shape Paul hankered to get involved. One day I told him he'd have to jump now, because later I might find it difficult to slot him in without it looking nepotistic.

He said nothing, but the following day he called me and told me that he and Claire had been talking and that they were prepared to take the punt and move down with their young son Oscar. He would need survival earnings but was quite prepared to cut his salary by two-thirds. We offered him a derisory amount to work for Eden, funded by Heligan. Paul was going to play a big part in shaping our future, carving out a role for himself through his willingness to try anything and his easy charm with journalists.

1995 and '96 are best described as the creation soup period of the project: endless events, visits, talks, presentations and two hundred-odd meetings in

Eden's evolution. The period saw us go through a rite of passage, from amateur enthusiasm to the harsh realities of creating the largest construction project in Cornwall's history. If rejection mortified us, it also pushed us into realizing the sheer volume of work expected from us to turn the project round.

Our first meetings with the professional team were in the late spring of 1995. Ronnie and Jonathan were obviously familiar with the roles and titles of a professional design team, and the jargon of contract and programme. I, on the other hand, was an innocent abroad, needing to have everything explained to me.

It works like this. The architects conceptualize a scheme to the point where the imagination has been captured and the client says, I like it. The engineer points out whether the concept can be built and the best technical way of doing so, tempered of course by considerations of cost. The quantity surveyor prices the concept to find out whether it is even vaguely affordable. The project manager lists all the processes that need to take place to construct the concept and sets out the order of events; this is called the programme, and gives a view on the likely timescale to take the building to completion. There are environmental engineers whose speciality is the creation of the living conditions – the heating, lights, mechanical operations, airflows and so on. They have sub-departments charged with making environmental impact assessments, studying the impact of the project on the general surroundings and local communities, and traffic boffins who find out what effect your visitors will have on infrastructure. Finally there are landscape architects. Their job is to create the hard and soft landscape designs, the land shape and plantings if you like, which set the context for the buildings. The Eden Project is unusual in that the landscape and its treatment were themselves integral to the project's mission, giving the role an importance far beyond what is normally expected.

I use the word 'concept' deliberately. The problem with innovation is that if something has never been done before there isn't a precedent for cost. If you want to build a domestic house, prison, hospital or shipyard there are industry benchmarks to give you a rough-and-ready costing acceptable to a third party. For us this would be impossible. More to the point, architects do drawings in stages called RIBA Stage A, B, C, D and so on. It is only at Stage D that a design is priceable with any accuracy, but by this time you are already well past halfway in the design process, which on a job as large as this represents a massive investment of time and money by the professionals – several million pounds, in fact. To invest this amount with no certainty of a go-ahead from the Millennium Commission would have been madness. Not to get somewhere close would have guaranteed failure. The words rock and hard place come to mind.

The Jonathan Ball Practice design, the 'Cobra Heads', had been for a flat plain. The first sketches our design team came up with were for the Goonbarrow crusty wart, and featured a netted structure, that is to say steel cables under tension which hold up the roof from pylons stretching high above it – rather like the eventual design of the Millennium Dome, oddly enough. Much of this work was done by Anthony Hunt of the engineering practice that bears his name. The team had come down mob-handed to see the site; they had been startled by how far away Cornwall was from London, and positively alarmed at the violence of the Clay-Country landscape after the bucolic beauty of Devon. They were soon won over by the toys for boys (and girls) working away in the pit – it was almost impossible to keep their attention on the job in hand. Giant Tonka trucks reach the little boy inside every man.

Anthony Hunt,
modern engineer

Anthony was the antithesis of what I expected a modern engineer to be. Especially in that alien landscape, he was strangely reminiscent of Doctor Who, brainy, eccentric, slightly foppish and dreamily distant, with an unnerving ability to bring himself back into sharp focus when required. He is regarded by his peers as one of the finest engineers of his generation, and has gathered around him a team of supremely able colleagues; together they have worked on some of the most challenging and impressive modern buildings.

He would often joke at the expense of the architects – with whom he enjoyed very cordial relations – that Brunel didn't see the need for architects and neither did he. Underneath lay the gentle barb that today's architect is seen as the sex symbol and creator of great works, when perhaps too little credit is given to the engineers, whose attention to detail and elegant problem-solving is often misattributed. What impressed me was that he was as prepared as anybody to get his hands dirty. In fact I think that was when he was at his happiest – I've never seen anyone look more ill at ease in meetings.

Nicholas Grimshaw and Partners were the architects. Their challenge was unequivocal: to create the first world-class conservatories in history that were good for plants and not a monument to the vanity of architects. Although Nick would get involved from time to time and was very supportive, their team was led by Andrew Whalley, one of the partners, and David Kirkland. Andrew was bearded, soft-edged and friendly, often sporting an expression of mild surprise; David, lean, chiselled, bookish, intense and inspired by the whole concept of Eden. David was later to contract a serious illness that required him to take things easy, but he, more than anyone, was to set the tone for the project design and the cooperative spirit that infused it.

Quantity surveyors, or QSs as they are referred to in the trade, revel in the reputation of being the hard bastards who have to mop up after everyone else, administering heavy doses of realism to the dreamy creatives. The top guys earn more than almost anyone else in the construction business. The reason is that while everyone else usually has to work at risk, if you want your project to pass muster with a bank you need a QS's sign-off as to its affordability. Ours were Davis Langdon and Everest, probably the biggest and best company of their kind in the world. Their team leader was Richard Baldwin, known affectionately to others as Bunter for what were then obvious reasons, although he married halfway through the project and became half the man he was. I disliked him instantly because of his nonchalant arrogance as he lectured us in a been there, done that manner. The annoying thing was, he had. Over the years I came to like and respect him; under the veneer, he was as prepared as anyone to go the extra mile to make the project happen. In hindsight I can also see that we would have done well to listen to some of his early advice instead of ignoring it.

It was going to be Davis Langdon's judgement call on costs that would determine whether we could create a viable project. I was struck by the integrity of the operation. Why couldn't they put a finger in the air and pronounce the price we needed to get approval? It was explained to me, on the dozens of occasions when I tried to

The architects: David Kirkland *(l)* and Andrew Whalley

twist their arms, that reputation was everything. Their role was to serve both the client (us) and the funders; to do the job, they needed to be trusted by both.

The project managers were Davis Langdon Management, close relations of the above but offering a different service. Their leader was Derek Johnson, an extremely able man with a droopy moustache that made him seem constantly miserable. He wasn't of course, and luckily for Eden he too was passionate about the project. Derek's team had to put in a huge amount of work before the project could be regarded as credible, much of which would be the sort of administrative paperwork that would give third parties confidence in us. Once in, DLM were the only ones who had no exit strategy other than to put the whole project at risk by stopping work. In the early days I persisted in seeing this role as horribly bureaucratic: bring on the men of action, I would say. What an idiot I was. Once you get serious, to drive the process forward you need people to formalize the meetings, ascribing responsibilities and actions to the parties present, chasing the laggardly for the promises they made, praising those who have met their agreed targets, and so on.

A good project manager will always appear like a Gradgrind, if only because his or her job is to keep everyone on their toes; highlighting achievement is important, but even more important is concentrating on present failings and anticipated hurdles. It is the PM who liaises with constructors and keeps the job to programme, or if it is slipping tells the client why. In short, the project management team form the logistical and administrative hub of the client's operation. If, like we were, you are operating in partnership with many others, their job is crucial in keeping everyone truthfully informed. Fact: you cannot be successful with poor administration, because once you lose control of the order of events the remainder of the team cannot do their job. Alexander the Great needed a good project manager.

The environmental engineers were Ove Arup and Partners, again industry leaders in their field. Their team leader would be Alistair Guthrie, a blond boffin. Nobody ever told him there were only twenty-four hours in a day; he was always harassed, coming and going like a revolving door. Luckily he had a sense of humour. Arup's job was to design the basic services like heating, climate control and lighting systems throughout the project. This would be a great challenge because, if they failed, our plant collections would die and so would they. No pressure there, then.

The landscape architects, who joined the project a little after the original crew, were Land Use Consultants. Their team leader was Dominic Cole, a friend from the earliest days at Heligan, where he had supervised the restoration plan. He is one of the country's foremost experts in historic landscapes, but has long been an admirer of the bold styles advanced by modernist designers such as the Brazilian Roberto

Dominic Cole,
three-dimensional
thinker

Burle Marx, whose impressionistic plantings and hard landscapes include such bravura projects as the Copacabana in Rio. The challenge was to create three-dimensional soft and solid geometry that worked both at an intimate and at an epic level. Not many landscapes have to work successfully from above, below and on the flat. The attraction of Dominic's work for me was that I felt we both wanted to create a landscape that gave the impression of a civilization newly discovered. This would need to be informed by a historical perspective liberated of cultural references, demanding flair, a love of colour and the confidence to paint a big picture that worked as a whole.

As the project progressed Dom would often come and stay, and over a convivial dinner and several bottles of wine would act as an interpreter for the work of the rest of the design team. This was sometimes the source of slight resentment in others, who feared that my ear would be bent to their disadvantage. In truth he kept me sane, encouraging me to push for quality whatever the odds, and convincing me, probably wrongly, that I understood what was going on. The others had nothing to fear: with few exceptions, he had the utmost respect for the very special team we had drawn together.

Creativity is not restricted to those who can hold a tune or use a pencil. The biggest shock to the system was our brutal introduction to project finance from Mark Bostock of Arup Economic, the project development arm of Ove Arup Engineers. I can't remember the exact date we met him, but it was like meeting a buffalo on a narrow street. Jonathan and I went to see him at the invitation of Alistair to seek assistance with the development of a business plan. Business plans are normally fantasies created by optimists (you) for the scrutiny of pessimists (banks). It says what you're going to spend, on what and why, and how you are going to pay for it through what you bring in over however long a period you need to do it. In other words, are you flush or going bust? Can you pay your bills, or are you doing the washing up? The only business plans that are accurate are those written in hindsight.

I had drawn up dozens of these for my businesses through the years, but nothing had prepared me for the rigour that Mark insisted on. He appeared to me to be horribly pessimistic, not to say aggressive, in his demand that in the big world assertion was not enough, justification was everything. If you say that visitors will pay £x to visit, £y for refreshments and souvenirs, where is your evidence? If you say you can rely on *x* visitors turning up, where are the comparators? How do you know you have enough staff? Why do you think you can get away with spending less on marketing than other places? Mark was to influence all of us greatly because for the first time we faced someone who was not prepared to give us the benefit of the doubt, not prepared to get excited about changing the world or building one of the great global icons.

He was in fact all of these things, but he was to say to me later that he felt as if he was watching an accident about to happen. He forced us to address all the issues and do some real work on researching what was going on elsewhere. He had to pretend that we weren't special despite his belief to the contrary. He knew that one day soon we would be up against tough bankers who would ask difficult questions. If we weren't prepared for them our dream would be over.

By early 1996 Mark had dragged me kicking and screaming into a way of thinking that was getting somewhere. Philip had done the budgets for the horticultural teams and had made some guesses at running costs extrapolated from examples elsewhere. Peter Stafford had supplied the operating costs and revenues from the Lost Gardens of Heligan as well as the analysis of seasonal visitor variation that would provide the backbone for the business plan. The visitor numbers Eden would require to establish that it was viable would depend on its costs of construction, operating and financing. In other words, the break-even point would be largely dependent on how much money we had to borrow, and hence pay back. Obviously, the more free money or grant we could secure, the less onerous the revenue projections needed to be. In those two years most of the

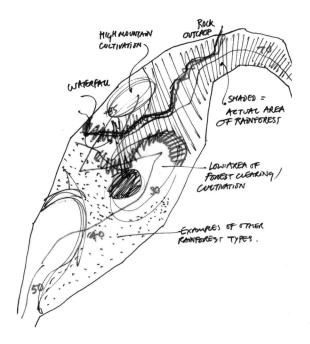

The Humid Tropics Biome: early sketches

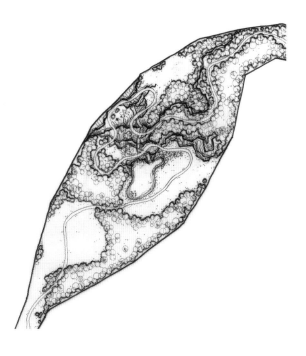

other projects we heard about were wildly overestimating their visitor projections, simply so that their business plan could 'afford' to pay back the huge sums they wanted to borrow to make their dreams live. You can't necessarily blame them, but you wouldn't want them running your business for you. We weren't going to be allowed this luxury, nor did we want it. Our ultimate aim always has been, and will remain, to protect our independence.

A sensible person would look at the most visited local attraction, Land's End with 500,000 visitors, and set that as a reasonable basis for what we hoped would become an international attraction whose must-see element might attract as many again. At the time Heligan was heading towards 300,000, and we believed that most of them could be tempted to Eden. We would run our business plan on three visitor scenarios: 500,000, 600,000 and 1 million. Our project was going to cost about £106 million and with the best estimates of the time we could count on raising only the maximum from the MC (£50 million) and – optimistically – maybe £20 million from other agencies in matched funding. This would leave a significant chunk to be found from private funding or sponsorship.

Privately I raged at these conservative constraints, because I believed that we would be creating the equivalent of a Sydney Opera House or Eiffel Tower in terms of drawing power, irrespective of location. Besides which, around nine million visitors come to the West Country annually, all in holiday mode, and they want to party. I think it was at this time that we first came across the word isochrone, meaning that you take a compass and describe a circle denoting the maximum distance that people can travel in two hours, then you add up the number of people within that circle at any given time and Bob's your uncle, that's your isochrone – in simple terms, your potential audience. Leisure experts swear by it and as a result bankers believe it too. I maintained that a must-see would break the rules; I would travel a long way to see something special, and have often done so.

But it's pointless arguing with experts who provide funders with the evidence that enables them to complete 'due diligence'. This is a technical term meaning simply that the assumptions have been checked against industry norms, and if you pass muster the banker can't be fired if he or she backs you. Just to be on the safe side, though, they will take an extra 20 per cent off your assumptions, no matter what your figures say, because everybody lies. If the project still stacks up they will lend you the money. By this time your project is so ordinary you might as well do something else; who but the desperate wants to go and see the mediocre? The culture of risk aversion has two inherent flaws. First, if said funders thought about it for a moment they would agree that they would not visit something average, but would pay to see the exceptional. Therefore they are assuming that lesser mortals might feel differently; never a sound judgement. Second, the system itself encourages a culture of over-assertion. If you know in advance that a bank will automatically slash your request by 20 per cent, you will simply cook the books so that you end up with what you need. In effect it institutionalizes deception.

Things were looking pretty bad for us until we discovered that Edinburgh Castle, which had the same isochronic population as Eden, attracted around a million visitors a year. We would use this as our benchmark, even though there are dozens of decent castles in Britain and nothing like Eden. The bizarre effect of such dogma is that projects based in the industrial heartlands of Britain are able to claim huge visitor numbers based on a pencil and a compass, yet hardly anyone goes there on holiday. Anyone knows that you don't make much use of the visitor attractions in the place where you live. Why don't people trust their instincts?

Back to Mark. Some people defy all attempts at pigeon-holing, and as I got to know him I found that he wasn't nearly as fierce as he pretended. A big man with glasses, City-issue suits and a limp, the result of a nasty accident while playing squash, his City savvy had an air of almost academic superiority about it. His playful terseness implied that any disagreement with him could only be the result of woeful ignorance on your part. He would rehearse the argument once more, only this time slowly, and let you know that he really wasn't keen to have you waste his time. It worked a treat. He came to Cornwall fairly regularly in the early stages, and while complaining that he couldn't really afford the time, gave the impression that this was actually a bit of a treat. Complaining made him feel less guilty enjoying himself. His idea of a holiday was to go on canoeing trips with his wife down the Zambesi every couple of years. They had once been capsized by a hippo. I asked him whether he'd been terrified, and he replied that he knew he should have been, but what had distracted him most was the surreal sight of his toothpaste being carried away on the current.

He told me a lovely story. He had been an anti-apartheid activist in his youth. His father, a missionary, had retired to Streatham in south London. One day in the early nineties Mark had been working in Germany when his father had called, sounding anxious, asking him to return home. Naturally Mark took the next plane and arrived back in Streatham at nightfall and let himself into the house. To his astonishment his father was sitting at the kitchen table with Nelson Mandela. Apparently, shortly after Mandela's imprisonment Mark's father had pledged 10 per cent of his annual salary to a fund to look after him, and told no one he

Mark Bostock: '...he felt as if he was watching an accident waiting to happen'

had done so. Almost immediately after his release Mandela had made a private pilgrimage to thank those who had made sacrifices on his behalf. That was why he was there. Mark had known nothing of this, and even as he told me this story, which I'm sure he'd shared many times, his eyes welled with pride at what his father had done – and mine came out in sympathy.

With the design team and Mark we felt that we were making strides towards putting a plausible proposal to the MC. There are degrees of credibility, however. Let us assume that we could design something that looked great, cost it, put fantastic plants inside it and have a business plan that could convincingly demonstrate our capacity to run it profitably. There were still a couple of rather glaring gaps. One, the site we had was wrong, with no suitable alternative on the horizon; and even if we had one, we didn't have planning permission. Full stop. Two, we hadn't identified with any certainty the source of the money we would need to match the MC. The funding gap was so great that we would need at least a million visitors to cover the interest on the loans we would have to take out, were someone to let us. While we believed this to be possible, nobody else appeared to share our conviction, Edinburgh Castle notwithstanding.

All of a sudden a number of things happened at once. Bill Rickatson found me a site and everybody immediately fell in love with it. While we would have

'Site, yes…'

to wait for Goonvean to effect the transfer, we were able to agree broad terms and convince ourselves that there was more certainty there than we had any right to. We couldn't afford to buy Bodelva, after all, and they were a commercial operation, no matter how kindly disposed to us they were in theory. Since they owned it they would keep working it until we paid up. No matter. The liberation of having the perfect site within reach got the creative juices going. The architects could get fired up designing, the engineers could take a look at the ground conditions, and the QSs could at last start to price something real, however rudimentary.

We had a little money left over from the grants made to us by our supporters. Jonathan and I allowed ourselves to be talked into putting some of it into the creation of a model in cross-section of the newly sketched conservatories. David Kirkland and Andrew Whalley had developed a concept, looking vaguely gynaecological and loosely referential in style to the design of the Waterloo International Terminal, with ribs curving from the bottom to the top of the pit. It was nearly a kilometre long and consisted of three conservatories, and the links that joined them together, hugging the south- and west-facing slopes. On the eastern side of the pit there appeared to be a conning tower, topped by an aerial, that denoted the putative visitor centre. The concept was topographically

challenged, in that the architects hadn't really taken account of the natural growing habits of plants, especially crops, and neither had they really considered the life-threatening possibilities of a landscape so precipitous that it would have been impossible to build on. But from little acorns…

The model was made of chicken wire and plastic, and contained lifelike trees, humans, their villages, a splendid waterfall, and walkways through the canopy of the rainforest. The people were to scale, and for the first time the awesome size of the conservatories hit home. It was splendidly encased in perspex, and we loved it. Everyone who saw it got excited, in spite of its practical shortcomings. Nicholas Grimshaw entered it for exhibition at the Venice Biennale. Jonathan and Paul went over with the design team and created quite a stir; the regional press gave it heavy-duty coverage, soon to be followed by the nationals, who were immediately taken with the ambition of the idea. The design would change later as problems revealed themselves, but at long last we had a site and a concept that for all its practical flaws captured the imagination. Site, yes. Design, yes(ish). Money, no.

chapter 6

hurt money

The business plan Mark Bostock had put
together was a good first stab, considering that
he was herding cats. The next stage was going
to be very difficult, however, because we would
have to begin dealing with the agencies that
we hoped might provide the matched funding.
One thing was clear. The process would be
a long one. The obvious target for big money
was Europe, which had designated Cornwall as
having European Development Fund 5(b) status
and had allocated roughly £150 million to the
area to assist with infrastructure improvements
across a range of categories: environment,
regeneration, small and medium-size business
support and so on. The documentation
outlining the conditions had been drawn up
by a crossword compiler having a bad hair day.

Consequently very few people or organizations had made significant inroads into the fund. We would eventually make a very large bid, for £12.5 million; most of this would turn up two and a bit years down the line, but it would feel like a decade. To kick the process off there was absolutely no doubt that we needed an expert interpreter. We went to Exeter to see Jonathan Johns, a senior partner of Ernst and Young, one of the so-called Big Six accountants.

Jonathan should not be an accountant. His body language screams artist at you; his wardrobe screams Cuban gambler chic, *c.*1955. In drink he will confess to being a poet and enjoying what passes for Devon café society; he talks with a manic enthusiasm that defies all preconceptions of the greyness of the number cruncher. In the four years I have known him I have never seen him at an official accountancy function. He has an alarming tendency to invite you to one and then fail to turn up, claiming some exotic business elsewhere. He may look like a roué, but he's inspired. Just when you think he's completely lost the plot, with some interesting digression or scurrilous tale of the city, he hits you with a lateral thought that opens up an opportunity.

Jonathan is intensely proud that he has worked his way up through the ranks; not a silver spoon in sight, but unusually no chip on the shoulder either. A remarkable man, he has carved out a niche in pioneering the funding of alternative energy projects, is passionate about the future of the South West and, most importantly for us, is prepared to put his firm's money where his mouth is. He agreed to work for us at risk until we had secured the funding we needed. He had complete faith that the project would go ahead and created great confidence in everybody with his assurance. He would lead a team to work up a business plan that met the European requirements, which inevitably were completely different to what a bank or the MC would need. (This unnecessary duplication of effort caused by the differing requirements of state agencies was the most shameful waste of time and money we encountered in bringing Eden to fruition.)

Then we went to see English Partnerships, the state agency charged with regeneration projects, particularly converting brownfield sites into a usable economic condition. We immediately hit a snag: while we were undoubtedly dealing with a brownfield site, the assumption was that they occurred in cities, not in rural areas. We would have been in danger of finding ourselves ineligible if it hadn't been for the tireless championship of our cause by the south-west team of the agency, led by Nick Harrington. Like all our other friends in the region they would come up trumps when we needed them most.

We were running out of the sort of chunky cash that you can do things with when we received a generous donation from Tarmac, whose chairman, Sir John Banham, a Cornishman and at the time also the chairman of the private-sector economic development group South West Enterprise (SWEL), was a big supporter of the project. Whenever possible he had promoted us, and both SWEL and now Tarmac were getting behind us. Alongside the money, we were offered the services of Robert Osborne, their director of special projects, and Simon Hipperson, who would help us develop a procurement strategy – construction-speak for establishing the form of contractual arrangement that would deliver the project. They had a great deal of experience in PFI, the Private Finance Initiative, which encouraged partnership between government and the private sector. They felt that Eden might be able to benefit from the models they had developed. We gratefully accepted the donation and help on the clear understanding that we were not bound in any way to choose them as our contractors. This they accepted with good grace, and their help was to move us on significantly over the coming months.

Meanwhile the Trustees were getting restless. We all knew that we needed bank support, as sponsorship and grant aid weren't going to be enough to bridge the funding gap. Right at the outset we had discussed the various funding opportunities that might be available to us. All were agreed that in an ideal world the Trust would have no need for private-sector involvement except perhaps in the form of sponsorship. As the enormity of the fundraising task dawned on us it became clear that all strategies ought to be explored, including equity finance. The one essential condition required by the Trust was that it should be impossible for its mission to be usurped by investors, and that control of its assets should pass to a third party only in the direst crisis. Tentative approaches to potential sponsors from the Trustees were getting nowhere because there was no guarantee of a successful outcome; they had no desire to see their money disappear into a hole, with no specific part of the project bearing their name. Venture capital was another avenue altogether, but enquiries of both the MC and Europe illustrated the limits of private/public partnerships. All sorts of barriers were put in the way, such as an insistence on the capping of returns. If you were a venture capitalist and someone said you can put your money at total risk but you can earn only a maximum of £x if the project is successful, the response would be pretty terse. We were left with no short-term alternative but to seek bank lending. Reluctantly the Trustees agreed, and Ian Hay Davison worked extremely hard to set up a beauty parade of City suitors. Three merchant banks came to see us, all completely uninspiring; one wished to take matters further, the other two wished us luck. Very soon it became apparent that the remaining suitor wasn't exactly our style, and we settled into a mood of quiet despondency.

In desperation I phoned a very good university friend called Rolf Munding. He and his wife Linda and family had moved to Cornwall two years previously and had bought a derelict pair of cottages at the bottom of the Lost Valley at Heligan. Once converted, these cottages were still

Rolf Munding, man of the world

reachable only in a four-wheel drive or on foot. This contrast suited Rolf, for his business life was hectic to say the least. His family roots were Swedish, Norwegian and German, and he spoke several other languages as well; the term 'man of the world' could have been coined for him. With interests in various states of the former Soviet Union, a flat and office in Prague, where he had an interest in a ski resort and a brewery, he had become extremely successful and a Freeman of the City of London. Rolf is not to everyone's taste, because he knows his mind and is so big that he can be unintentionally intimidating. But if it was 4 a.m. in Aberdeen and my life was in ruins, I'd call him and I would lay odds that he would be on the way in minutes. I have known him since we were both nineteen. From that day to this I have never known him tell a lie, save for a forgivable exaggeration about the quality of some of the beer he imports.

Rolf has another extraordinary characteristic: he acts instantly. You might ask him at dinner if he knows somebody who could be useful for something. He will immediately get on the telephone and fix a meeting there and then. You have no scope for second thoughts, which is at once alarming, exciting and exhausting. I called Rolf and explained the problem, and he came up to the office at Heligan immediately. He made calls to friends at Hambros and the Canadian Imperial Bank of Commerce (CIBC). He primed them on what was needed, sent them documents by special delivery, spoke with the chairman of Trustees, and arranged for the banks to make a presentation at the chairman's club some days hence.

In a week we had a bank: not necessarily a very willing bank, more one that had been mugged. Shell-shocked though they might be, CIBC would help us make a massive leap forward. The reason was the extremely clever if somewhat pugnacious Martin Peck. (His boss, Douglas Hogg, always liked to tell us that his main claim to fame was involvement with the Channel Tunnel. Bearing in mind that our chairman, Sir Alcon, had at one time been involved with the development of Concorde, this was not necessarily the most reassuring omen for our budgetary controls!)

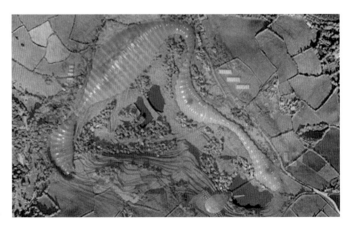

OVERFLOW PARKING
870 No. CARS

'It was nearly a
kilometre long...':
early Eden

TROPICAL RAIN
FOREST

ADMINISTRATION
ACCOMMODATION

DESERT

LAKE &
MARGINAL
VEGETATION

MEADOW

STAFF PARKING

SUB-
TROPICAL

TEMPERATE

MEDITERRANEAN

LAKE

BACK-UP
GREENHOUSES

KING
CARS

ENTRANCE

COACH & CAR PARKING
245 No. CARS,
15 No. COACHES

GATHERING &
BUS DROP OFF

SCREEN PLANTATIONS

THE EDEN PROJECT

LAND USE CONSULTANTS

To see your dream put under the microscope of analysis, shorn of all romance or benefit of the doubt, is a real shock. If Mark Bostock was Baloo, Martin was a sort of small Shere Khan, prowling round our flock of ideas knocking them off one by one and respecting no sacred cows at all. We were to have some fearful disagreements as he bulldozed and harried, the greatest of which centred on his faith in the professional advice he was getting from the construction industry about costs as opposed to his disdainful disregard for the professional advice he was getting from our horticultural team that they could produce the plants and that they would live. He wanted proof, but none existed except in the confidence of the team.

He tore into our assumptions, insisting on worst-case scenarios and introducing me to the concept of 'hurt money'. If his bank was going to fund the project, the principals, meaning Jonathan and I, the contractor and the operator, were all going to have to put up money. Hurt money simply means that in the event that the bank has to take a bath then they at least get the satisfaction of knowing that those charged with running it properly feel the pain also. His view was that we

Tim Carter, ace
project manager

should go down the path of having equity stakes in an operating company controlled in some way by the Trust. This wasn't ideal, but was a situation that could instantly be revisited in the event that monies were made available that obviated the need for this route. Martin was to have a hard time with the Trustees, who were never convinced that this was his real intention and always suspected it would all end badly. However, they had to swallow it as there was no alternative.

We didn't have a contractor or an operator, although Martin had assumed that Tarmac would be the constructor by dint of our relationship with them. In April 1996 Jonathan, Paul and I had been introduced by Derek Johnson of DLM to our first top-ranking project manager. His name was Tim Carter, and he had been in charge of the construction of the Nynex Arena in Manchester before coming down to London to take charge of the late James Stirling's No. 1 Poultry. The job was nearing completion, and Tim gave us a vertiginous tour of the scaffolding so that we could enjoy the view from the top. Paul and I shut our eyes and felt our way down like blind men. The explanations were excellent, and he described the process with a clarity that made it seem comfortingly easy.

In June, to our great pleasure, Tim became Eden's project manager. His first task was to lead a newly formed management group to draw together all the strands necessary to make a submission to the MC in December, which was their final deadline for Landmark projects. We would meet every fortnight at the offices of Ernst and Young in London. The team would comprise Tim, Rolf, a Trustee, the bank in attendance, lawyers in attendance if they so wished, Ronnie Murning, Jonathan and me.

Just before Tim formally came on board three things had happened. First the MC had indicated that they liked the project in principle after all. Their regional project director, Bill Alexander, had come down to meet the whole team and give us a lecture on how the process would be handled and the standards he expected us to reach. He was a tough Scot, and we were extremely nervous of him; we had been told that his opinion counted.

Subsequently Michael Montague and Patricia Scotland, Millennium Commissioners, had both visited and offered their encouragement. Michael had later written to Jonathan and me saying how impressed he was with the idea, and how confident he was of its success. He had recently been to Buchart Gardens on Vancouver Island, which were attracting a million visitors a year. Finally Jenny Page, then director of the MC, had also paid us a visit with MC staff. We put on lunch for her in our stripy crusader tent on Flora's Green at Heligan to try to thaw her out. She was a consummate professional and asked all the right questions. There are not many people who put me on the back foot, but there was something challenging about her; impress me, she seemed to be saying, and don't think it'll be easy. Our Trustees came down for the event and she took a delight in probing me about why we had chosen them. It transpired that events elsewhere had left her jaundiced at the number of the Great and the Good who signed up to projects and then didn't deliver anything but their names and past reputation. Luckily for Eden, our Trustees would be of a different mettle.

For me the day of Jenny Page's visit was memorable for another reason. During a quiet moment I was given some advice by the MC's national project director, Doug Weston, that would have a profound influence on the way the project would conduct itself. The crucial thing you must understand about working with civil servants, he said, is that once they are committed they are likely to remain so. They operate in a different way from the private sector, however, in that if there is bad news you must let them know immediately; their terror is not the news itself, which they can deal with very easily, it is the not knowing, which exposes them and potentially their ministers. This advice would colour our every move, and we would never be disappointed in the trust we showed. It created a true partnership.

June was a great month for a further reason too. She was a tough, attractive blonde, northern and a bit bolshy; everything was sharp about her – bones, glare and wit. She was also completely unimpressed by me – a situation not helped by my having been double-booked on the scheduled date of our first meeting. Paul had seen her in my stead and invited her to join a tour of Bodelva pit with the Green Team, Peter and Philip's horticultural think tank. A Marilyn Monroe dress

(overleaf)
The coconut grove at Eden

and designer sandals were not appropriate dress for an interview in a windswept, muddy pit in driving rain. Paul warned me afterwards that maybe it hadn't been a good idea. Anyway, undeterred, she came to Heligan as a one-woman inquisition to determine whether I was the right sort of person to benefit from her talents. She had been running management courses for Cornwall College in Redruth, the county's largest further education provider. Its principal, Dr Alan Stanhope, and I had been friends for some time. He had been very supportive of Eden's aims and objectives, and could see its potential as a unique educational resource. So when I bemoaned the fact that I was drowning in an organizational ocean he suggested that I might like to meet Kary Lescure.

I was immediately aware that this wasn't a normal interview. She left me in no doubt that we would be equals or nothing, although in public I might be allowed to wear the trousers. She had an expressive face, a profound sense of the ridiculous, a healthy disrespect for 'boys' games' and a prodigious appetite for work. She had another side to her as well, one which we referred to as the mother hen, not in jest but out of genuine appreciation for her intuitive understanding of how people were feeling. She could sense when people were under pressure and when they needed a 'stroke and a sugarlump', as she would put it – she is a horse-lover. She may be a hard taskmistress, but her instinct has always been to nurture, protect and support, often to her personal cost as she takes on further work to shelter those who are temporarily drowning. When I look back to the roots of the Eden culture I can see what a debt we all owe her. As we drove ourselves to the brink of exhaustion and beyond in the pursuit of our dream, it was Kary in the background, with sealing wax, Sellotape and sticking plaster who made sure we didn't fall apart, while in the foreground she was forging relationships that would be of vital importance to Eden's future.

It didn't take long for all those dealing with the project to recognize that she was a safe pair of hands and that they could just as easily deal with her as with me. It also didn't take long for the team, by now growing by the week, to realize that here was someone who would look after their best interests, someone who was unimpressed by power and authority. She knew that sorting out the expenses for a volunteer was as important as securing a massive European grant, because she understood that what would enable Eden truly to deliver on its promises was not the glitzy architecture, the glad-handing of the Great and the Good, or even the public acclaim. These would all be as nothing if we hadn't created the true foundation on which all else could be built – the team.

I digress – we were talking about the bank and their demand for 'hurt money'. This was defined as a financial investment from the constructor and the operator, their involvement being deemed essential to underpin the assumptions in the business plan. In other words, the credit committee of the bank is given the assurance that professionals are on board from the two key risk areas, construction (to see that costs don't overrun and leave them vulnerable to having to lend even more money to complete the project) and operations (to guarantee that the visitors will come and spend enough to enable a profit to be made and so pay back the loans). If they fail, it will cost them dearly.

Construction is a funny business, not to be confused with building. Constructors are a breed apart. Early on in the construction of the project I made the mistake of remarking to one of the managers that I was hugely impressed, having watched work going on for more than an hour, that no one seemed to be wasting time or sloping off for a fag break. He grunted and said, we're not builders, these men's pleasure is to construct things, it's what makes them get up in the morning. He was right.

Kary Lescure: 'dispenser of strokes and sugarlumps'

Tarmac had given us some money in the full knowledge that we accepted it with no strings attached. Nonetheless there was a hope that through early involvement they would find themselves on the inside track. The Millennium Commission and the Government Office for the South West, our regional brokers for European money, informed us that the construction contract would have to be tendered in open competition, as is the case with all projects using public money. We would have to advertise in the European construction trade journal and properly interview a shortlist. There was no obligation to accept the lowest bid; the client can set the criteria, which might include, as was the case with Eden, the requirement to invest a sum of money in the project. But it is important that all bidders should operate on a level playing field. Indeed nowadays it is quite common for the client to choose the middle bidder, simply to discourage unrealistically low tenders that might lead to problems later on.

So we placed our advertisement. The replies were whittled down to six: Tarmac, Hierry, Kier, the Sir Robert and Alfred McAlpine Joint Venture, Costain-Hochtief and Bovis. All would be invited down to Heligan and then escorted around the pit prior to formal presentations from them in London some weeks later. We put together a brochure for them, giving the basic project information and mentioning that Tarmac were sponsors. Big mistake: all the other bidders wondered whether they were just there to make up the numbers, and it was a hard job convincing them to come. But come they did, in the end. Kier, Hierry and Bovis had all the pzazz of marketeers and came over very impressively, whereas the other three were grey. McAlpine's were so grey and apparently uninterested that I was certain they would drop out; if they didn't, I was sure we wouldn't want to work with them.

How wrong can you be? We assembled in London to interview the six after they had had time to work up a presentation. Kier, Hierry and Bovis made the most stylish presentations, but were found wanting in the investment department. This would count against them as far as the bank was concerned. This left the other three – Tarmac, McAlpine's and Costain-Hochtief – as the front runners. To our amazement we all found ourselves drawn to the rank outsiders, the McAlpine Joint Venture, who without fuss simply said they were interested because they liked to build things and this was the ultimate construction project. The speaker was Barry New, a project director famous in the South West for managing a remarkable feat of engineering, slotting a huge segment of flyover into the main Plymouth bypass. After all the glitz, there was a seriousness of intent about these people that demanded closer inspection. As it turned out the negotiations dragged on a bit and it wasn't until February 1997 that we were able unofficially to let McAlpine's know they had reached preferred bidder status, and not until June would they get a letter to that effect.

Simultaneously with all this we were hunting for an operator, because the bank was insisting on it. I hated this process. My experience at Heligan had convinced me that it was far better to run all your own catering operations; you had one team with no split loyalties, and it was more profitable into the bargain. My final argument against bringing someone else in was that food itself was central to what the Eden Project was about. The idea of having outside caterers doing their own thing without our being able adequately to control price, quality or sourcing filled me with gloom. But the bank was adamant. So where would we find an operator we were happy with?

Again I called on my friend Rolf Munding to assist. Over a weekend Paul, Kary, Rolf and I put together a brochure that cannibalized lots of other documents but looked just about professional in an amateurish sort of way. Rolf sent it to most of the caterers in Britain that could operate at the level we intended. These were Granada, who owned the Compass Group, Gardner Merchant, Vardons and Scottish and Newcastle.

We were desperate; time was running out. We'd met all of them bar one and had been totally unimpressed. The feeling had been mutual. One gloomy afternoon we assembled at the bank to wait for the representative from Primary Management, the project development arm of Gardner Merchant. Martin Peck, Rolf, Jonathan and I were sitting rather self-consciously in a massive boardroom with a splendid view over the Thames when our guest was announced. In walked Evelyn Thurlby, immaculately dressed in an expensive yet understated way, with short dark hair, glasses and an aura of quiet authority. Once pleasantries had been exchanged, she took the meeting by the scruff of the neck, analysing our figures and deconstructing them in the light of her experience at the Royal Armouries in

Leeds. She was sceptical of the Heligan model but prepared to look more closely if we wanted to take things further. We were very impressed. We liked her, but more importantly if she liked us we would have our operator. In due course she visited us at Heligan and we were in business. Although we didn't know it then, she would profoundly influence the course of the project over the next few years.

What a game of smoke and mirrors it all was! Just to summarize, we needed a constructor and operator who would invest 'hurt money'. The bank would consider giving us a letter of intent for our borrowing requirement if these things were in place, or at least likely to be so. The Trustees hated the path we were going down, but felt they had no choice. The funding gap was actually enormous, and we would never be able to finance the project unless we could identify matched funding from Europe and various other agencies. Even then the borrowings were terrifying.

In December 1996 our final submission went to the MC, although we would adapt it over the next few months. In the New Year the Management Group met for its regular get-together at the offices of Ernst and Young. We were faced with a stark decision. The quantity surveyors had done a rough pricing, and there was no way they could recommend proceeding with the current scheme. They proposed drastic cuts in both scale and provision of facilities. Philip and I talked at length about the impact of such a decision, and we came to the view that rather than cuts across the board we should stick to our dream of having the largest conservatories in the world. Philip suggested putting the sub-tropical oceanic exhibitions inside the rainforest house and forgoing the sub-tropic house, leaving us with two major conservatories and a large temperate parkland outside.

It was the wisdom of Solomon and it would keep us in play. We could still proceed with the other house later if we could find the funds, but if we shrank the conservatories now it would be the end of our dream.

In March 1997 the bid in front of the Commissioners was for a capital project to construct two giant conservatories and a designed parkland, with visitor and educational facilities. Its total cost was £74.3 million. The amount of documentation was awesome: there was a scheme proposal, a costing, a business plan, an environmental impact assessment, and supporting documentation about the constructor and operator which had no contractual force but which derived a sheen of credibility from the bank's letter of support indicating that if certain conditions were met they would provide funding. There was a mass of other assumptions about money we might receive from Europe and English Partnerships as well as guesstimates about sponsorship, not to mention small details like purchasing a large clay pit and obtaining planning permission for same. If you said it fast enough it seemed totally reasonable. Bearing in mind that no one had ever done anything like this before, the act of faith that enabled so many people to sign up to Tinkerbell Theory was a testament to the spirit of Eden taking hold.

chapter 7

performance

A mountain of paperwork, a design team from
heaven and some up-country big cheeses count
for nothing in Cornwall without local support.
This meant carrying the local and county councils
with us, which in turn meant that the local
communities had to be behind the idea or else
their councillors would have felt unable
to champion the cause. Paul Travers was to
be the ringmaster for an exhausting but
entertaining campaign of presentations which
took us to village halls across the clay district.
Bugle, Roche, Trethurgy, Tregrehan, St Blazey
and many more hosted the touring circus of the
model, which fitted in the back of the
Volvo with no room to spare.

The ice would be broken by our incompetence at manœuvring it through the doorway, which usually led to a degree of audience participation. The model may look naïve now, in the face of the real thing, but at the time we had the feeling of being participants in a Victorian travelling show. Audiences were always bowled over when they saw the little people to scale against the giant dome. The statistics became ever more fantastical. First it was big enough to contain the Leaning Tower of Pisa, then it could contain thirteen Truro cathedrals, then twelve double-decker buses one on top of the other. Nick Grimshaw came up with a great one: it could contain 6,000 domestic greenhouses in volume. This caused great confusion with the public, some of whom latched on to the bizarre notion that we weren't after all going to fill it with plants.

The halls were packed. People were generally very excited about the idea, although for many it was pure fantasy and would never happen. You could see it in their eyes. The giant conservatories in a pit were never going to be a problem, except to a very few people who were agitated that this sort of money was to be blown on something like this rather than a hospital or some other socially worthwhile structure. In the main the concerns centred on traffic, and following on from that the need for a new road. We were sometimes told that it was pure hypocrisy for an environmental project to be encouraging the use of the motor car to visit it.

The travelling model: 'Audiences were always bowled over...'

In the autumn of 1996 we had submitted an application for outline planning consent to Restormel Borough Council. For those unfamiliar with the process, what happens is that you submit your plan in sketch form with outlines of the buildings and an approximation of the areas involved. This is the domain of the Borough Council. The situation is complicated by the fact that certain functions have to be approved by the County Council, whose jurisdiction covers highways and minerals as well as anything proposed that lies outside the County Structure Plan – the forward-planning strategy document which provides the framework under which planning is decided. We faced frightening odds against success on a number of counts.

There would be strong objections about the road access, which at present involved a tortuous meander through narrow country lanes between the arterial A30 and St Austell. In many places there was not enough room for cars to pass, let alone coaches. The nearest safe A-road for access to the A30 was more than three miles away at Carluddon. Even then many argued that the increase of traffic in the clay villages would pose a serious hazard, especially at school dropping-off and picking-up times.

There would also be resistance within the clay industry to any decision to sterilize a resource at Bodelva, for reasons given earlier. It would need the County Council Minerals Department, with the authority of the executive, formally to waive their right to regard the land sale to us as a precedent. Furthermore the clay board, representing the two major companies in the area, would have to agree to the sale.

Before putting in our planning application we had begun an environmental impact assessment, funded by Europe and English Partnerships. This was a monumental piece of work which covered all the environmental aspects of the pit itself and also concerned itself with the proposed access routes and the impact each would have on the area. This assessment was led by Ove Arup, doggedly chased in London by Ronnie Murning, who could see that if any stone was left unturned it might eventually provide the pretext to send us back to the drawing board, thereby making the delivery timescale slip, and allowing the cost to escalate to the point at which the project became unworkable.

So the pit was given the third degree. It was drilled, poked, observed and sampled to within an inch of its life. We knew every bird, bat, badger, fox, field mouse and dragonfly by name. We knew the geological make-up of the spoil and the core of the pit itself, and could say that this or that bit wouldn't slip, could drain or, most importantly, wasn't polluted by any minerals or chemicals. The water would be discharged into this leat or that brook and it wouldn't contain more than the permitted sediment, nor would it be of such a quantity that it would cause flooding further down the watercourse. The coring activities resulted in an amusing cat-and-mouse game between us and the owners, Goonvean, whose supplies of the precious white gold were running out. If our boring company had hit a lode during one of their forays Goonvean would have been in there with the machines as soon as we'd finished. The architects back in London were in despair because every week the pit changed shape, making their work insufferably difficult. They had never ever worked in conditions like these before.

The engineers then began to look at potential road access and surveyed all the possible routes for structural soundness, ease of work, water-table impact, wildlife and archaeological remains. They determined what the traffic flows would look like and the noise and pollution impacts of the cars. Strong objections were already being voiced by those living alongside the country lane that led to us from the west, but help was at hand in the shape of English China Clays and Councillor Joan Vincent.

Joan Vincent lives in Stenalees, at the heart of the clay district and right on the main road that would bring traffic to Eden. Although married to a former clay man, she has been a mighty thorn in the side of the industry for many years. Many's the time I saw hardened clay executives slump at the mention of her name. Joan liked the project, and she and Roger Preston of English China Clays came up with the solution simultaneously. The Clay Country has a superb network of roads and railway lines that keeps the works traffic off the public highway. The most impressive road by far was the dirt track known locally as the Burma Road, not far from our site boundary, that carried the giant trucks and dumpers from Carluddon to Trebal. The land between the Burma Road and us was either in ECC's ownership or that of a couple of local farmers. English China Clays agreed to sell, and Joan Vincent agreed to support the strategy and promote it as a bypass for the local village. By this time Joan and Paul had developed a very friendly relationship because the beach near his home provided a constant supply of washed-up cuttle-fish, the staple diet of her beloved budgerigars, which she bred. He would often drop off a sack as a peace offering. There would remain issues about badgers and dragonflies, not to mention whether we were going to tear down miles of ancient Cornish stone hedging and lay waste to historic trees, but… we had a solution. The Highways Agency travelled the length of all the local roads and conceded that they too could support the plan.

Bodelva gets
the third degree

Paul drove hundreds of miles with the agencies up and down all the roads that could conceivably be used in getting to us. This was crucial because it was one thing getting their support, quite another to get away scot-free without financial penalties. County councils everywhere are keen to extract funds from developers for road improvements, on the grounds that the impact of your development requires amelioration. We would eventually agree to make contributions to traffic-calming measures, traffic lights and cycle and bridle paths.

But the hours of scouting and village hall visits were beginning to pay off. I remember a remarkable evening in Bugle, which would be the most affected of all the villages. The county planning officer, local councillors, County Highways, Paul, Kary and I were all there to answer questions from the villagers. They were supportive, but worried about traffic. Matters became quite contentious when the audience demanded a zebra crossing. The Highways man stood up and said that in built-up areas more people were killed on zebra crossings, because they thought they were safe, than on the open road. His intervention carried the day.

Further afield we faced other community issues. The main road from Plymouth goes through the village of Dobwalls, at which point you fork left to St Austell via Lostwithiel or go straight ahead to Bodmin and on to the main A30. County Highways decided it was better to send traffic down the A30. Within days a furious letter had arrived from the town council of Lostwithiel demanding the decision be reconsidered, on the grounds that a straw poll taken in the town indicated that local people were massively in favour of Eden and welcomed the traffic as an opportunity to sell the town. The decision was rescinded with much scratching of heads. The poor man from County Highways said he had never in his life had a letter from a community demanding more traffic.

In St Blazey, Eden's local town, Paul and I met a very frosty reception; several of the more vocal protesters had chosen this particular meeting to express their views. The issue of the hypocrisy of attracting cars had to be met head-on. I said that while we recognized the inconsistency, we believed that on balance the good the project would do outweighed the negatives, that those in cars would have been in cars somewhere else and we were providing a reason for them to stop driving. (In hindsight, this was perhaps a little disingenuous.) We were not our brother's keeper. If we had to police all aspects of the environment nobody would ever build anything. I hate to have to duck and dive to pay lip-service to the agendas of others, so I admitted that I loved my car and said that so did almost every car owner in the world. The issue wasn't the form of transport, it was the way it was constructed and fuelled, and that was a government issue. Anyway, I said as a parting shot, had they ever tried making love in the back of a bus? Collapse of stout party.

In truth, I agree we use cars too much and that the industry hasn't done enough to curb emissions or regulate the standards of construction. All Western

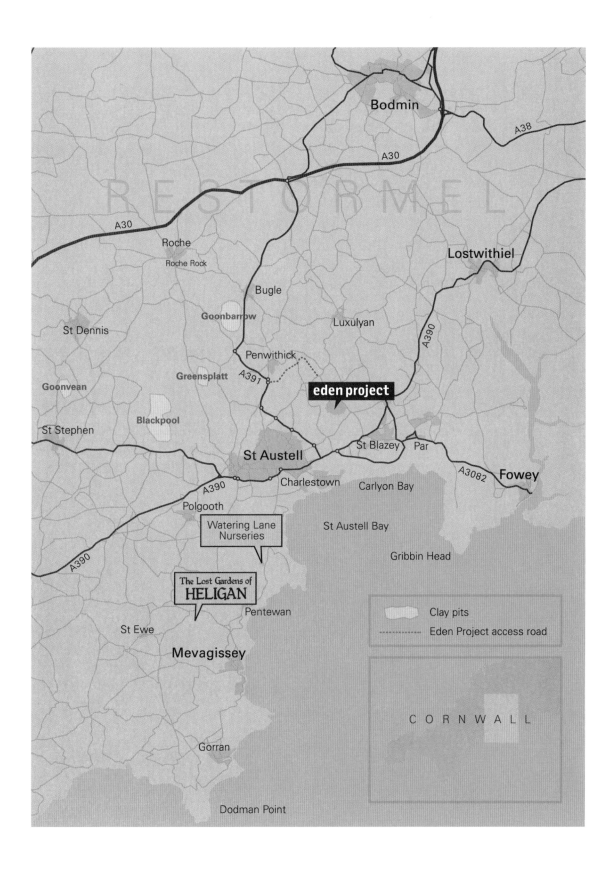

governments are guilty of being craven in the face of the most powerful lobby group in the world. Eden does encourage buses, and we are developing innovative schemes to encourage people to come by train; at the time of writing Eden attracts 20 per cent of its visitors in coaches, a statistic unmatched anywhere else. However, those projects which actively discourage arrival by car have found people voting with their feet, so to speak. The Earth Centre near Doncaster charged those arriving by car extra for a while, so people either didn't come or got cross. The same happened at the Royal Armouries in Leeds, where there is a parking charge. The urban park-and-ride schemes such as Oxford are still far from successful. The argument for a car-free zone is extremely hard to make in Cornwall, since the local provision of services is lamentable; in fairness such services would have to be massively subsidized to provide a credible alternative to the ease of the car.

The use of the car was one thing, the heaviness of the traffic was another. There was a tendency to imagine that all the vehicles would arrive at the same time, which they don't. One of the most remarkable things at both Heligan and Eden is that the visitors seem to spread fairly evenly across a week. There are fewer visitors at weekends because of changeover days for holidaymakers, who tend to peak on Tuesdays, Wednesdays and Thursdays, but nonetheless I have always found it remarkable that they don't all decide to come on the same day for some reason. Why? The Heligan experience was a useful one in countering the fear of gridlock, but the killer statistic was arrived at by the transport consultant from Arup's, Hugh Collis, who pointed out that Eden's busiest day would still be less busy than the least busy day at the nearest out-of-town supermarket. This appeared to still many of the concerns.

There were other criticisms. A local headmaster was vehemently opposed to us on environmental grounds, and also because he felt that the project was too big for Cornwall and would be like a cuckoo in the nest. He was a very honourable man; he came to see me at Heligan and told me that he would use every means within his power to derail the project, including asking questions at meetings and writing to the press and the government. However, once a decision had been made one way or the other, we would shake hands and it would be over. You can't be fairer than that.

There were other angles on the project. One man wrote a very moving letter expressing the view that we would be successful, because it was a great project, but he was going to object, albeit reluctantly. In his view Eden would attract so many wealthy visitors to Cornwall that they would buy up all the houses and raise prices to a level unaffordable on Cornish wages, which are among the lowest in Britain and indeed in much of Europe. This is a difficult argument because it is in essence true; but then it always has been. Even now there is genuine despair at how local youngsters will ever be able to afford to live in the county of their birth, especially with job prospects so bleak. I argued that this was defeatist; the only way out of this vicious circle is to create jobs which pay well and break the cycle. Heligan began employing staff on a significant minimum wage, because we wanted to. Local employers complained that we were skewing the local economy, but we argued that any business paying such bad wages deserved to go bust. Good wages mean respect, which in turn means better performance and improved productivity. End of story. Funny how within weeks all the local businesses competing for labour found they were able to raise their salaries.

The most virulent protestors were the least expected: the Green Party. We would have thought that a project providing an international focus on many of the issues dear to their heart would have won their grudging support. They chose to be purist, much to the chagrin of Jonathan Porritt, whose help I tried to enlist to broker a truce. A litany of evil was laid before the public: our roofing foil was poisonous (it isn't, it is in fact bio-degradable); we were going to employ German labour (why?); we were going to research genetically modified crops (we weren't); we would chop down ancient trees to make our new road over prime farmland (we didn't and it wasn't); we were encouraging cars (well yes, in a way we were, but they chose to make their banner protest against us by driving to the site and saying so); and we had cut down our proposal from three conservatories to two, thus proving that we were a theme park. The logic of this last accusation was difficult to follow, but in any case we had always thought one of the conditions of sustainability was economic viability. We couldn't win, so we ignored them.

All of this activity culminated in a giant public meeting at Penrice School in St Austell, on 22 January 1997. George Down, the chairman of the Planning Committee, had persuaded all interested parties to make a public presentation at which the mood of the meeting would be tested before taking the project to Planning. The press would be there, the protesters would be there, and also a battalion of experts for the public to question. I don't think I have ever been so nervous in all my life. The radio had announced the meeting, and the papers had been full of it. There was certainly no excuse for not knowing it was happening. Paul was organizing the event like a military tactician, checking that the dimmers worked, the slide projector was greased, there was water on the tables and the public address system was set up, as well as making sure that all the speakers knew what they were doing and what the running order was. He was aided in this by Angie Rowe, who knew that this could be our Waterloo.

As people assembled I paced around outside the back of the hall. It was dark and drizzly, and raindrops kept fizzing on my cigar and putting it out. All I could hear was traffic and the murmur of people. Every so often I took a peek round the corner and became increasingly alarmed at the size of the crowd. I am a fairly confident public speaker, but my throat went dry, my heartbeat raced and I felt short of breath.

I couldn't remember a word I was going to say; nothing would stick. Eventually it was time, and Paul came to track me down. I felt sick and sweaty, and wanted to run away. I was going to talk gibberish and splutter to a halt with the whole world looking at me.

You'll be fine, said Paul, guiding me down the corridor with a smile on his face. My God, it was packed, even the standing room was full. As my eyes adjusted to the light and I walked slowly towards the stage at the far end of the hall, where by now all the experts and councillors had settled into place, I heard voices saying hello and saw people giving me the thumbs-up. Everywhere I looked I could see people I knew. There were literally hundreds of Friends of Heligan, many of them old and extremely frail; there were dozens of people who had come to our presentations. Right in the middle I recognized the faces of some who were not so kindly disposed. It was a humbling thought that all these people had come out on a cold, damp winter's night, many of them without cars who would have had to walk or take taxis. I had a lump in my throat as I walked on to the stage.

George Down made the introductions and set us all on our way. I know I spoke, but I can't remember a single thing I said. Apparently I paced the stage like a man possessed, and talked so fast that most people probably couldn't understand me; whatever it was I was saying, I appeared to be passionate about it. The transport consultant was next, followed by a superb presentation by County Highways, and finally David Pollard, the county planning officer. It was time for questions; now, surely, it was going to be difficult. A lady got up and waved a petition. For a moment I thought the protesters might have outflanked us, and my heart sank. But no: Shirley Polmounter, representing the local Chamber of Commerce, brought us God knows how many hundreds of signatures in support. A few detailed local points were raised, and I believe one protester made a mildly negative comment, which was greeted by silence.

Then, right in the middle of the audience, a lady stood up and introduced herself as a Cornish bard. She admitted that the Cornish were often against things on principle, but tonight she had come because she felt she had to. There followed an impassioned speech about the future of Cornwall and how anybody who opposed the project was betraying the first glimmer of a prospective new dawn for her children and grandchildren. She sat down to a roar from the crowd. Astonishingly there were no more questions, and when George Down asked for a show of hands to give the meeting a sense of the public mood only the tiniest number were raised against.

The meeting broke up amid a cacophony of good wishes and waves from friendly faces in the crowd. I saw a number of the Heligan Friends happily making their way out into the night, job done. The home team was still on course, and I felt tears welling and gave Paul an enormous hug. This was his triumph, he had orchestrated it. It was also George Down's night; he had done the right thing in hosting the meeting and we all congratulated him. As George, David Pollard and I reflected on the evening's events, David said, this is probably the largest public meeting of its kind ever held in Cornwall and you know, in all my long career I have never attended a public meeting like this where people were in favour of something – quite extraordinary. Shaking his head, he departed with his team from Highways, who themselves deserved great credit for their attitude. As we were to find so often, people who would have found it a lot more comfortable to say no were doing their damnedest to say yes.

There was a huge significance to the evening which we hadn't even dared talk about before. When a project is mooted that falls outside the County Structure Plan, it may be considered, but if it is at all contentious it will be 'called in' by the Department of the Environment for consideration. Once you've fallen into that maw of bureaucracy you can say goodbye to your project. Tonight we knew that the likelihood of that had receded beyond our wildest dreams. Only a real problem with the new road could stand in our way with the authorities. There would remain difficulties with badger passages and dragonflies, but they could be ironed out.

The MC were delighted by the outcome of the evening, and everyone was on a high. That lasted about twenty-four hours, before the bank told us that the finance team at the Commission was insisting that there should be much stronger evidence of matched funding from partners than our say-so. There should be real commitment. We had logged our basic application for European funds, which had so far seen us get a contribution towards the environmental impact assessment, but this process would be very slow indeed; there was no hope of achieving anything more solid before the next meeting of the Commissioners. The same held true of all the other agencies. The next few months drifted past in a frenzy of meetings and applications. The business plan was being modified by the week as costs were tweaked, contributions rated up or down, or assumptions tightened up. Evelyn Thurlby was beginning to take a bigger role with the bank as the revenue streams from operations were put under the microscope. The visitor-number assumptions were crucial. We were still at a million visitors, and the MC were going to test this to destruction after the fiascos at other sites.

Heather Couper,
Sir Alcon
Copisarow, TS

There would be a meeting of Commissioners some time in May 1997 and that was the likely time for them to take a proper look at our proposal. Before that we had to demonstrate that we had other partners. We were once again to be lucky in our friends. Many months before, Paul, Pete Stafford and I had stayed up all weekend to help rewrite a strategy document for the Devon and Cornwall Training and Enterprise Council. Malcolm Bell and Cairns Boston, who were behind the venture, were trying to win a competition for funding called Regional Challenge, worth somewhere in the region of £6 million to the tourism industry. The bid document had been put together by consultants as a cure for insomnia, and with the deadline days away Malcolm had begged us to help. We rewrote it in readable English and added a few touches, and they won. Trebles all round, and we were glad to have been able to help.

When our turn to beg came round Robert Davies, their finance director, pulled every favour he was owed to get people in the right place at short notice, and they were not found wanting. The TEC turned round the grant request in forty-eight hours and we were able to show the Commission that we had their support. In parallel with this we were urging our friends at English Partnerships to make a bigger commitment to demonstrate regional support. With something like six hours to go before the deadline for the MC papers to go out to the Commissioners, Nick Harrington, the local director of the agency, with the support of Richard Beattie, his boss at head office, signed off their offer letter for around £500,000.

While all this had been going on I had been writing a book. *The Lost Gardens of Heligan* came out with a big press fanfare in March, alongside the Channel 4 documentary of the same name, and by early May the book was top of the *Sunday Times* bestseller list. On 17 May I went to London, where Hatchards, the magnificent old bookshop on Piccadilly, had asked us to create a window display of old tools, forcing pots and so on. I was trying to park outside the shop in the busiest street in London, blocking a bus lane and access to a construction site, when my mobile phone went. Flustered, I said I couldn't talk and could they ring back in a few minutes. A voice I recognized said, I think you'll want to hear this now. It was Doug Weston, the MC project director. You've got it, he said: the Commissioners have made a conditional grant of £37.15 million. You have to stay shtum for a week until the formal announcement.

The conditions to be met before any money would come our way were that we must finally identify the matched funding, must rewrite the

'...and that's what it's all about...'

business plan and have it signed off by their consultants, and get planning permission. In the wave of euphoria that washed over me these seemed like mere details. We were there. Later on, it would really hurt as we tried desperately to meet their conditions. For now I was a firework. I even told the dumper-truck driver who was trying to get me to move out of the way because there was a crane with big lumps of steel hanging above the Volvo. I moved and phoned Sir Alcon, who was delighted, and would tell his fellow Trustees. I phoned Jonathan, who was as exuberant as one would have expected. Paul, Kary and Sam Tancock, our excellent project secretary, were all in the wooden hut at Heligan and there was much whooping and screaming.

I suddenly felt strangely empty. It's horrible having good news and nobody to dig in the ribs in delight. I dropped off the stuff at Hatchard's and drove home as fast as I could. Never before did crossing the Tamar feel so good.

The formal announcement took the form of a celebration on the main lawn at Heligan on 23 May. All the Trustees, funders, design team, consultants and the Eden core team were there, as were the Heligan mob, who were as caught up in the excitement as we were. A sunny day, a crusader tent, lovely food, lots to drink, nerves that meant you couldn't eat anything, a rostrum, speeches from Sir Alcon, Jonathan and myself and of course the main attraction, the delightful, bubbly Professor Heather Couper, the Millennium Commissioner charged with delivering the news that we had received the award. She said that Eden was 'Mega brilliant. The scale is absolutely mind-boggling. It's the most breathtaking thing I've ever heard of, a unique facility which will benefit not just the ecological movement but the whole world. It's a truly grandiose mission … I think it is truly marvellous that a project of this environmental scale is coming out of an environmentally scarred landscape. We are putting back what we took away, and I think that is the truly marvellous thing about the Eden Project.'

There was a quote from the Heritage Secretary, Chris Smith: 'Eden is a world-class landmark project and a bold statement for the future.' Heather, Jonathan and I were pictured out on the lawn doing what looks like a hokey-cokey. Radio and TV interviews followed, and then it was over. The rest of the world now thought that all we needed to do was start building, that we had all the money. We didn't, and the next two years were going to be the most difficult of all.

You see, there comes a moment in all great ventures when the talking has to stop. We'd created the constituencies, we'd talked the hind legs off donkeys, we'd been snake-oil salesmen with attitude and a dream to peddle, but turning a dream into reality needs iron in the soul, money in the bank and military organization. Now we would have to crank up a gear. Now we had more to lose than our own time and money; we had the hopes of the region on our shoulders, and those are some heavy monkeys.

chapter 8

...and some fell on fertile ground

With all the effort being expended on matters legal, financial, contractual and political, it was important to keep reminding ourselves why we had begun this journey. We had started with the idea of four conservatories representing some of the key climate zones of the world, and one further conservatory that would demonstrate the widest possible range of productive plants from these regions. This then evolved into four conservatories containing both their wild and productive flora. By December 1996 we were looking at three conservatories: the Humid Tropics (broadly rainforest), the Sub-Tropics (islands) and the Warm Temperate (Mediterranean climate) with an external designed parkland that would tell the story of our own temperate climate.

This meant that in Cornwall we could grow plants from sources ranging from the Himalaya and Australasia to open British moorland. After our submission to the Millennium Commission, we decided that the debt burden would be too great with three, and merged the Sub-Tropics with the Humid Tropics, leaving us with two giant conservatories and the external landscape.

The history of great conservatories is mixed. Their graceful elegance and classic proportions led to them becoming fixtures at most of the great houses and palaces of Europe and at the great botanic gardens. In truth none of them was particularly good for growing plants; they were monuments to the vanity of architects. This remains the case to the present day.

So if you're going to build the largest conservatories the world has ever seen in a sterile pit, other than the construction itself what sort of problems will you encounter? The first will be that there is no earth on site. While you may garner some spoil from work outside the pit such as road-building, a quick and dirty estimate, taking the area of the pit and the depth of soil required to give plants a chance of establishing themselves, gives you a figure of around 90,000 tonnes. That's a lot of lorries and a whole heap of dirt. Cornwall, with few major road or construction projects on the go, just didn't have it. The Midlands was the closest hunting ground, but assuming you could find it there would be no guarantee that it wasn't contaminated, and neither would it all be in one place. We would need at least 3,000 lorryloads and the coordination of a well-drilled army foraging all over the country.

Let's assume that we could somehow get hold of enough soil. We then meet the water problem. Drainage in pits is always an issue. They become huge sumps for all the local springs, and require constant pumping out. Bodelva would be no different. Plants need water, and in a controlled environment it has to be clean. It mustn't be thick with sediment or it will pollute the new soil, leave a residue on the leaves and clog up the fine nozzles of the spraying systems. Another worry is that water lying still within an irrigation or air-conditioning system is a breeding ground for bacteria, including the notorious legionnaires' disease. Water needs to be distributed throughout the site, to the roots and leaves of the plants and, within the conservatories, into the air as humidity. It will need to be evenly spread and will have to be monitored accurately – plants suffer as much from excess as they do from drought. Just to make things more difficult, the project is committed to recycling all but the drinking water.

Having parked soil and water, we need to populate the space with our precious green charges – the plants. As well as soil and water, they will also require nutrients to keep them growing. When they first move in there will be no leaf litter to supplement their diet as in nature, and many of the tropical plants feed by microrhyzal association, by which a carpet of benign subterranean fungi linked to

'Drainage in pits is always an issue...'

the roots of the plants break down the goodness in the soil for them. Establishing this system will be a key to the success of the enterprise, and the fungi are acutely sensitive; the control of pests and diseases will have to be largely biological so as not to upset the delicate balance.

Pests and diseases will be a great concern. The introduction of pests on imported plants is inevitable, no matter how carefully quarantined and treated they are. Native pests too, if introduced without a balancing number of their predators, can multiply alarmingly. The experience of other conservatories will be valuable, but the sheer scale of Eden presents its own problems, not just in terms of manpower and monitoring capability, but also in terms of the impact of the public. What might our visitors bring in with them?

Every conservatory in the world suffers from cockroaches. Even the strictest régime of cleaning and sterilization is no match for the sheer survival power of the roach, that armour-clad lumberer with a passion for things dirty. So primitive is it that you can cut its head off and it will survive for up to a month. Many curators become obsessive about them. If it kills roaches, eats roaches or even if it only discourages roaches, they'll have it. Other than geckos and ground quail not many things like roach as a main course.

Should Eden introduce any wildlife? If so, what? We would have to consider pest control through the introduction of predators such as lizards, birds and insects, and within the waterways fish and invertebrates to act as system filters. Was there an argument for birds, butterflies and other creatures to provide public enjoyment, or would this move us unacceptably close to theme-park territory? What about the insects that would be needed for pollination? Should we risk their introduction without fully understanding *their* predators, and possibly end up with the world's greatest collection of twigs? It is an extraordinarily complex debate, and highlights how important the science of ecology is, and how much more we need to discover. The romantic notions that everything has its place, and that when a butterfly sneezes it has an effect on the other side of the world through a mystic web of inter-connectedness, are beautiful thoughts … but not a lot of use to us.

Plants turn sunlight into food, for themselves and for all living things, either directly or indirectly. To be really healthy they need to have the optimum amount of light across the whole spectrum that is available outdoors. Of course each species makes its own adaptation according to which niche it inhabits. Some plants need hardly any light at all, while others flourish in the full glare of the sun, just as some plants need rich soil and others thrive in the poorest. The essential thing is to provide the best quality light and as much of it as you can. Traditional glass cuts out a wide range of the spectrum, including ultraviolet. You might sweat to death in a glasshouse but you won't die of sunburn. Glass is heavy and in a modern conservatory, using thicker glass for health and safety reasons, heavier still. Its weight will need to be supported by a massive steel or concrete structure that in turn creates shade. That is why, despite their glamour, traditional conservatories are not ideal homes for plants. This was perhaps our greatest challenge if we wanted to show plants in their full productive glory.

Having addressed issues of soil, water, pests, diseases and light, we will be left with climate control as the last physical condition to be brought under the spotlight. Eden, unlike Biosphere 2 in Arizona, would not be an enclosed system. It would not therefore be susceptible to the build-up of gases from decomposition and an artificially high carbon dioxide level that would encourage the plants to grow so rapidly as to lose all strength in their stems. The conditions at Eden would still encourage extraordinary growth, however. For instance, in the Humid Tropics, the heavy rains would be reduced to a mist, so that whereas in nature the nutrients would be washed away, here they would be contained and augmented, and growth rates would greatly exceed what would be expected in the wild. This would affect their strength and susceptibility to disease.

What could we do to encourage the movement of air, and thus provide fitness training for our plants? Would we have to hug our plants in turn, shaking them to build up their stem strength? Eden's conservatories would be naturally ventilated, but huge. It was estimated that on a sunny day with the vents closed it would take roughly twenty minutes for the steel struts in the roof to get so hot you could fry eggs on them. What we didn't know was what would happen on a cold day. How long would it take for a catastrophic temperature drop to occur? What

Climate control systems, part 1...

sort of heating capacity would we need? What effect would the granite cliffs that formed the rear walls of the conservatories have? Would they be an effective heat sink? Could we create rain, not just to water the plants but to capture the rising heat in its droplets, bringing it back to earth and creating a cycle? Was the volume of the biomes so big that, just as at Cape Canaveral, they would develop their own weather systems inside? Should all the systems be computer controlled or should we insist on manual overrides?

Once the physical issues had been considered we would then need to address the plant collection itself. We had quickly squashed the idea that we could recreate ecosystems, which would be a nonsense and scientifically impossible. We intended to represent and interpret climate zones which exhibited the maximum impact of man on the environment, thus providing a canvas on which to explore the widest range of issues. We wished to recreate certain habitats to inform and entertain the public about human dependence on plants, and in so doing create a predisposition to effect or support positive changes in the way we live. We didn't want to be worthy or preachy, seeing entertainment and an optimistic outlook as the best starting point for engaging the interest of the widest possible audience. There was widespread acknowledgement within the team that we would have to be brave in pursuit of the common touch. Scientists as a breed are famous for their contempt of colleagues who deign to make their subject more accessible, less mysterious or indeed less serious.

Right from the start we could see the pointlessness of building a new foundation that preached to the already converted. In the UK alone about three million people are affiliated in one form or another to organizations that could loosely be described as having an environmental bias, from environmental activists at one end to the National Trust at the other. What interested us was how we could reach the other fifty million who weren't involved in any way. Surely they, and the billions around the world like them, had to be the prize? How we would tell the stories, and marry the twin aims of entertainment and the application of science for change, would be the subject of impassioned debate.

Peter Thoday had gathered his prize ex-students around him and created, with Philip, what was to become known as the Green Team. Initially an informal gathering, meeting irregularly to discuss some of the generic issues raised by Eden's ambitions, it became more focused on problem-solving and highlighting issues for others in the design team to resolve. This work would prove invaluable when it came to developing the final brief, and these remarkable people gave their time freely, with no expectation of reward, and travelled great distances from all over the country.

There was David Rae, whose majestic Ph.D. on the condition, aims and ambitions of the botanic gardens of the world would enable us to define what our ...and part 2 unique contribution could be in taking the tradition forward. He observed that most botanic gardens, other than those with significant financial backing, were in decline and often in a very poor state of repair, relying heavily on the commitment of a few people to keep them going. Most suffered from a crisis of direction. They were set up as exploitative branches of the state or commerce, and in the modern political climate were having to rewrite their history and mission to take account of conservation as their primary remit. They were moreover largely set up along departmental lines, leading to a culture of inter-departmental competition for resources rather than one that encouraged cross-disciplinary collaboration. This Victorian baggage held within it the seeds of their potential destruction. The international agencies were increasingly becoming the largest providers of research funding, and they demanded a modern multi-disciplinary approach to problem-solving. The botanic gardens would have to adapt or die.

Tony Kendle

Other members of the Green Team included David Miller, the master commercial grower from Guernsey, who brought with him his expertise at high-quality industrial horticulture; and Paul Hadley from Reading University, an expert in light transmission through plastic and also the man in charge of the Cocoa Transit Centre. (Extraordinary but true: many of the great crops such as cocoa, cotton, sugar and bananas have their plant transit centres in Europe so as to prevent epidemics spreading through direct contact with other growing areas and possibly wiping out the livelihoods of whole nations.) There was Simon Fowler, an entomologist specializing in tropical pests; James Hitchmough, whose subject was prairie and wildflower flora; James Wilson, a landscape designer who had been involved in a number of the garden festivals; Mike Maunder from Kew, who brought a wide expertise on development issues; and Judith Teasedale, a landscapist and project manager who would knock some sense into us concerning the targets we would have to hit to bring the project off horticulturally. Four others who would leave an even deeper imprint on the project would, in due course, join it.

Tony Kendle is a most unusual man. Round, blondly balding in a wispy way, with a ready shy smile, he is softly spoken but, when you can hear him, totally brilliant. A man for whom a suit looks like a jail sentence, his natural camouflage is a dress code best described as sub-Oxfam. This diffidence disappears with a vengeance at party time, when he reveals his alter ego, the king of the dance floor. Who can forget his arrival at the Eden Christmas party fancy-dress ball, a pink brush taped to his head and an industrial binliner clinging to his form? Unusually for a scientist, he has the ability to write with great clarity, wit and poetry for Everyman; he wears his passion for his subject lightly. He is an unashamed champion of the killing of sacred cows, and his air of benign reasonableness as he leads you gently by the nose of your own prejudice into a brick wall leaves no rancour, only a wry recognition of your own sloppy thinking. Well read across many subjects, he too believed that our fledgling foundation should be anti-departmental and that our house style should be unashamedly populist. But, and this was the crucial but, there should be a method of accessing deeper knowledge easily for those who wanted it. Tony's commitment to education is total; he sees it as a great liberator at all levels and at any time of life. He rarely gets irritated, but the suggestion that education is just about schools and colleges infuriates him. He is hugely attentive to the students in his care and would allow no engagements of his own to get in the way of his duty to them.

Perhaps my most vivid picture of him comes from a night at Peter Thoday's house in Box, when after an entire evening of talk without any contribution from Tony save the occasional nod, he summarized all the arguments in a few minutes, added some pepper, salt and gunpowder, lit the blue touchpaper and left. Philip remarked on the way home that it was exhilarating to be forced into thinking by the quality of argument. It could be uncomfortable to argue with Tony, but the sense of danger would be essential if we genuinely wanted to stimulate new ways of thinking and doing. He would remain at Reading University for a while longer, but we had no doubts in our mind that Eden was a stage tailor-made for his talent.

Tom Keay and Helen Rosevear are partners, and had been students of Peter's at

Helen Rosevear, Tom Keay

Bath. Helen's family lived in Porthpean, near Heligan, and that's where I first met her when as a student she accompanied Peter on one of his trips. With her mane of fine honey-blonde hair, great bone structure and lips that you pay good money for in California, she was every inch a Pre-Raphaelite model. She had a studious, worried air about her that belied her ability to corpse into giggles with little encouragement. It was Helen who would make the very first model of Eden out of bent bits of plastic and pipe-cleaners. She is one of those people you trust implicitly to do the best job she can with a diligence that is at once humbling and immensely comforting.

She would be party to many of the Green Team meetings, joining the project formally with Tom in July 1997 to coordinate the landscape design work.

Tom is a very different character, lean, mean and serious, with short dark hair, thick glasses and something of the look of a student radical about him. He is a first-class horticulturist with a special interest in the plants of the Warm Temperate. Tom's determination to succeed is awesome. This makes him demanding, but he is harder on himself than on anyone else. He takes criticism through gritted teeth, but never makes the same mistake twice. He cares about what he does with a passion, and as the project unfolded he and Robin Lock (whom you will meet later) had to take on board skills and responsibilities that I don't believe have ever been asked of anyone in horticulture before. Tom has a charming ability to thaw suddenly into a smily character when the pressure is off. He is another of the team who is completely comfortable with the breakdown in departmentalism, although you can sometimes almost hear him sniff the air to see whether he can smell hype or sense the first stages of backsliding.

Ian Martin comes from a completely different mould. In his placement year as a student at Kew he decided to go and work in South America, as opposed to the usual humdrum garden-centre jobs favoured by contemporaries. He never looked back, and after qualifying ended up in Malawi, where he married a local girl and worked on a number of development projects. I hope he will forgive me if I describe him as having the appearance and demeanour of a slightly otherworldly vicar. He loves plants, and delights in telling their stories to adults and children alike.

Ian once brought a Green Team meeting to order by chiding us for Western oversimplification on the issue of conservation. He explained that most African languages have no word for conservation. The gods in their pantheon are the providers of all worldly needs. The problem Ian faced in Africa was that he had to

promote conservation in the communities in which he worked in a way that made sense to them. First of all he had to convince the witch doctor that as he grew older he would need to walk further and further to find the ingredients for his medicines, and that it was therefore in his interest to promote the growing of these plants in all the back gardens of the village. Later he employed the same tactics with the women whose daily chore it was to collect firewood. Before long village plantations were in place. Ian

Ian Martin,
nursery supremo

joined the team as our nursery manager at the same time as Helen and Tom.

Outside the Green Team we had been advancing our relationships with other institutions in the quest for help. Philip and I had begun in February 1995 with the Natural History Museum, who were polite in a patrician manner but didn't take us seriously. They showed us the door and never got in contact with us again. Later that year Philip and Peter established very strong ties with the Royal Botanic Gardens in Edinburgh, where the director, Professor David Ingram, was a big supporter. He encouraged his team to get involved where they could, and it was they who introduced us to BG Base, the Botanic Gardens computer-based plant cataloguing system. It is crucially important for a serious institution to know what plants it has, where they are located and where they originally came from, as well as much other information. We would soon be cataloguing thousands of specimens and seeds, and without a coherent system we would become a shambles. If we were unable to monitor our own collections effectively, our participation in conservation studies and the trade of information with other serious institutions

Inside the nursery

Professor Sir
Ghillean Prance

would be jeopardized. We owe them a debt for their generosity.

In 1994 I had by chance bumped into the director of the Royal Botanic Gardens at Kew, Professor Sir Ghillean Prance, and his wife Anne, who were visiting Heligan during a stay with their daughter, a doctor at Treliske Hospital in Truro. We exchanged cards and pleasantries and they invited me to come and see them at Kew. The following year Friends of Kew and Friends of Heligan entered a reciprocal arrangement to allow each other free access and this cemented the warm relations between us. I was to meet Ghillean on a number of occasions over the next few years, sometimes on my own, sometimes with Philip and again with Jonathan. The more I got to know him the more I hoped that he would join us in some capacity.

Initially the approach was designed to forge collaborative links with Kew itself, but in truth, while Ghillean was keen, some of his staff were a little wary that we might represent unwelcome competition – not in terms of attracting visitors but in the pursuit of research funding. Kew is heavily dependent on obtaining research grants from government and non-governmental organizations (NGOs). Our problem was that no one told us of their concerns, and more than a year was to go by before we could make our peace and explain that Eden didn't want to have an independent scientific research facility, and neither did it want to engage in any area where others were already pre-eminent. Relations subsequently warmed considerably, and we like to think that they see us as partners.

Ghillean and I stayed in touch, and I never missed an opportunity to put him under friendly pressure to come and join us. Eventually he succumbed and offered to become a Trustee if that would be helpful. Circumstances were to conspire to prevent this happening because as the project gathered momentum we were to have much greater need of his hands-on experience, and he would ultimately become our first director of science. But that still lay some time in the future.

Our Trustee Sir Ralph Riley was meanwhile trying to help us develop relationships with some of the international organizations with which he was involved, most notably the Food and Agriculture Organization (FAO) and the International Food Policy Research Institute (IFPRI). Ralph was passionate in his belief that Eden was important because it sought to bring together environmental activists, conservationists and agribusiness in the search for solutions. Through his involvement with the Rockefeller 20/20 Vision project he was becoming ever more convinced that divisions between conservation and agricultural interests needed to be healed

if the debate was going to be based on scientific observation and best practice, not knee-jerk emotional responses. Interestingly, although he might have been expected to favour the agriculture lobby, he was as keen as we were that Eden should be apolitical, advancing the arguments or positions of all sides so as to inform the public. He wanted us to host professional seminars with the same aim in mind.

In October 1997 Ralph invited me as his guest to attend the Rank Prize Funds Symposium in Bournemouth, a gathering of some of the world's leading scientists working in the development field. I went with some trepidation, expecting to be out of my depth. It turned out that it wasn't just scientists attending; there were some NGO executives and civil servants from what was then the Overseas Development Agency (ODA). To my great delight the first people I bumped into were Anne and Ghillean Prance. My delight began and ended there. Ralph was the host, so I wasn't going to see much of him, and after an incredibly dull black-tie dinner followed by an eggbound speech from the guest of honour, I realized that there were two completely different interest groups in the room. There were the idealists who were in the business of using their skills to improve the lot of their fellow man, and there were the hard-nosed snouts-in-the-trough boys who knew a good angle for soft money when they saw one, and enjoyed offices in Rome, Geneva or New York and the lifestyles to go with it them. In the bar on the first night I felt as if I had been inducted into a Kafkaesque secret society that spoke only in acronyms. The knowing civil servant, his vanity afire with drink, explaining how to get round this and that and what the real agendas were for governments, and the international scientist who needed only a few million dollars to crack the code of this or that, appeared to be two sides of the same cynical coin. At breakfast I spoke with Ghillean about this, hoping that I'd got the wrong end of the stick. He implied that I wasn't completely off beam, but urged patience until I'd heard the lectures.

I'm not qualified to comment on some of the technical presentations, but the whiff of special pleading hung heavy everywhere you eavesdropped. Then on came a man who spoke with passion and commitment, and the unmistakable smell of cordite. He was Gordon Conway from Sussex University, who would go on to run the Rockefeller Foundation. The gist of his speech, although dressed up in masterfully diplomatic language, was that scientists shouldn't bury their heads in the sand; there was no point in pretending that their suggested solutions were worth anything at all if they wouldn't acknowledge that their influence was negligible in the face of the pressure of globalization and global poverty in all its forms. I can't remember much of the detail of what he said, but its impact was electrifying.

Back in the bar consciences had been pricked, and the tenor of the evening was completely different from that of the night before. The issues of the day were being discussed in a new way. Salinity of the soil, the bane of so many developing and developed countries, was talked of as a compound problem caused by the 'Green Revolution' and the attendant over-irrigation which reduced water tables, Western demand for prawns leading to the wholesale destruction of the coastal mangrove swamps to create prawn pans, and so on. There was an interlude in which I asked my new friends who they most admired. The unexpected answer from many of them was Bob Geldof, because he showed respect. A lot of money was raised by Live Aid, and there was temptation to set up a new organization to distribute it. Instead he listened and took advice and used existing routes. This was exceptionally good for morale, and Live Aid itself raised the profile of their work in the eyes of the public and with governments.

The evening became increasingly revelatory. These people told me that they were fed up with working in isolation without the world understanding what they were trying to do, and having to spend most of their time fighting for diminishing sums of money because governments needed to justify their expenditure to their voters. If it was difficult for governments to understand, what on earth would the public make of it? Bob Geldof had made a simple moral proposition and people had been moved and had seen the importance of what needed to be done, but the faceless acronyms in Geneva, Rome and New York couldn't drum up the passion or the commitment. All that remained was to knuckle down and do the best you could, having had your Andy Warhol moment.

I had come to the conference as a cynic and wannabe rebel, and I left it having realized that underneath the veneer most of the people there believed in the sort of things I did. The difference was that many of them, worn down by the politics of development, were consumed by a sense of powerlessness, so chose instead to focus on the smaller, albeit still important issues they had some control over. I got the distinct impression that they would love to get fired up again, if only someone or something would give them a reason to believe that real change was possible.

I remember returning home from the conference and talking to a journalist who asked me to sum up in one sentence what the Eden Project was about. It was the same question I'd been asked a hundred times by other journalists, banks and consultants. If you can't sum it up in a phrase, you haven't got a product, was their view. For the first time I felt angry with myself for playing the game. It was H. L. Mencken who said that nobody went broke by underestimating the intelligence of the public, or words to that effect. I think he was wrong: if you show respect you get it back, and if you fail while being true to yourself people will forgive you, because they know you tried. Why, for God's sake, put yourself and your friends and family through years of grief to build a crappy theme park so that some smartass can define it in a sentence? Too many people were putting too much of themselves into this. We weren't for sale. Eden wasn't a product, it was a place in the heart.

chapter 9

when pips squeak

The conditional award from the Millennium Commission in May 1997 was the beginning of the end of the old way of doing things. We were left in no doubt, once the bunting had come down, that unless we delivered a business plan the Commission's consultants believed in, Eden would disappear into limbo. There were a number of difficult conversations to be had both with the bank and with the Trustees. A Trust is normally set up to look after the assets or activities of a known quantity, a fund or an endowed activity, or a place. Much credit must go to the Trustees for taking on the responsibility for something that was being defined by others on an almost daily basis.

Its development was truly organic, like a jellyfish; it gained mass and strength with each new person or idea that joined. At the same time, however, there began to be friction over the leadership of the project. For all the right reasons the Trust wanted to monitor what was going on, and deliberate on the options available to it. The Trust never wanted the private sector to take equity in its operating company, seeing this as a watering down of its control. They rightly perceived that should the project have teething problems there was a chance that they could lose control of a huge asset to a minority stakeholder.

At the same time the bank was becoming impatient at what they saw as a lack of support from the Trust. In the absence of any other source of funding it was futile to suppose that there was an alternative. They suggested a compromise which would require the Trust to proceed along the equity route, but with an option to buy out the investors should funding materialize from elsewhere. In the business these are known as preference shares. The Trustees were wary, because they didn't see how this stratagem squared with the bank's other reason for taking equity – performance guarantees from the investors, in this case the operator and constructor.

Times had changed, however, and we now had a constructor and operator impatient to conclude contractual negotiations. Our design team was becoming restive, having by now worked for two years for nothing save small fees from feasibility studies. We were also beginning to address the way in which the constructor and the design team might work together, and a number of exploratory meetings were taking place under the direction of Tim Carter.

Tim is perhaps the calmest man I have ever met, which considering the pressure he is always under is remarkable. What Tim brought with him was integrity. A few

Colin Weekley

minutes in his company convinced you that here was a man who believed the best of human nature and refused to look for the worst, and it influenced the attitude of all those who came into contact with him. I spoke to him for ages about why contractors and designers always fall out and why budgets always overrun. On the constructors' side we were dealing initially with four people: Cullum McAlpine and his deputy, Colin Weekley, from Sir Robert McAlpine; and Derrick McCormick and Martin Miles, managing director and commercial manager respectively of Alfred McAlpine. Cullum and Martin would play important roles later on, but initially the main points of contact were Colin and Derrick. This was the first time that the two McAlpine companies had worked together in a major way for many, many years.

Colin was suave and tanned, looking rather like an Argentinian polo player. Derrick presented the more traditional picture of a constructor, very robust in his opinions but also hilarious in his world-weary powers of observation. They both deserve a lot of credit for keeping open minds throughout the process of negotiation. Obviously they wanted to make a profit, but they instinctively understood when to play the hard contractor, if people were getting a little precious, and when to allow the design team to fly. They were concerned that costs would overrun horribly if they didn't control the design team. For their part the design team were terrified that once under the wing of the contractor the project would turn into a design-and-build contract that would result in Eden looking like an industrial building.

Britain has too many constructors chasing too little work. The result is a culture of bidding too low in order to secure the contract; sometimes these quotes will be below the actual cost to the constructor just so that the work comes in. The trick then is to have a running

battle with either the client or the architect to prove that the job the constructor is actually having to do is bigger than that for which the original quote was made – hence the development of the culture of 'extras', without which all constructors would have gone bust years ago. It is a culture that depends on warfare and fault-finding and is not compatible with partnership. Salvation was offered in the form of what was known as the New Engineering Contract (NEC), which I believe Eden pioneered, at least on this scale. We were all nervous, but both the designers and the constructors believed that this might be the way to create a great piece of work without all the attendant programme and budget overruns. It was simple in concept. One agreed a profit in advance with the contractor, obviating the need

for them to find fault with others in order to prosper, and then the contract would be run on an open-book basis, meaning that all costs would be open to scrutiny from both sides. The scary thing was that for it to succeed everybody needed to work with the utmost good will; however, this would turn out to be one of the best decisions we ever made. We would also invite McAlpine's on to the board of the Trust's operating company, Eden Project Limited. This would cement our relationship even further.

Derrick McCormick and Ronnie Murning went off to start negotiating the contracts for the design team, while back at Heligan Kary, Paul, Sam Tancock and I were managing the relationships with the other major funding bodies from the wooden hut. We were joined here by Evelyn Thurlby, who commuted weekly from her home in Winchester. She took the responsibility for developing the operational business plan and took over the contact with the bank from me.

Other changes at the wooden hut saw the arrival of Neal Barnes. Neal had been the local councillor at Tregrehan, adjacent to the Bodelva site. He had attended the council meetings and the local village hall presentations. We'd first met to discuss ways in which we could give comfort to various local interest groups. Neal was a lecturer in health and safety, explosives and various facilities management subjects at St Austell College. He wasn't enjoying the work that much and was fascinated by Eden, and asked whether there might be a job for him. Having no money we embarked on our usual course of action, which was to persuade his college to second him to us. Neal is a very large, friendly, bearded man with glasses. Our office was very small. Neal would take over a lot of the planning and land acquisition coordination for us. As we moved through the summer we had to identify all the landowners who lived along the route of our proposed road, and check that all the agreements with English China Clays were properly marked as the area is notoriously lax with its land registrations – perhaps unsurprising since it moves so much.

We were looking for £12.5 million from Europe. Four top bods from the European Commission were coming to Cornwall to decide whether to award us the money, and for reasons that escape me now I was the only one available to drive them into the pit. Imagine the situation if you will. It is winter, it is dusk, everyone else has gone home. You have loaded four men in Armani and Gucci into a four-wheel drive and are descending into a pit where it has been raining solidly for a week. The mud is four feet deep. Right at the bottom of the pit the vehicle comes to a grinding, crunching halt. I have contrived to park on top of a granite boulder hidden under the mud. I rev the engine and the wheels spin. There is silence among my passengers. How am I going to tell them that they will have

Evelyn Thurlby: the view from the Wendy Hut

to get out and push? Suddenly, a moment of inspiration: a childhood memory of a John Wayne film, *Hatari!*, I think. Game warden stuck in a river rocks vehicle and lets clutch out when a wheel hits solid ground. I pray. I instruct my passengers to rock from side to side. They think this is some kind of bizarre English party game and they all, especially the German, think it highly amusing. Thud, engine screams, lurch, launch like a cork out of a bottle. Lots of hearty cheering and I take the plaudits for a most enjoyable visit. There by the grace of…

By August 1997 there was a moment of calm, and I decided to take a holiday in Italy. The day before I was due to leave all hell broke loose as the Government Office for the South West decided that now was the time our full application for money from Europe should be presented. I had no option but to go to Italy or I would have faced a family insurrection. I was allowed a mobile phone on condition that I turned it on only in the evening. Kary was on her own and she asked Evelyn to help. While I was sampling the delights of Romeo and Juliet country in the Valpolicella region, north of Verona, they were desperately trying to put the final touches to our bid document. My memory of the period is of an excruciatingly painful marble seat in the Verona Coliseum watching *Madam Butterfly* and wishing I was anywhere but there. Kary and Evelyn's memories are of filling in forms full of tortuous Eurospeak about additionality, wishing they also were anywhere but there.

My other great memory is of visiting the Giardino Giusti, a fantastic garden built in a quarry hidden behind the gates of a Verona townhouse. An ivy-draped walkway cut into the cliff face leads you upwards to a central tower, at the top of which you emerge to take in the view of the garden below; to marvel at the mathematics of the *parterres* and the symmetrically placed statuary, highlighted by the shadow play of cypresses. I wished that the team were all there to see it, to take inspiration for our pit. I wrote to Dominic Cole in a lather of excitement at my moment of revelation, only to be put in my place on my return. Not only was he well aware of it, but he had already developed some ideas in sympathy with the perspectives that had so excited me.

Kary and Evelyn made a magnificent job of the Euroforms and managed to submit them just before the deadline – horror of horrors, that turned out to be the same day that Princess Diana died in Paris.

I ought at this point to say that the Trustees were pushing for a proper chief executive to take over the delivery of the project. I was considered to have political, big-picture skills, undertaken with a maverick gusto. They wanted a more traditional executive to take us forward in line with the rigour demanded by the bank and the constructor. I couldn't disagree – there was far too much to do to worry about the vanity of titles – but there was no money with which to pay this fabled beast. Mr Micawber took control of my mind and Heligan paid for an advert

in the usual places to solicit applications for a chief executive for the Eden Project, salary to be negotiated.

Two things had happened recently. First there had been a General Election, in which the Labour Party had swept to power, and secondly there had been a defence review. That was how it came about that Kary, Paul and I ended up in the living room of my house with a bottle of wine and a mountain of three hundred job applications, the majority of which seemed to be from former MPs or brass hats. Our hearts sank as we sifted through the names. By the early hours we had about six we considered worth forwarding to the Trustees, of whom two looked more likely than the others.

Meanwhile, back at the wooden hut in Heligan, Evelyn broached the subject of the chief executive post and enquired whether it was worth her while applying to the Trust for an interview. Go for it, we said, having been impressed by the way she had stepped into the breach with the European grant crisis. Evelyn had been seconded to us by her company as part of their investment in the putative operator's contract. She was like a breath of fresh air, very dynamic – she always gave the impression of being in a hurry – incredibly focused and good fun to be

Picasso meets the Aztecs, part 1

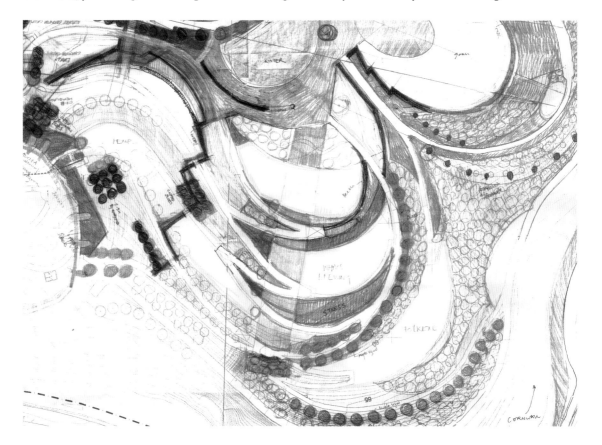

with; her only vice, like many of us in the team, was smoking. There was an ever-present tension in her, and even when she laughed you'd sense a slight edge. She didn't suffer fools gladly, and adjusting to our organized chaos was a culture shock, a test she passed with flying colours. She worked unbelievably hard, and as she headed off into the night you felt for her.

The interviews for the job were held in two stages in September. The interview panel consisted of the Trustees, Jonathan and myself, Peter Thoday, the McAlpine representative and the then boss of the Millennium Commission. The military men were fine, but when it was Evelyn's turn she was streets ahead. She had recently completed a start-up, and gave an aggressively professional presentation of what had to be done. She was chosen, and it was arranged that she would take up her position formally in October. Her company would continue paying her for another six months, and Mr Micawber had come up trumps.

It would be disingenuous of me to deny that there were tensions in the project. I won't dwell on them, but a slight distance had arisen between Jonathan and the rest of us simply as a by-product of the level of work now hitting us every day. He was in Bude and the project was based in the wooden hut at Heligan. The ambassadorial role had become less important, and his practice appeared to me not to want to engage in the nuts and bolts of developing the technical side of the project, even though Grimshaw's had indicated that they would have no objection. Jonathan and I talked about it; he felt he was being frozen out, although this was in no way our intention. When he, Paul and I met at the Crown at St Ewe just before the announcement of the MC award it was to discuss media coverage of the big day, but also on the agenda was Jonathan's unhappiness at being deliberately excluded from the media limelight. Paul explained that the success of Heligan, which at the time was riding high on TV and in all good bookshops, led them to focus on me, no matter what he tried to do to persuade them otherwise.

This unhappiness was compounded by the Trust's inability to address issues of past and future reward for the risks taken over a period of three years in developing the project to its present stage. The Millennium Commission for their part had been robust in saying that they felt payment for services rendered was totally appropriate, and in private acknowledged that the unusual nature of the project might permit the Trustees to make a recommendation as to a small premium to recognize the risks taken, but that future royalties or equity in the operating company would not get their support.

In hindsight it is a pity that these issues were not addressed head-on at the time. In our defence, life was so busy that it seemed somehow inappropriate to be discussing personal terms and conditions at a time when there was no certainty that the project would proceed. Jonathan said balefully to me that if personal conditions weren't sorted out now before new people came into the project it

would be only a matter of time before history was rewritten and we'd be airbrushed out. I couldn't see it that way at all.

The project hit its first major crisis in September 1997. It had been brewing for some time. Philip had said many times that while the Millennium Commission and the banks might work in terms of financial years, plants worked in seasons. If we didn't begin the propagation of our collections this autumn we would have to kiss goodbye to one season, which in turn would put back the delivery of the project by a year. This would be a disaster. The project had no money, and the Millennium Commission would advance us none.

We had found the ideal site for the Eden nursery – Watering Lane at Porthpean, roughly halfway between Heligan and Bodelva. During the summer Philip had entered discussions with its owner, Roger Noyce, who was a supplier to Heligan. (Indeed, he had once been involved at Heligan with a view to taking a stake in it during the early years.) His nursery was probably one of the best in Cornwall, clean and with a large area under glass, and Roger, being a man of foresight, had also laid down the infrastructure for its future expansion. His problem was that he was bored with running a nursery. So when Philip approached him he was a willing vendor. We had it valued, and there we were in limbo. I approached the McAlpine team, who were initially encouraging, but after contracts were sent a deafening silence fell.

One evening Peter Stafford put through a call from Cullum McAlpine. We talked about the nursery and he said bluntly, you buy it, you're in this business, we build things. It was a case of put up or shut up. Heligan had already spent a small fortune by its standards bankrolling part of the project payroll and its running costs. Rolf Munding told me straight that I should think twice about doing this. He said, you are still a young man, but John Nelson is coming up to retirement. I know you control the company, but remember your responsibilities to him. He was right and I knew it, but quite simply Philip and I recognized that if we did nothing the project would be finished.

Peter Stafford was a pillar of strength. You must do this, he said; I will make sure that the company isn't put at risk by it. What on earth would you say in a couple of years' time, that you'd got this close and bottled it? The next day Peter spoke to the bank, the estate agents and Roger, and the deal was done; we had a nursery. It had a bungalow where Philip could set up the library, it had rooms that could be converted into offices, and a couple of bedrooms for staff who could double up as security people.

Philip sprang into action like a man possessed. Helen and Tom would move into the offices, and he asked Emma Cummings, a volunteer, to become his PA and move into Watering Lane with a view to setting up a secretariat for the

Emma Cummings

Green Team and preparing the place for an invasion of people. Ian Martin was summoned and told to get ready to start propagating immediately. Winston Woodward and James Treseder, prize students at Duchy College, where Philip was a Governor, were told to prepare themselves to volunteer for weekend working, because he had plans for them. Carload after carload of books and papers were transported from Philip's home and the Heligan offices to start off our library. If Philip had had any doubts about the outcome of the project he had none now.

There were two other effects of the purchase. The first was that McAlpine's had called our bluff, we hadn't been found wanting, and they respected this. It would give them the confidence to go a few extra miles themselves if necessary. This confidence was amply demonstrated in a memorable board meeting some years later. We were beset by a massive funding gap, and our biggest creditor was always going to be McAlpine's. We had a legal responsibility to call time on the Project if there was a reasonable doubt that we would be able to meet our obligations. Gay produced the monthly figures demonstrating that we'd be all right with a following wind, but there'd be a judgement call to make. Many of the directors were uneasy until Cullum McAlpine looked up from his papers and said simply, 'I'm still here.'

The second consequence was that immediately Evelyn was appointed chief executive she insisted that the team should move up to Watering Lane. She believed, rightly, that for Eden to come of age it needed to come out of the shadow of Heligan and develop its own culture and working practices. She wanted independence. For her own office she selected a garden shed, which was soon christened the Wendy Hut, and she asked Kary to start organizing the office equipment with Emma. We would move as soon as we could.

(overleaf)
Watering Lane, plant wonderland

A number of other issues needed resolving. Evelyn asked for a meeting with Jonathan and me to discuss our future roles. I would take on the title of project director and would sign a contract with the company. My task was to continue creating the Eden culture and developing the relationships with the funding agencies. Evelyn would take charge of all the contract negotiations with the Millennium Commission, the bank, the constructor and the other funders. She would also further develop the business plan. We could work together.

The conversation with Jonathan was less conclusive. He didn't want to work at Watering Lane; he had commitments to his practice and wanted therefore to remain in Bude. She offered him a 'hot desk' at the nursery for three days a week. This was also declined. It was left that he would write a job description for Evelyn to consider. When it came she was unhappy with the wide brief Jonathan had given himself in areas where she was unconvinced that he had the requisite expertise. A compromise was reached. Jonathan would become corporate affairs director, in charge of various initiatives for fundraising and promotion, but payment would be made on results and there would be a review in six months. Jonathan was not happy, neither was he thrilled that the Trustees had announced that he and I should no longer attend Trust meetings, since Evelyn

The Wendy Hut:
Watering Lane
nerve centre

was the representative of the company. At some point in the middle of all this change Jonathan decided to register the name The Eden Project as a trademark belonging to him. Although disconcerted, we felt that kicking up a fuss just as a new chief executive was getting her feet under the table seemed an overreaction; surely we would be able to resolve the issue amicably.

In November the big move started. Kary, Paul, Sam, Neal and Evelyn moved out of a wooden hut, travelled a mile up the road and decanted themselves into another wooden hut. A stray cat made itself at home, which cheered Evelyn up immensely, since she was missing her cat back home in Winchester. It was lucky, she said. Eden suddenly felt very grown-up to me, and I wasn't convinced I liked all this change. But no doubt it would be for the best.

chapter 10

rollercoaster

Evelyn was just what the project needed: tough,
driven and focused. While her full-blooded
approach made me swallow hard on occasion,
and her impatience to dispense with pleasantries
sometimes felt like fingernails running down a
blackboard, she was right that the project needed
to become professional if it was not to disappoint
all the hopes that the previous years had raised.
What drove her mad were the myriad connections
that were nurtured for no immediate gain, with a
view to a bigger picture at some indefinable point
in the future. Where I saw a campaign, she saw it
broken down into individual battles that had to
be won along the way. The truth was that we
were both right, and without both tactics being
employed in tandem we would never have
made the progress we did.

She was a fabulous cook, and would entertain the troops on a regular basis at her lovely flat in Fowey, bought shortly after becoming chief executive. Here one would see a different Evelyn, the warm, convivial hostess interested in everything under the sun, looking after us in a style to which we would have loved to become accustomed. For a moment there would be a great thaw, and we would talk about the wider issues and get excited about the opportunities over the horizon. I think she resented the fact that pressure of work made it look as if she didn't care about such things, and that I had all the fun without the responsibility.

Having worked with Kary for the first period of her secondment, Evelyn knew that she was wasted working just for me. Kary was immediately promoted to become the project co-ordinator, charged with managing just about everything – nothing new there except the title. Kary's role was to be central because the crucial strength of any project is the team and its morale. During that first difficult year of cultural change her mother-hen-meets-sharpened-sabre approach was to keep us afloat, and her management of Evelyn, reinterpreting demands for action into more diplomatic requests, was masterful.

Kary's final task as my PA was to select her replacement. Again I was interviewed and put through my paces, and luckily I came up to scratch. So it was that Carolyn Trevivian consented to join me. She had worked at the Tate in St Ives and had followed that by acting as a personal assistant to a lady trying to revive for the stage a thirteenth-century mystery play cycle in Cornish featuring a cast of several thousand. Caro, as she is known to all, is Cornish through and through and lives down west, but commutes in a vehicle with a formidable track record of failure. Hugely well read, and with a flamboyant ignorance of the advances in time-keeping afforded by the watch, she has many of the characteristics of a cat. One day I remonstrated with her for her lateness, and she sympathized with me and observed that if she was me she would fire her. It was only a matter of weeks before colleagues and outsiders alike realized that my PA was Cornwall's equivalent to Victoria Wood and began phoning her in preference to me. I was once told that she had been invited to a royal function and had been asked if she would like to bring me along. Her deadpan humour is matched by an Amish-inspired dress code that perfectly demonstrates her independence from normal working practices. She was, and is, priceless. She, like Kary before her, passed through my life and enriched it before moving on to better things, of which more later.

The key to our eventual success was always going to be the management of our finances. Evelyn, though financially

Paul Travers,
media maestro

literate, knew that we would have to bring in a first-class finance director. For reasons beyond imagining every public agency in Britain and Europe insists on developing its own procedures and payment mechanisms. A vast secretariat is needed to deal with the paperwork this generates. Hundreds of man-hours are spent turning the same information into different formats, filling in slightly differently worded questionnaires, and disbursing and receiving funds at variable times. Add to this the knowledge that all the funding bodies will have their own experts or consultants whom they will insist on sending down to ask you the same questions as the previous lot, and you have a recipe for impatience, to say the least. The most irritating factor was that the consultants were so pleased to be in Cornwall that they didn't want to rush things. This was work and pleasure to them. A by-product of all this complexity was a small rainforest's worth of legal documents, and lawyers don't come cheap.

It was a bleak November evening outside the School House Restaurant in Pentewan when I first met Gaynor Coley. She had come to meet Evelyn and me to discuss the possibility of her joining us from Plymouth University, where she was the finance director. Professional yet casual, self-contained yet warm, she was a latter-day Lois Lane, not at all the typical fusty number we had been expecting. Plymouth University was a big operation, with a turnover in the region of £80 million a year, itself involved with many of the major funders we were hoping to attract. She was tired of commuting and wanted a new challenge. Evelyn and I proposed taking her on, initially as a seconded consultant, later as a fully fledged team member. She joined the board as FD-in-waiting in January 1998, taking up what was supposed to be a part-time position in March. It soon turned full time in all but name as the pursuit of the various funding threads hotted up.

At the end of the previous year, at Ronnie's suggestion, we had started a courtship with Imagination, the London corporate imaging company. As usual we went to see them cap in hand to persuade them to work for us on a promise. Previously Marcello Minale, a friend of Rolf's, had generously had his team at Minale Tattersfield experiment with a corporate image, but although the designs were beautiful none of them seemed to hit the mark. A series of meetings at Imagination's iconic HQ couldn't have provided a starker counterpoint to what the Eden Project was hoping to stand for. This was an all-singing all-dancing temple to the gods of style and consumption. But when it came to substance we found ourselves battling to explain that we weren't after gloss, we

Gaynor Coley: not your common-or-garden number-cruncher

Imagination man:
Peter Hampel

wanted soul. Eventually, after some translation, we fixed on our major requirement, a lettering for our name that said serious, not worthy, practical, not affected, scientific, not theme park. To give them credit, we used what they came up with and are very happy with it.

The bright side of the exercise was that we met Peter Hampel, who was Imagination's accounts director and a regular visitor to Cornwall, where his family had a holiday house and where many of his friends lived. Over the next few months Evelyn persuaded him to decamp and come and do a proper job with us. Peter has a languid charm that belies his passion for what he does. His job would be to develop a consistent approach to interpretation at Eden across all media. His effortless conviviality was also in big demand when it came to the schmoozing that any project needs to do in order to woo its potential supporters.

Paul Travers and Peter became firm friends and they hit on the idea of using the Imagination building for a launch party in the capital. We invited all the major supporters from Cornwall and the potential sponsors, banks and institutions in London who might not have been tempted to take the long haul down. There was a lot of speechification, from us and the MC, an exhibition, eats, drinks and oodles of confidence. It was a great success, and after the ball the Cornish contingent had to be decanted back into the sleeper before they turned into pumpkins.

We needed to secure the pit and we needed planning permission. Derrick McCormick from McAlpine's and I had begun the negotiations in the knowledge that although we had no money, we had to agree a price or else we wouldn't know the sum we needed to raise. To our great sadness Bill Rickatson had passed away eighteen months previously, so we no longer had a champion at Goonvean. The company was now headed by Andrew McGowan, who was quite rightly trying to secure the best price, and was concerned over the implications for staff

Result: Robert
Bradford's
Bombus the Bee

morale if he set in train the mechanism for purchase and transfer and we then pulled out. Evelyn became involved in a bruising series of negotiations that appeared to be going nowhere. A further complication, alluded to earlier, was that the land registry documentation left a lot to be desired. The slip of a felt-tip pen on the plans had turned the site into a hostage to fortune, with other landowners appearing to own the rights of access that we would need to bring in our new road. Our lawyers were going quietly mad as a whole raft of searches and legal agreements were being drawn up in an uncertain landscape – literally. Disaster loomed.

Evelyn and I were frantic because we had in theory got all the funders we needed to enable the MC grant to go live, but getting them to commit to paper was like herding eels. McAlpine's were getting jittery, and the design team were so stretched they could snap at any time. Progress was essential. Under the auspices of the Government Office for the South West a meeting was called of all those involved in the funding process – GOSW, representing the European money, English Partnerships, NatWest, McAlpine's and the MC – to take place in Plymouth on 14 September 1998. It was another of our Waterloos, the most serious yet.

Two days before this, my wife Candy's parents came to stay and Chris, my father-in-law, offered to cook a curry. I was distracted and ate my supper dutifully before going to bed. To cut a long story short, the following day I had stomach-ache. By evening I was doubled up and by midnight, after hot-water bottles, bicarbonate of soda and recourse to the foetal position had all failed to alleviate the agony, the doctor was called. It could be pancreatitis, she said, and the ambulance was called. Hello, Tim, said the cheery driver, whom I knew from his visits to Heligan, never expected to have you in the back. Don't worry about a thing, we'll get you there at top speed. True to his word, he put his foot down as we hurtled through the narrow lanes that separate my home from the hospital in Truro. His assistant meanwhile was tapping the back of my hand for a vein and inserting a needle for administering fluids. The ambulance was in rally mode and I hate needles, and suddenly I felt really bad. Noticing at the last moment that the assistant was wearing a hat, I grabbed it and was sick as a dog.

Hearing the noise in the back the ambulance came to a halt and there was silence. The assistant was dumbstruck – I'd filled his hat. After a brief pause he said, you been eating curry? Ah. At the hospital a nurse ripped my clothes off to put me into a gown without noticing the needle in my hand, which was duly wrenched out. There was blood everywhere. It turned out that my father-in-law had used an entire tube of vindaloo paste in the curry rather than the recommended two teaspoonfuls.

Despite the discomfort I had insisted on taking some smart clothes with me for the meeting the following day, even though it seemed unlikely that I would make it. When I arrived with Evelyn and Gay on Monday morning for this make-or-break showdown I was besuited but bandaged and dripping blood. The mood of the meeting was serious, and not for the first time NatWest and McAlpine's acted in concert, stating that the much-vaunted private/public-sector partnership, of which Eden was supposed to be a shining example, was on the verge of collapse. If the pit could not be bought now, and the promised funds from the public sector were not released from the bureaucratic logjam, they were pulling out and the project was over. The pressure was intense, and Doug Weston and Jerry Michel of the MC promised that they would push the Commissioners on their return to London. It worked. By the end of the meeting we had guarantees from all parties that we were now their highest priority. At last we were within sniffing distance of the money we needed to get construction under way.

What the Millennium Commission did for us at this point represented as massive a vote of confidence as we could ever have hoped for. Jerry and Doug intervened at Evelyn's request and persuaded the Commissioners that unless the logjam of land ownership was cleared up, the project would never go ahead. Our grant was supposed to be conditional, and we hadn't secured all the matched

TS, Evelyn Thurlby

funding. This represented a huge risk. An elegant solution was found, and one I still find hard to believe: Goonvean lent us half the purchase price, thus providing the matched funding that would enable the MC to provide the other half. Even then it was a gamble, because the small print in the contract said that if we hadn't completed the transaction by a certain date the deal would be forfeit and Goonvean would be able to keep the MC money and have the pit back.

The purchase of Bodelva was to be our liberation. The details of decommissioning had to be sorted out, and we needed Goonvean people to manage the pumping operations that prevented us taking over a lake, but on 17 October 1998 we owned the pit.

We had received outline planning consent just before the MC award in 1997, but it came with a sting in the tail. The devil was truly in the detail. We

would have to identify, secure and raise a bond to create a brand new road, which in turn meant that prior to any consent being given we would have to have sorted out the tangled web of land tenure and purchased the little strips from a large number of owners, any one of whom could have baulked our progress. Paul and Neal had been on a charm offensive for months, being hugely attentive to the desires of each and every one of the landowners. McAlpine's came up trumps with the bond for the road that would guarantee to the County Council that it would be built as soon as permission was granted – because, as Cullum would say, their business was construction, not plants. Unbelievably, despite all the risks, we succeeded, and in November 1998 we all trooped into the planning meeting at Restormel to hear the debate.

It was extraordinary. The meeting lasted around an hour, of which fifty-five minutes were spent on the road and only five on the massive project in the pit. We could have been building a nuclear reactor and no one would have noticed – the road was their only focus. We got our permission, subject to a number of conditions relating to the road which would finally be satisfied just before Easter the following year. We were deliriously happy, in an understated way. We thanked the councillors, especially George Down, who had nursed the project for more than two years, and decamped to the pub for an evening that stayed resolutely sober despite our best efforts.

The Imagination relaunch of the Eden Project had been the start of our courtship of the high street banks. Martin Peck at CIBC had been honest enough to say that when we cut the project from £106 million to £74.3 million the amount of money we then needed to borrow represented small beer to their operation and was unlikely to get the support of their credit committee. Evelyn and Gay set up a beauty parade of the big banks. They were invited to come and spend a day with us, first at Heligan, then at the pit, ending with presentations at Watering Lane Nursery. It was a refined form of masochism: legions of suits poring over business plans they didn't understand, trying to look interested when they knew from the start that they would never be able to persuade head office to swallow the tale. I know it's an old joke, but the Bank that Likes to Say Yes said No, and the Listening Bank went deaf.

There are times in your life when you feel that someone is watching over you. Just days after our project first broke in the press I received a phone call from a young man called Mark Price, who had recently been promoted to look after corporate banking at the Truro branch of the NatWest. He was totally open about the limits of his influence, but he treated the whole idea with respect and enthusiasm and simply told me to keep in touch. He phoned me every month, never pushy, just interested. When CIBC became our preferred bank, he called and wished us luck. Stay in touch, he said.

When we held our beauty parade, there he was with his boss, Dennis Spencer. Dennis was a member of that dying breed, the old-fashioned bank manager completely rooted in his community. He knew his patch and everyone in it. He loved rugby, golf and a good pint of beer. He was humble about his achievements, loud in his self-deprecation. He was nearing retirement, and he'd been around so long that the new rules taking away local autonomy were still slightly grey as far as he was concerned. He loved the project and felt comfortable with it; he had known Gay from her Plymouth days, and hit it off with Evelyn immediately. He came at the project in a way that was different to everyone else. Mark had obviously been keeping him informed, and he said straight away that he would love to have this project as his last great deal. Moreover, he believed that it was exactly what the region needed.

No high street bank should have been interested in us. None of them was, except Dennis and Mark. There would be a painfully long way to go, because the sums of money involved were significant and the regional corporate director would have to be on board. Evelyn worked like a demon with Gay and our friends at Ernst and Young in Exeter to knock the business plan into plausible shape. The cuts were scary, and threatened to leave us relying on ingenuity rather than cash to fit out the eighth wonder of the world. No matter.

In the summer we heard that the regional boss was playing hard to get. We were terrified because if this didn't work we were stiffs – there was nowhere left to go. The man came to see us. He was called John Brett, and is one of the most extraordinary

The NatWest deal: Dennis Spencer and Gay Coley do the business while John Brett, Lindsay Bridgeman, Toby Stroh and Evelyn Thurlby *(r)* egg them on

men I've ever met. How he came to be working for a bank remains a complete mystery. He had a passionate love of opera and a Goon-like wit. He was warm, he was childlike, he loved punning and wordplay, yet his intuitive understanding of the nuances of business at every level would have earned him respect in any boardroom. He had an unnerving way of allowing conversations to weave crazily off course until we were in paroxysms of laughter, and then suddenly interjecting a question of brutal severity. He put Evelyn through the mill, but you got the sense that this was a rite of passage. She knew her stuff and he knew she did, and she also confided in him about where the problems might lie ahead. You could see him relax; it was the right call. He didn't want to work with people who were trying to pull the wool, and she hadn't. He would back us. So began a friendship with the project that launched him on a path that, two years later, would see him champion our cause in a different arena, so far beyond the call of duty that we would have to admit that this man is an entrepreneur. But more of that later.

In February 1999, after being due diligenced to death once more by another lot of consultants and after Evelyn had spent many sleepless nights first understanding the loan contracts, then dealing with lawyers, she and Gay would finally sign the deal for Eden in a low-key ceremony in the library at Watering Lane. Afterwards Evelyn invited the Eden and NatWest teams back to Fowey, where she had prepared a celebration meal. Paul brought with him the first Eden video, which we played in total silence. When the credits rolled John and Dennis were obviously moved. This wasn't about business, we all knew that.

Another strand of the campaign, discussed in the previous chapter, involved persuading Europe to give us £12.5 million. The process had begun in 1997 when we had lodged an application for said sum with the Government Office for the South West (GOSW), whose then boss, Steve McQuillan, was a big supporter of the project. The context was unfortunate. The most disadvantaged parts of the South West had been awarded a grant of £150 million from Europe to spend on regeneration projects. The effect was to set neighbour against neighbour in pursuit of the funds. A committee of local notables, representing all the areas concerned, had been set up to be the final arbiters of where the money should go. Obviously our request was significant. At the time there was one other large bid, for a proposed university near Penzance. The politics were tricky because any Cornishman, if asked whether he supported such an idea, would have felt treacherous saying anything other than yes. The problem was that it was actually a no-hoper for reasons outside Cornwall's control, but nonetheless it appeared to the other counties that Cornwall was trying to monopolize the pie.

In February 1998, Evelyn and I had gone to Brussels to meet up with John Mills, the then chief executive of Cornwall County Council, Steve McQuillan, Malcolm Bell of the Devon and Cornwall TEC and Angie Rowe of Restormel Borough

Council, who had all travelled over to lend their support to the project. We were, as I recall, the guests of the region's Euro MP, Robin Teverson, and were going to make a plea to one of the big cheeses in the Commission. It was an extraordinary meeting that began with us having to listen to this man giving us a lecture about fat cats and private enterprise raping the assets of the people. This was followed by horse-trading over how much he would allow us to have. In a completely arbitrary way he told us that he would support £10 million and not a penny more. The implication was, as always, that we were sure to have asked for more than we needed. But we hadn't. If the committee were to approve this we would be short.

If a week is a long time in politics, try project development. The next few weeks were a nightmare. First, it appeared that a move was afoot to halt the project on the grounds that if we received the money it would end the hopes of others. Secondly, it was November of the year after the original application, which was supposed to have been processed in six weeks. Imminent in Eurospeak has an entirely different meaning in translation. We were by now so close to the wire that a failure at this hurdle would kill the project. Decision day dawned and we could concentrate on nothing else.

What actually happened that day was told to me in hushed tones later that evening, so unusual had been the turn of events. The meeting had begun in the usual way with neighbour bashing neighbour. That was to be expected, and would generally be resolved by bargaining in corridors. However, the Cornish contingent had managed to present a less than solid front on this occasion, and the fruits of more than a year's lobbying, paper-pushing and lecturing were about to come to a spectacularly ignominious end. Then the miracle happened. The leader of Somerset County Council, Humphrey Temperley, stood up and made a speech of Churchillian stature, as unexpected as it was welcome. I had met Humphrey a year before, when lecturing at Hestercombe Gardens to raise funds for their Trust. Hestercombe is also Somerset Fire Brigade's HQ. He told the meeting that Eden was so important for the future of the region that all differences should be put aside, that he was confident we had wider interests at heart than narrow local ones and that he would withdraw one of Somerset's projects as a symbol of his support. Apparently (I say this because this is what I was told), this so electrified his colleagues that others reconsidered their opposition and came out in favour. Thank you, Humphrey, for rising above politics and setting us all an example.

The build-up to the build-up is now nearly over. Most of the characters have made their appearance, and I am sorry if you are having trouble keeping track of them all. But that's the point, you see: Eden never was about plants and architecture, it was always about harnessing people to a dream and exploring what they are capable of.

chapter 11

designed for life

On a personal note 1998 had started on a high.
A glad-rags bash at the Hilton for the National
Book Awards, where I thought my book was there
just to make up the numbers, ended with Ned
Sherrin announcing that *The Lost Gardens of
Heligan* had been chosen as Illustrated Book of
the Year. So unexpected was this that I was
sloshed and had no speech prepared. The
audience was rather dazed by my rant against the
iniquity of gardening as a middle-class fad while
horticulture as a profession was dying for lack
of respect. I stumbled off-stage to have my
photograph taken with Dickie Bird, the
cricket umpire. 'Upsetting the allotment
holders again,' he said with a wink.
Marvellous man.

A taxi deposited Candy and me at Paddington just in time to catch the sleeper back to Cornwall. On the train we found ourselves next to another of the Awards guests in black tie, looking as if he couldn't wait to rip it off. It was Pete Goss, the round-the-world sailor who had rescued a Frenchman from certain death in the Southern Ocean and been awarded the *Légion d'honneur* for his bravery. We settled down for a nightcap in the bar and four hours later we felt as if we'd known each other for years. He was a genuinely humble, inspiring man, completely matter-of-fact about his heroics, implying that he was only doing what anyone else would have done. He told us about his latest venture, to build the fastest catamaran in the world at a yard in Totnes. We talked of the advances in composite materials stronger than steel and lighter than carbon fibre that he hoped would herald a design revolution. We agreed that at some point Eden and his team should collaborate to demonstrate what could be achieved.

The philosophy of Eden had evolved over four years. What had begun as a project to exhibit plants from around the world and show how we had domesticated them developed into a far deeper strategy to use plants as the common backcloth against which all human life is led. Wherever in the world we lived, plants were adapted to broadly similar uses, be they for medicine, fuel, shelter, cosmetics or food. To these social, cultural and economic perspectives would be added an exploration of perhaps the most vital aspect of all, the spiritual. Not in an overtly religious sense, but from the standpoint of examining how, in many cultures, the conceit has taken hold that we are apart from nature rather than a part of nature. We felt that in understanding and addressing this aspect of ourselves we could best create a constituency for change. If the majority of people are unaware that all the air

Hemp and wheat,
August 2001

we breathe and all the food we eat comes directly or indirectly from plants, how could we persuade people to see interest in them as anything more than the enthusiasm of specialists? Eden would be dedicated to inspiring people to reflect on the vital role of plants and come to understand the need for a balance between, on the one hand, husbandry – growing them for our use – and, on the other, stewardship – taking care of them on behalf of all living things. The approach we would encourage towards stewardship was a difficult one. If conservation at all costs was the end, I suppose whatever means you employed would be justified. However, the idea that conservation is good simply because it guards us against forcing important crops into extinction before their usefulness is discovered seems to miss the point: we are part of nature, and nurturing it is our responsibility as the predominant species. Failure to do so will ultimately lead to our own extinction. If that happens, good riddance; we wouldn't deserve any tears. We are after that essential balance – conservation and stewardship with sustainable use.

Thus plants at Eden are a metaphor for working with the grain of nature. They provide the symbolic ties of common use that link all cultures, as well as illustrating, in part, the scope of possible futures for us all. One of the most striking aspects of the conversations we've had over the years with people at both ends of the supposed environmental debate is the general acknowledgement that common sense indicates we are missing a massive trick. Who hasn't felt humble in the face of the power of the natural forces of the oceans, the winds and the sun, and known instinctively that the future lies in their harnessing? Whether you are a captain of industry or a peasant farmer you will have felt this. Views may differ across a whole range of other issues, but this, most of us will share. Were we to be able to harness that power, many of the other problems we face might seem surmountable. If cheap, environmentally friendly power forms part of the solution, then achieving a balance between the successful husbandry and the stewardship of nature, and of plants in particular, also forms a major part. No businessman, politician or social activist can deny that the greatest issues of the day are global poverty and inequity. These are becoming the engines for environmental destruction, as globalization creates heightened expectations anywhere that the media's tentacles can reach (and that is just about everywhere). Only through a re-evaluation of industrial and agricultural practices, and exploring the synergies between the two, will there be a chance of satisfying our aspirations without consequent terminal damage to the environment and ultimately ourselves.

First it is necessary to create awareness of the part we play in the natural world. Exploring the problems and potential solutions comes next. Engaging people's interest in pushing for change is a function of the first two stages combined with convincing them that their efforts can make a difference either individually or

May 1999
Sketch by Richard Carman for LUC

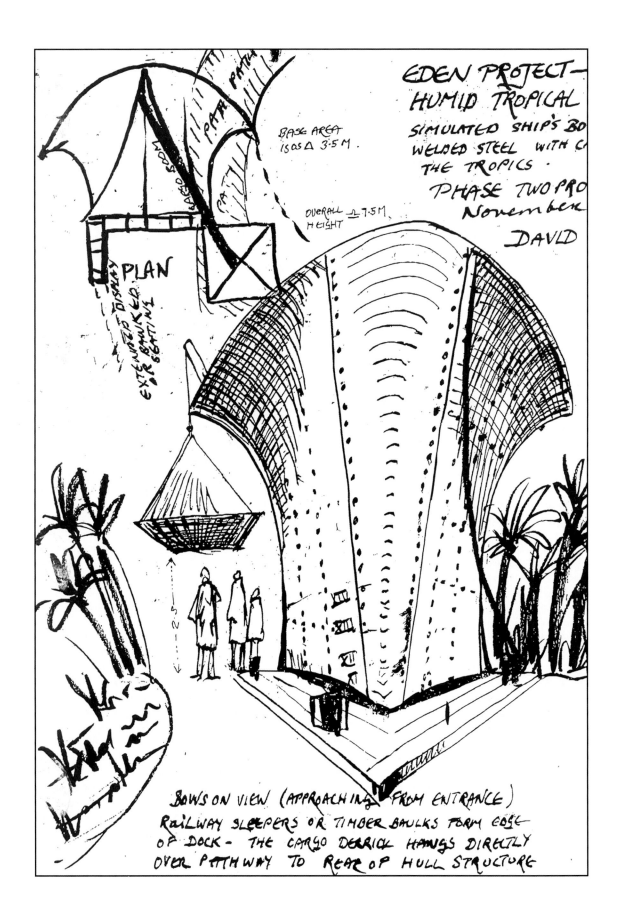

EDEN PROJECT —
HUMID TROPICAL
SIMULATED SHIP'S BO
WELDED STEEL WITH C
THE TROPICS.
PHASE TWO PRO
November
DAVID

BASE AREA
ISOS △ 3·5 M.

OVERALL 17·5 M
HEIGHT

PLAN

CARGO BOOM

PATH PATH

PATH

EXTENDED DISPLAY
OR SEATING

BOWS ON VIEW (APPROACHING FROM ENTRANCE)
RAILWAY SLEEPERS OR TIMBER BAULKS FORM EDGE
OF DOCK - THE CARGO DERRICK HANGS DIRECTLY
OVER PATHWAY TO REAR OF HULL STRUCTURE

collectively. Apathy is often simply a by-product of powerlessness. Empowerment can create a tiger.

When I was sent to England to enjoy the character-building virtues of prep school, my early schooldays were blighted by inherited asthma and a sickly disposition all round, which meant that my main companions lived in the imagination of writers. Of course much of that companionship – G. A. Henty, Sir Arthur Conan Doyle, Rider Haggard – can now be seen for the imperial twaddle it was, but the sheer richness and variety of human experience, told in a language that made me feel as if I was taking part, seems as vivid today as it did then. My only other luxuries were a precocious interest in reading *The Times* from cover to cover, listening under my bedclothes to all Mohammad Ali's fights in the early hours of the morning – and, of course, collecting stamps in my own random, purist-infuriating way.

There are two types of stamp collector. There are the anal retentives, whose need for control of their world leads them to want to own every single stamp in a series, in mint and used condition, of every denomination, with every vagary of watermark, just for the sake of completion. A schoolfellow called, I think, Bevan (whose treasured collection once suffered the appalling fate of being hurled out of a dormitory window by school bullies) was one of these; it was his ambition to gather together every single stamp bearing the head of Queen Elizabeth II.

I fell into the second group, those who saw stamps as calling cards from exotic locations, each with a story to tell, each licked once upon a time by someone with a name and a life to go with it. These silent monuments spoke volumes to me across the years: Rhodesia and Nyasaland, Swaziland, Kenya, Uganda, Tanganyika, the Cape of Good Hope, the Sudan, Burma and so on; Magyar Posta, Suomi, Helvetia or – a really prized possession – a stamp from Czechoslovakia bearing the postmark of the occupation swastika. So many stories, such a big wide world, and yet I could slip these little lozenges of delight into a thin vellum-backed volume, to be brought out in those quiet, homesick moments and opened like Pandora's box to take me to faraway places. I never wanted a complete set of anything, because somehow that would spoil the romance of what might be waiting just out of reach.

So what do stamps have to do with plants? Simply this: just like my stamps, each plant is the repository of a story rather than something collectible in its own right.

Plants need champions to tell their stories. That was the purpose behind poaching Peter Hampel from Imagination and Jo Readman from television. Their brief was to develop a contemporary language and imagery, free from the unimaginative and dry jargon usually associated with science, and which would be indistinguishable from popular media while offering the widest possible audience easy access to deeper knowledge if they wanted it. Jo joined as education officer in

Humid Tropics Biome: sketch by David Kemp for his Tropic Trader

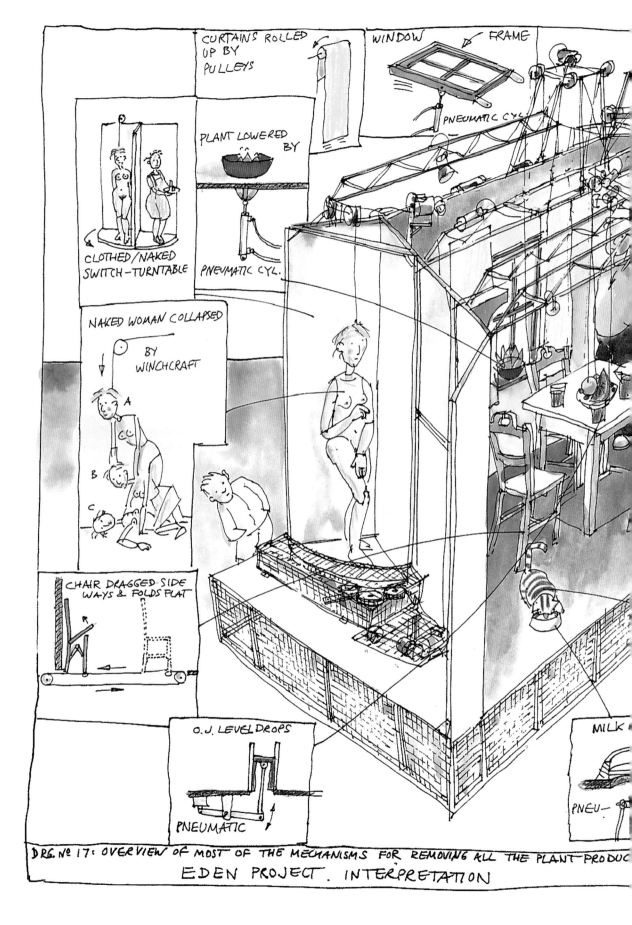

CURTAINS ROLLED
UP BY
PULLEYS

WINDOW   FRAME

PNEUMATIC CYL

CLOTHED/NAKED
SWITCH-TURNTABLE

PLANT LOWERED
            BY

PNEUMATIC CYL.

NAKED WOMAN COLLAPSED
        BY
        WINCHCRAFT

A

B

C

CHAIR DRAGGED-SIDE
WAYS & FOLDS FLAT

O.J. LEVEL DROPS

PNEUMATIC

MILK

PNEU-

DRG. No 17: OVERVIEW OF MOST OF THE MECHANISMS FOR REMOVING ALL THE PLANT PRODUC

EDEN PROJECT. INTERPRETATION

CALENDER FLIPS

BOOKS FOLD INTO THE WALL

FIRE = SILK RIBBONS + LIGHT + FAN

RUG = ½ FABRIC ½ BARE FLOOR

TURN TABLE

NEWSPAPER FLIPS OVER

CHAIR WINCHED INTO CEILING SPACE

A

B

C

CAT COLLAPSES PNEUMATIC-ALLY

TABLE FOLDS INTO RECESS IN FLOOR: PNEUMATIC

99.	DRAWN BY	P. SPOONER
	APPROVED BY	W. JACKSON
	AMENDED	

Mongrel Media's 'Plant Takeaway', aka 'Dead Cat' – drawing by Paul Spooner

February 1998, thanks to the same generosity that had brought Kary to us, through job sponsorship courtesy of our friend Dr Alan Stanhope at Cornwall College. Charged initially with developing programmes for schools but with the understanding that education at Eden was for everyone, she was to play a significant role in creating our interpretation strategy. Jo would work with Peter Thoday, the Green Team and a number of part-time researchers, developing the common themes and individual plant stories to inform and entertain our audience. Peter Hampel meanwhile would oversee the development of a palette of artistic works or stage sets that would complement and expand on the stories where words of themselves failed to capture either the subtlety of the intended message or the excitement of the story. As well as this he had to ensure the aesthetic integrity of all the interpretative media on site. To add complexity to this already difficult process, Helen Rosevear had to coordinate their work with the plant collections to create a visually coherent whole within the overall Landscape Master Plan designed by Dominic Cole.

I would be lying if I said it was easy, but the confusions and frustrations of the early years were to stand us in good stead later on. The problem with scientists is that they have no idea how stupid the rest of us are, so when you ask them to make something simple it's still several levels above the average person's head. This I had discovered at Heligan. Add to that a creative team whose job it is to pretend to be denser than they are in order to force the scientists to react, and you have a recipe for both humour and rage. The researchers initially delved into everything far too deeply, moving us forward at a snail's pace, not realizing that we couldn't be all things to all people on day one.

You would have to have spent the last twenty years under a stone not to have appreciated that the world is now being interpreted in a post-imperial way, and that any form of interpretation can be a sensitive matter. For example, any important cash crop comes with a large amount of baggage about environmental degradation, labour conditions, economic exploitation, cultural imperialism and the social context from which your exhibit is derived. That is without discussing the nature of the crop itself. How you tell the story is of necessity political. This is a problem when your ambition is to be apolitical.

Bringing partners who could corroborate all our stories into the fray brought us into contact with the non-governmental organizations (NGOs), who are to acronyms what Ireland is to Guinness. Add to that a tendency to inclusive political correctness and you have a recipe for total constipation. The sustainability debate dumped lashings of rhetoric on our heads. We had the benefit of a sustainability adviser, Brian Spooner, for over a year, alongside IIED, Plantlife and English Nature, who helped us see the wood for the trees. While their contributions opened our eyes to the breadth of the subject under discussion and the agendas of each of the players, we came to realize that we would very soon drown under the weight of other people's expectations, and would never deliver a project at all. Working on an environmental project leads to your being regarded as your brother's keeper on every subject under the sun. If you fall into this trap you will lose the fire that inspired you in the first place, and forget what it was you wanted to say. You will turn into a camel and do everything badly. You will also commit the cardinal sin of boring people to death.

As well as partners, we were under pressure to find sponsorship. Through Peter Hampel Evelyn met one of his former colleagues, Dave Meneer, at that time in a high-flying job at McCann Erickson, looking after a number of obscenely large advertising accounts. Dave had an Achilles heel. He was Cornish and hankered to return to his roots. His father had run a pub in Redruth and his mother still lived nearby. Bearded, affable to a fault, he could talk the hind legs off a donkey, not to mention show off his encyclopaedic knowledge of pop music lyrics. We all liked him immediately, and thought that he might be the right man to front our approaches to the corporates in the search for sponsorship. He took the job and moved down with his wife Anna, a TV producer who would later direct much of the filming at Eden, and their two young children.

Dave Meneer

The issue of sponsorship was quite contentious. The MC were demanding it, and we had to pretend to be committed to the process while being privately appalled at what projects elsewhere were doing. We made lists, went to see people and made dozens of presentations, without much in the way of results. To tell the truth, neither Dave nor I was at all convinced by the sponsorship approach. If you were trying to create an apolitical foundation, why would you accept money from companies engaged in activities that were difficult to justify, unless, that is, those companies were prepared to allow us to discuss their activities dispassionately and free from interference?

A second issue cropped up early on. Many companies enter into so-called sponsorship deals on the understanding that they get the exclusive right to sell their products at your venue. I'd come across this at Heligan, and it is nothing more than an upfront loan against a product that eventually you end up paying a premium for. What would you do if one of the world's largest ice cream and soft drinks manufacturers were to offer you a huge sum of money on those conditions? How about an internationally famous fast-food brand? Eden believes in local sourcing and quality local food production. How would we have faced our neighbours, who make possibly the finest ice cream in the world, if we had done such

a deal? A once-in-a-lifetime local opportunity thrown to strangers with no investment in the future of where we live? I think not.

It was at this point that we started to develop our own policy about sponsorship,
which we have adhered to ever since. We will accept sponsorship from individuals
and companies provided that we are not expected to advertise them in the main
site. Part of the attraction of Eden is that hoardings or name checks don't assault
your senses at every turn. We will accept money or help in kind only from individuals, companies or foundations whose ambitions are in line with ours, whose
activities are in sympathy with the Eden mission, and with whom we will have an
ongoing relationship. Interestingly, no one complains about our conditions
because they are the same for everyone. Dave and I were later to take a certain satisfaction from the fact that when put under pressure to accept what we thought to
be inappropriate sponsorship instead of asking the agencies for a larger contribution to our costs, we were able to say, here are the keys to Eden, you do it.

Jo Readman for her part was playing the whirling dervish. She consumed work,
talking to teachers' conferences, schools, even the Association of Girl Guides, as
she developed her unusual education programme. Her idea of a good time was to
be put in a class with the least responsive children and given the opportunity to
turn them round. She first tried out her ideas at a school in the clay district in the
summer of 1998. She persuaded Heligan and the Eden Nursery to lend her tropical
foliage plants to line the walls, and took with her a tape of rainforest noises and a
slide projector with a wide-angle lens that would throw a picture of the rainforest
along one wall. The children were led blindfold into the darkened room, and then
suddenly launched into a blaze of rainforest sights and sounds. They learned to
make blow-darts and to explore what you could and couldn't eat in a game of
survival. At lunch they were told they could have a drink only when they had
made themselves a cup from banana leaves. Some might have gone thirsty, but
they learned to respect another culture. After the first day of this week-long course
children with a long history of truancy started to come and ask whether they
could join in. I wish I'd had a teacher like that.

The interpretation strategy was coming together in theory, but it would be
Dominic who would have to make it come alive by providing the three-
dimensional stage for it. Dominic would stay at my house and show me the
designs on which he was working. I had said that I wanted a samba beat, that I
wanted wow factor 11, that it had to be Picasso meets the Aztecs in glorious
Technicolor. We talked for hours of the drama that we wanted to unfold, of how
unsuspecting visitors would be drawn towards us, catching no more than a tantalizing glimpse of what lay in store. Once at the arrival point they would walk
down to the Visitor Centre from where for the first time they would see into the
bowels of the crater, where stretched beneath them would be a civilization the like

of which existed only in the imaginings of romantics. We wanted them first to be awestruck at the sheer bravura of the architecture and landscape design, and then, all cynicism put aside for a moment, wonder why we did it. They had to be David Livingstone to our Victoria Falls; 'scenes so lovely must have been gazed upon by angels in their flight' was what he had said on first seeing them. Under these circumstances maybe, just maybe, people would be in the right frame of mind to be humbled by the power of plants to shape our destinies.

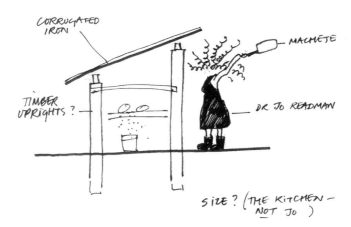

CORRUGATED IRON

MACHETE

TIMBER UPRIGHTS ?

DR JO READMAN

SIZE ? (THE KITCHEN – NOT JO)

Jo Readman plays the whirling dervish

The ability to imagine in three dimensions is a gift given to few, and certainly not to me. I would look blankly at the intricate tracery of Dominic's work, the scimitar-shaped beds that mirrored the strange geometry of the pit rim, their sharp terraced outlines forming a pattern of great complexity, bold and sinuous, playing hide-and-seek with mystery and revelation. The impression needed to be of a complete culture, reflecting the myriad activities and functions that might have been carried on there; the production of food, brewing, a place of public entertainment, works of art that hinted at unknown gods or icons of the age. It should not be a place of grand botanical displays, of pleasure grounds. It had to become the canvas on which people like us painted our lives, or, to be more accurate, the people we wished we were lived out theirs. We wanted it to mean something, to inspire others to want to be here and, yes, maybe even be buried or remembered here. We wanted to create something that was instantly recognizable. In this location the architecture would look fabulous, but it would have no meaning if not set in a cultural context all its own; it would not have been alive. I will never forget the emotion on Nick Grimshaw's face when he first looked into the pit as the magnificent structures rose from the crater floor and he could start to see for the first time how the landscape and structure would work with each other. He began to try to intellectualize it, but his voice trailed off as words failed him. He shrugged his shoulders and said, It's bloody brilliant.

'...to think in
three dimensions
is a gift given
to few...'

The model was sent for a wind-tunnel test in April 1998 to see whether it could cope with wind in the pit, and as many other natural conditions of unnatural severity as could be dreamed up. There was an early misunderstanding, happily picked up by Anthony Hunt: the testers apparently thought they were testing not to gale force 12 but to Mach 12, which would have blown the model to smithereens.

The tests showed up the need for a redesign of the structure. The original had a passing resemblance to the Waterloo International Terminal. The ring beam that described the outer parameters of the footprint of the structure hugged the bottom of the pit before curving sharply at both ends to climb the cliff face, until at about three-quarters height it curved again, carving deep into the cliff to meet in the middle. The supporting ribs of the structure rose from the base in an arc as a single span of varying heights and lengths to accommodate the natural growing habits of its putative inmates. The wind-tunnel test demonstrated that the ribs would move beyond a safe range of tolerance. Oddly, the reason for this was not the direct effect of wind hitting the structure, but rather the suction effect of wind passing over the top of the pit.

It was back to the drawing board, but this was, as in several other instances, a good thing. There was another problem: working in three dimensions with a ground relief of such extremes was unprecedented, and the architects themselves were finding it difficult to understand the internal footprint, with its combination of sheer slopes, gentler rising ground and rather limited flat areas. Their targets for percentages of the ground that could be cultivated properly, rather than stage-set by climbing plants, were on the edge of what was possible.

I remember meeting Jonathan in a hotel in Truro in 1995, and he pulled a handful of leaves out of his pocket and gingerly placed them against one another. Wouldn't it be good if the structures themselves could mimic nature, he said. Grimshaw's came up with an alternative design that perfectly echoed the sentiment, if not the inspiration of leaves. Their starting point would be an exploration of geodesic structure, made famous by Buckminster Fuller, who himself had designed a geodesic dome called the Climatron at Missouri Botanic Gardens in the USA, which looked like a giant steel *boules* ball. The concept provided for least weight and maximum surface area on the curve – with strength. The scale of Eden was such that the pentagons favoured by Fuller would not suffice, but the ideas acted as an inspiration. Analysis showed that the strongest structure at this magnitude would be made of hexagons of various sizes.

The reason they came up with this design is interesting. We were having difficulty securing the funds to purchase the pit; in the meantime we were carrying out the environmental investigations by taking core samples, which the mining company were keeping tabs on so that they could spot where previously undiscovered reserves of their precious clay might lie. The effect was that the pit was being worked erratically and the architects had to design on a site that was constantly changing – they literally had to build on shifting sands. This was when they hit on the idea of soap bubbles. If you play the children's game of blowing soap through a little hoop and watch the bubbles settle, you will see that no matter what surface they land on they adapt to it. Just as importantly, you will notice that where two or more bubbles land adjoining each other, the line of join is always exactly perpendicular. By using this model one can see that it is possible to develop a design that can adapt to whatever the surfaces beneath it are doing. This was the big breakthrough. Soon a model was created variously described as mimicking a dragonfly's wing, a fly's eye or the simple honeycomb. The moment we saw it we loved it, because it felt natural – a biological response to our needs, but forged in materials that would allow us to explore the cultivation of plants in a way never before attempted.

Elsewhere in our Eden we were trying to address the vexed question of the construction contract. We had agreed the philosophy of our collaboration and had hit on a contract that would, we hoped, minimize the potential for conflict while engendering a sense of ownership in constructor and design team alike. However, the trigger for the contract being acceptable to the constructor was a degree of

certainty about the final costs of the project. Bearing in mind that there were no detailed designs, everything was based on best-guess costs. This did not afford the constructor a great deal of comfort, nor us, the client, either. On his own admission, the constructor would have to build in a margin that would guarantee that if the costs of one aspect of the job overran, this could be compensated for elsewhere.

You will remember that at the time of the award from the MC we recognized that our costings were 'ballpark' to say the least. In fact what we had done was to work out the most money we could afford prudently to borrow from a bank on top of the public-sector grants, private-sector sponsorship and soft loans we'd secured, and had squeezed our project into those parameters. I won't bore you with the details of the dozens of meetings that took place as a result of the costs soaring as we got a tighter fix on the design. Our dread was that cuts would mean a loss of quality, and the consequent death of our dream to create an icon of beauty and power.

The task of reaching a point of agreement on costs was given on our side to Davis Langdon and Everest, our quantity surveyors, and for McAlpine's to Martin Miles, their commercial manager. Evelyn was as passionate about protecting the dream as any of us and she and Martin had the most enormous ding-dongs when she took his realism as a personal attack. This was unfair; he was trying desperately to make something work that his bosses could sign up to. Having subsequently got to know him, I realize that he stretched plausibility as far as his professionalism would allow to make it work for all of us. In a cautious industry used to litigation, overruns and clients who get flaky when the chips are down, a designer-led glamour

'The moment we saw it we loved it...'

project driven by idealists was perhaps as big a gamble as it gets, especially when they are asking you to put down some of your own money for the privilege of working with them and haven't even raised all the finance necessary to complete the job. Other than that it was a dream job. One mustn't forget that the only other millennium project McAlpine's were working on, Hampden Park Stadium in Scotland, was causing a lot of grief through no fault of theirs.

Anyway, we were going to have to cut costs. This would turn out to be the best thing to happen to the project because it created a moment that was to bond the team. The first target was the Visitor Centre. In its original design it looked not unlike two bits of the Thames barrage linked at one end. We called them the Steel Armadillos. They were going to cost something like £5 million. Signature architects are not known for their flexibility, and have a reputation for getting grumpy if the client questions the art. We explained the position to Grimshaw's and they got straight on a train, accompanied by Ronnie Murning at his most affable.

Designed on a napkin: Anthony Hunt and Andrew Whalley rough out the foundations

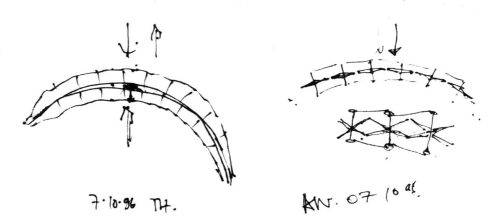

They brought with them something I hadn't seen in this saga until now – paper and pencils. They sat on the pit rim and sketched and paced, then sketched some more, and unbelievably at the end of a couple of intense days had designed something far superior to the original at less than half the cost. The truth was that the original design had been a concept long before Eden came along, and they had felt that it suited the milieu. Now they had really taken ownership of it, and it sang. The architects were pleased, and the constructor, who had thought the architects would throw their toys out of the pram, was impressed. The two sides realized they could work together. There was another pivotal moment when the architects asked McAlpine's for advice on a number of issues. This was to seal the collegiate approach we had all been hoping for, and would mark the start of a genuine team effort, where everyone contributed within the area of their expertise and comment was freely made without offence being taken.

The delivery vehicle for the Trustees was Eden Project Ltd, wholly owned by the Trust. Sir Alcon Copisarow was chairman both of the Trust and of the company, though the latter position he would subsequently relinquish. Evelyn was chief executive (CEO), Gay was finance director (FD), I was the project director, Jonathan corporate affairs director, Philip McMillan Browse and Peter Thoday were joint horticultural directors, Dave Meneer was marketing director, Peter Hampel creative director, and at long last we had landed Professor Sir Ghillean Prance as science director. We had Cullum McAlpine and Derrick McCormick from the McAlpine joint venture, with Colin Weekley and Martin Miles as their alternates in case one or other couldn't make a board meeting.

The discipline of having to report to the board was good for all of us, even if at times one was tempted to sympathize with Wellington, who, when asked to audit his operation while conducting the Peninsular Wars, responded, Would you like me to put my staff on accounting for every last loaf of bread or would you like me to pursue the enemy? Evelyn and Gay in particular rose to the challenge and took the board with them in their detailed explanations of how the project was progressing; and their professional attitude in the face of daily crisis was directly responsible for creating the confidence in McAlpine's to go the extra mile when it mattered. Led by Cullum, they took the view that the project had reached a point of no return and that provided we all did our jobs and didn't do anything rash, the funding would come. Bearing in mind that they were several million pounds into the job and without a signed contract (for the first time in their history), this was some act of faith, inspired perhaps by the fact that so many other members of the team had taken that gamble too: Tinkerbell Theory in action.

The construction contract would finally be signed in January 1999. We had drinks as much in relief as in celebration, at a signing ceremony at the offices of our lawyers in London. Once again the pressure was so great we just didn't have time to mark a historic moment properly, and to take a breather in the light of a very real achievement.

I need to pick up on a number of other developments. First, Watering Lane had undergone a metamorphosis from a domestic nursery to an international plant facility. Our loyal friends at Restormel Borough Council and the Rural Development Commission had clubbed together to find the £450,000 we needed to build two huge greenhouses for the large plants we were both propagating and importing. Early in 1998 Philip had given the job of curator of the Humid Tropics to a brilliant Dutchman called Robin Lock, who was welding a team, under Philip's tutelage, to gather together the collections that would be transported to Bodelva. He and Tom Keay, the curator of the Warm Temperate and Outside Temperate zones, would travel across Europe selecting plants from nurseries and partner institutions in Holland and Germany. Waggeningen University, Robin's alma mater, gave us a range of plants from their collection, and the University of Kassel, in north Germany, did likewise from their large tropical crop collection. Then they went to Italy with Helen and Dominic to select the individual specimen plants for Tom – Robin went because he speaks Italian.

Robin would later travel to the Iwokrama project in Guyana to set up our twinning relationship with them. He was accompanied by Jo Readman, who set up educational links which are already bearing fruit in the active twinning with Gorran School here in Cornwall. Later still he would travel with Ian Martin to the Cameroon to establish links there. Meanwhile Tony Kendle was setting off for the Seychelles to cement our ties with their government environment agency; later he travelled to St Helena, where he manages a research project which is now linked to Eden. The choice of partners, and the idea of mutual benefit, was beginning to emerge.

In October 1998 the construction of the great greenhouses at Watering Lane was under way in conditions reminiscent of the Somme. The whole horticultural team worked alongside the contractors in a fever of anticipation. The plants in the existing greenhouses were exploding out of their skins and hitting the roof. The team had to dig holes in the floor to accommodate them while we waited for the new houses to be completed. In the early spring there would be a celebration as stirring as any when Lady Mary Holborrow, the Lord Lieutenant of Cornwall and a great friend of the project, opened the new houses. She it was who introduced us properly to the Pennon Group, who had lent us their group finance director,

'...conditions reminiscent of the Somme'

Ken Hill, as a non-executive director, and would lend us £1 million and sponsor the waterfall in the Humid Tropics.

That same October we had taken over the pit at Bodelva. McAlpine's had been waiting for so long that when the moment came they were on a war footing. Lowloaders snaked through the countryside bringing their giant earthmovers, bulldozers and dumpers, all emblazoned with the moniker AMPL and brand spanking new because McAlpine's argued that the schedule was so tight that they couldn't afford downtime with repairs. These were unloaded and were instantly put to work levelling the waste ground inside the former works access to make the site ready for the arrival of the Portakabins, those ubiquitous temporary buildings which take on the appearance of permanence the moment they arrive. In came a legion of fixers and fitters to establish campaign headquarters, setting up services such as electricity, loos, phones, faxes and photocopiers.

Then a wave of caravans and mobile homes arrived to make up the McAlpine Village, where the team would live in shanty conditions with smart cars parked outside. Almost overnight tarmac appeared, creating the impression of instant civilization where previously chaos had reigned. Our first presence on site was the project manager's office, just inside the entrance gate. This would be the team's on-site HQ for more than a year. After a near-insurrection it was only a matter of weeks before another building appeared in the base of the pit. This was the café, where one could eat breakfast at virtually any time of day – and with its arrival we became a proper building site. For the next two months up to the Christmas break

Tonka heaven

the machines indulged in the wholesale destruction of all the old buildings save the water tanks, which we would recondition later and use as part of our recycling system. The eastern flank of the site was levelled to make space in what would become the works area for the rest of the equipment. I have never seen so many big machines gathered together in one place.

Christmas came, the New Year dawned, and then it rained. We had worked so hard to get to the moment when construction could begin, but it rained to break Noah's heart, the worst weather in Cornwall's recorded history. In January alone, 43 million gallons of water poured into the pit. The pumps were working at full capacity and barely coping. Every cliff face seemed to have springs spouting out of it, and we faced the unthinkable. Work stopped for ten weeks; machines up to their hunkers in mud could do nothing. We needed a party to take our minds off things.

Paul had been setting up all sorts of tasty morsels for the project, beginning with a very supportive broadcast from the pit in *Gardeners' World*. Local television covered us constantly, because Paul had taken the initiative of commissioning a stunt helicopter pilot to do a low-level assault on the pit. These stunning pictures would be worth their weight in gold; every network found them irresistible, and ten-second news items would be stretched to several minutes.

Paul had been working for more than a year with a friend of mine, Deborah Clark, who has a PR company in Truro. Deborah is extremely tall and imposing, and her career in the Wrens followed by television broadcasting makes her an unusual combination of bossy and sophisticated. Like me she hates being patron-ized by up-country operations which think they have all the answers. She took particular delight in running the PR for our Imagination launch from Cornwall. The array of foreign press and television people who attended had been invited by her, not the London agency employed by the MC. Point made. Deborah was and remains a trusted sounding-board for the politics of the West Country, and has an ear so close to the ground it's a wonder it doesn't have mud in it. Her heart is in Cornwall, and she nailed her colours to our mast right from the start – another of the team who worked for years without recompense.

Now Deborah and Paul had to arrange for the Secretary of State, Chris Smith, to turn the first sod. It was 9 February 1999. The finest precautions were taken. The guest list was checked and then double-checked to make sure no dignitary's nose would be out of joint. There was a marquee perched on the side of a spoil heap; outside caterers were busy and there was plenty to drink. A podium had been hastily constructed, complete with a working microphone. The press were all invited and as a final flourish Paul had hired two members of the Natural Theatre Company from Bath to arrive by helicopter at the appointed time bearing a spade for the turning of said sod. There was also a beautiful slab of Cornish slate inscribed with the details of the day. The minister was due at ten thirty; at eight

'...the wrong kind of photo-opportunity'

thirty a gale shredded the marquee, and was closely followed by rain. Paul could handle it; another one was delivered and erected just before the arrival time. There was some speechifying from the minister in which he was very kind about our prospects, a few words of thanks from our chairman and a reply from me in which I highlighted the support of the community and remembered the contribution of James Wilson, a member of the Green Team who sadly had died earlier in the New Year. The wind howled into the microphones, so probably no one caught a word any of us said.

Then we heard the mincing throb of the rotor blades as the helicopter hove into view, made a pretty dicy landing, and decanted the two actors bearing the ceremonial spade and wearing flowerpots filled with daffodils on their heads. Although the minister was quite obviously amused, his staff were anxious about the wrong kind of photo-opportunity. So I had to slide down the scree slope, accept the spade and climb back up in indecorous fashion to present it to him. He turned the first sod, into which we set the fine piece of slate as a memento of the day. After this he walked and talked among the canapés and then left. Within minutes of his departure a freak blizzard covered the site in a blanket of white and froze our staff and guests into an early exit. While February isn't Cornwall's best month, the early daffodils can be stunning.

chapter 12

Noah wore a shamrock

More than one hundred consecutive days of rain fell in the middle of Cornwall through that winter of 1998/99. The swing shovels, dumpers and bulldozers stood idle, the unwanted toys of giants who'd gone inside to play. The only noise was the throbbing pulse of the pumps working flat out and the tinkling and hissing of streams that seemed to burst from every rock face and crevice. At the aptly named Watering Lane Nursery, the roadway disappeared daily under a fast-flowing river, collected from the glasshouse roofs and decanted in torrents outside the Wendy House. It flooded the main office, which was barricaded with sandbags, then swept on down the lane. But work continued against the odds.

On the south-western lip of the crater the land had been cleared ready for the foundations of the Visitor Centre. The hillside below was a horrendous gloop of rust-coloured blancmange, and one morning it simply slid into the base of the pit. The Visitor Centre was now a flying freehold. The first emotion was disbelief, the second terror. The third was relief to be in the company of a genius, Jerry O'Leary, the site manager for McAlpine's. He was a large man with a ruddy complexion, an unflustered disposition and an optimism that verged on mania. He had a refrain: I've seen worse.

Jerry was due to retire in October 1998 after a life spent travelling around Britain constructing mainly motorways. He boasted that he could drive to Liverpool from Cornwall on roads in which he had played a hand. On hearing that McAlpine's had won the Eden contract he asked for the job so that he could finish with a flourish, with something to tell his grandchildren about. He had insisted on bringing his trusted crew with him rather than taking on local staff – that would come later. Trailblazing required nerve and you needed to know who was who when the pressure was on. Many of his team had been with him for upwards of fifteen years and were like family. While the majority were men, there was a fair-sized female contingent who were regarded no differently.

Evelyn, Ronnie and I had worried that we were being bounced into unnecessary expense through the McAlpine crew's insistence on using new vehicles. This was dispelled when in March 1999 work began again in earnest. Standing on a vantage point among the trees high above the northern lip of the pit, I watched mesmerized for over an hour one day as dozens of machines played out the most beautiful and intricate ballet in a triumph of industrial choreography.

Derrick McCormick told me something about these men at dinner one evening. They were a breed apart. Their lives were hard and they burned the candle at both ends. Their itinerant lifestyle meant that they depended on one another for everything, often going for months without seeing their families, although they would drive enormous distances at weekends to get home if they could. The men were charmingly in thrall to their wives and partners. When they went out it was never in working clothes, and swearing of any description was liable to have you ejected head first from the bar. They could drink with a vengeance, but they had a code of honour which meant that no matter how heavy a session they'd had the night before they would turn up to work on time. They took great pride in what they did. To watch the dozer drivers pushing spoil into the pit at speed, then slamming their machines into reverse just metres from a hundred-foot sheer drop, never ceased to create butterflies in the tummies of onlookers.

Jerry O'Leary:
'I've seen worse'

Jerry had superb intuitive organizational skills, and could judge with great accuracy what should be done and when. The joy of the Eden Project was that we were so up against the constraints of time and the vagaries of the weather that everyone instinctively put their faith in the crew as our only possible hope of salvation. These were men who thrived on trust. I'll never forget a story I was told by one of the McAlpine crew. One day a neighbour had phoned Jerry to complain about the noise of the machinery. Jerry was very courteous and listened intently as the lady told him that she had been woken at five past seven by the sound of engines roaring into life. What are you going to do about it? she asked. I'm going to give them hell, said Jerry. Thank you, said the lady. They should have started prompt at seven, said Jerry, putting the phone down.

'More than 100 consecutive days of rain...'

After Martin Miles, the McAlpine commercial manager, had evaluated all the project risks with our team it boiled down to two areas where there was any real sense of the unknown. The first was the earthmoving, or muck-shift as they called it. The volumes were vast. On the site's western flank a former spoil heap had to be moved and landscaped to create terraces for car and coach parking. The site of the Visitor Centre had collapsed into the pit and would have to be rebuilt painstakingly from the bottom up. The pit itself would have to be filled in places to create a landscape with sufficient flat ground for planting and easy visitor access.

'...a triumph
of industrial
choreography'

The second area of risk concerned the roofing material. The challenge, you will recall, was to find a material that was both lightweight and extremely light-permeable to create the ideal growing conditions for the plants. A light material

would save a fortune on steel as well. The architects had hit on a foil known in the trade as ETFE (Ethylene Tetrafluoroethylene), or clingfilm with attitude as we called it. No one had ever used it on the scale that we planned. It had covered a sports complex near Ringwood and the rooflights of the atrium at the Chelsea and Westminster Hospital, but that was about it in the UK. In spring 1997 the design team and some of the Eden crew had gone to Holland to see the largest clear-span example of the foil in action, at Burgers' Zoo in Arnhem, my father's home town and a favourite haunt for childhood visits with my grandparents. They were very impressed by what they saw: the plants were healthy, the quality of light good and the maintenance costs low. Over ten years only about 10 per cent of the material had needed repairs.

The zoo director reported only one problem. Arnhem is heavily wooded and has a large population of crows. One day a baby crow set off on its maiden flight, crash-landed on the roof and bounced up as if on a trampoline. All the watching crows thought this was great sport, and before long hundreds of them were at it. Something had to be done; the noise was deafening. The staff strung fishing line across the roof and the crows soon gave up in frustration.

The material is so light than an eleven-metre square is easily handled. To give a high insulation factor our hexagons would be triple-glazed pillows, the layers kept apart by compressed air. Should external temperatures be high, so expanding the air inside the pillows, they could be vented between layers; should they be low, more air could be pumped in. We would have a living building responsive to climate. The most frequently asked question concerned window cleaning. In fact, while we would train some of our staff to become abseilers, intrepid bubble climbers, the foil is antistatic and repels all dirt – except seagull droppings, which

The crew

have the consistency of glue, and have to be removed by the abseilers.

The muck-shift was going to be a visual feast for truck fans. It was a joy to watch the suits arriving at the site and being mesmerized, with beatific smiles on their faces. Work started on levelling the eastern side in preparation for all the works infrastructure. It was then that the rains came. Hunt's, the engineers, were beside themselves. Having designed drains that would cope with an exceptional, once-in-a-century storm, they found that they were looking at a case eight times worse than predicted. These were the only moments on the project when even I had a sneaking doubt about whether we would make it. The gloom was intense, and the temptation to find a darkened room and either howl or shoot oneself was great. But it was now that all those years of risk and team-building paid off. Quite simply, everyone was brilliant. The two Joneses, Martin and Alan of Hunt's, went back to the drawing board, Dominic Cole and his landscape team revisited the sculpting of the hard landscape and the McAlpine boys came up trumps. Apart from Jerry, from among the many others who played a

Barry Johnson,
capo di tutti capi

major part I want to single out Barry Johnson, Keith Titman and Keith Pizzey.

Barry was the *capo di tutti capi*, the project manager for McAlpine, Jerry's boss. His lived-in face was an emotional relief map honed by years of worry, not dissimilar to Walter Matthau's. His expression when off guard was always gloomy; years of waging wars to get jobs done on time had hardened him. He was old school: a consummate professional, always courteous with the client, prickly with the client's representatives, defensive of his company's reputation, always well turned out, usually with a tie except when reeling under the Eden dress code. When he smiled, it was glorious, like the sun coming out. I could never rid myself of the impression of one of those wizened Galapagos tortoises grinning. He and Tim Carter were to develop a huge respect for each other, but the thawing of old attitudes in an industry of hard knocks, used to a litigious backdrop, took a little while. The let's-sort-this-out-and-never-mind-who's-to-blame view takes some getting used to.

(previous page)
Standing on the
roof of the world

Barry would take every complaint personally and raise Cain to get it sorted. Ronnie Murning, who was now down at the site on a regular basis, had the responsibility for developing the briefs for each aspect of the project and then signing off the drawings presented to him by the architects as a result. A colleague of his was responsible for checking the work and creating a defects register, which in turn would come back to Barry in one of the endless meetings that make a project tick.

Tim Carter, our project manager, was a glutton for detail and produced a slim volume every month entitled the Project Monthly Report. Actually a weighty tome that seemed to grow with every edition, it began with an executive summary of events, followed by action points that reminded everyone of their failings. Each month that an action point remained in its place meant a public humiliation for the person who was supposed to have dealt with it. Tim was a great believer in management personality tests, and he discovered early on that I was of a species that wasn't supposed to get on with his. I admit my approach to life is intuitive, whereas Tim's is ordered, and I did feel that he was a bit of a nag. But as time went on I marvelled at my naivety; it escapes me how I could ever have imagined that a project as large as this could be organized without an administration that ran like clockwork. Tim was an easy butt of schoolboy jokes, but as he, later joined by Carol Bell, relentlessly produced documents, action points, works programmes and defects notices and in turn worked with the MC project monitors establishing the landmarks we needed to reach to draw down funding, and later still worked with the monitors from the bank who needed constant reassurance, I came to develop a respect for process and good management that I never would have believed I was capable of. Without the rigour of the constructor and our project managers we would have been headed for disaster.

I need to digress for a moment. The contract that we eventually signed with the constructor in January 1999, after they'd already been working for a considerable time at risk, had a GMP, a guaranteed maximum price, to which they pledged themselves. Any cost overrun, except such as might be directly attributed to the client (us) changing our minds about something, would be borne by them. This risk was offset by an understanding that any savings achieved by them would be split between us, but with a cap placed on the maximum saving bonus they could take. The bank and the public sector funders didn't wish to be exposed to risk and therefore passed it on to the constructor, enabling the constructor to drive a hard bargain, which on the face of it meant that they would do very well out of the

Carol Bell

project. However, as Martin Miles said to me after the signing ceremony, the irony was that by liberating the constructor from worry about profit, the arrangement meant that the McAlpine team could bring all their experience to bear on doing the best job, rather than possibly being forced to find their profit in the fault of others. This saved the project a fortune.

We didn't have an entirely blame-free culture, but we worked hard at it and matters were never allowed to become acrimonious. Tim and Barry would often tell me that they had never worked on such a rancour-free venture. The most important aspect of this pioneering contract, though, was that it enabled us to become one team, and I can't tell you how exciting it was to see the construction team as emotionally committed to Eden as we were. Maybe it was because we were all in Cornwall, where there is a close community and not many places to go for entertainment, but whatever the reason it wasn't long before everybody was drinking in the same pubs and inviting each other to parties.

Construction is an old-fashioned business, secretive by nature and deeply suspicious of the outside world, which it perceives to be hostile and unappreciative of the values it exults in. Constructors won't talk to the press; they loathe them as interfering busybodies who will accuse you of all sorts andl never give you a fair

'Even in a drought, water drained into it'

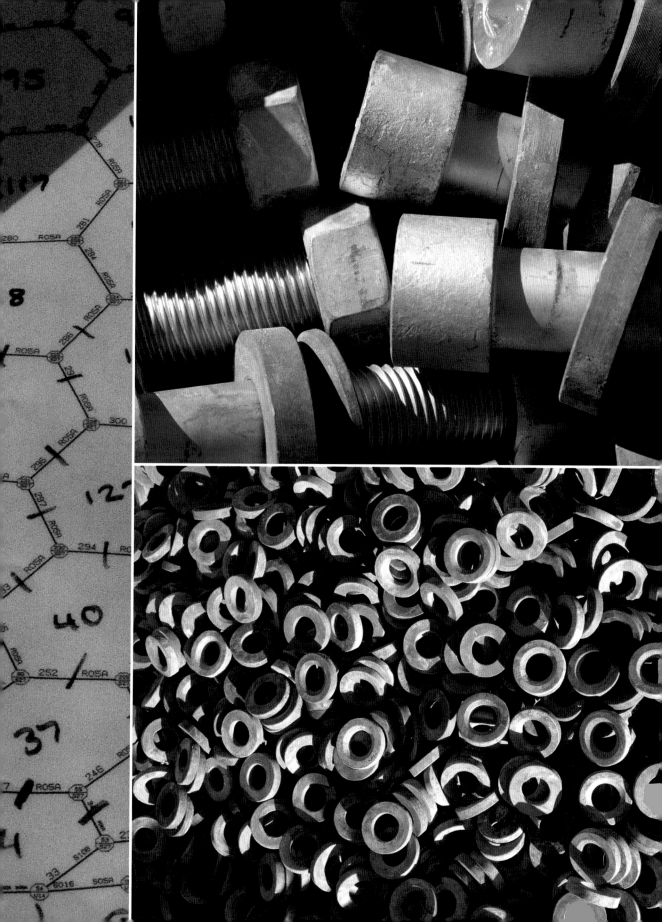

hearing. Under duress they might sponsor a profile in a professional magazine, but that would be the end of it. McAlpine's were notorious for being tight-lipped and, I believe I'm right in saying, had never had a marketing or PR department until recently. It is hardly surprising if construction is an underestimated profession.

Very early on in the job, as the muck-shift was gathering pace, there was an accident. A fuel bowser lost its brakes and careered out of control down the service road into the pit, hit a rock and overturned, throwing the driver out through the windscreen just before it crunched into nothing. The driver had a miraculous escape, suffering some major but not life-threatening injuries. The bowser ruptured its fuel tank and diesel gushed out. The construction boys were brilliant. In minutes machines were there, damming the stream into which the diesel was leaching and siphoning it off. The press heard about it and contacted Paul Travers. An uncomfortable time was had by all. Barry didn't want the press on the site. Paul, who had great relations with the press, begged Barry to relent and promised that it would be all right. Barry, having reluctantly agreed, was amazed to read 'McAlpine's save the day with swift action' in the next day's papers.

It would take a while – there would be battles over photographer and film-crew access to the site, and a reluctance to give interviews – but as the project unfolded the constructors relaxed and began to understand that sometimes the press wrote knocking copy because without cooperation from themselves there was little alternative. Maybe there *was* a bigger audience interested in the skills and challenges of building things; after all, holes in the hoardings round building sites are powerful people-magnets. By the end they took the media in their stride, and Barry turned out to be a most eloquent champion for his profession: weather-beaten salt of the earth meets passionate dream-builder.

The first four months of helter-skelter muck-shift were awesome. Dozens of machines hurtled around the site from sun-up to sun-down with hardly a break. The first major task was to put in the drains. The bottom of the pit was thirty metres below the water table. Even in a drought water drained into it from the myriad springs, broken adits, culverts and leats that litter this former industrial landscape, and the pumps had to work full-time to keep it dry. We wanted to recycle all our water, but this would be difficult because in a clay pit the water is constantly picking up sediment. If we simply put in normal drains it would be only a matter of time before the settling sediment choked everything up. In layman's terms what they decided to do was to lay drains across the site and then cover them with a monstrous sandwich comprising plastic sheeting and granite waste in alternate one-metre layers. The sheeting was clever stuff that worked by capillary action, allowing water to flow downwards through it but preventing it from rising. Thus the water would shed its sediment in the plastic and arrive at the bottom clear as a mountain stream. From here it flowed into a series of giant tanks where it could be held to serve all the site's needs except drinking water. At the start of the job enormous concrete collars were placed at various points across the pit bottom. As the layers of granite and plastic built up from the crater's floor the collars would be added to, metre by metre. These would become the drain inspection pits. By the time June arrived, removing the wooden protective covers that capped them would leave you looking into a vertiginous void seventeen metres deep accompanied by the rushing of water far below.

All the water in the pit had to be managed. The rainwater run-off from the roofs of the giant conservatories would be collected and decanted, just as the Victorians used to do it, into yet more tanks. Its purity was highly prized for plant irrigation. This would become a sealed system to ensure that no impurities could clog up the fine sprayers of the misting units once the conservatories were operational.

The dreadful weather was to test the site, quite literally, to destruction. The face that had collapsed into the pit had done so because long-dormant springs had burst into life and eroded the hillside from underneath. When the ochreous sludge had settled, the muck-shift boys had to clear it away, cut into the hillside, find the

The scaffolding begins to rise

springs, either cap them or channel them into the drainage system, and then begin the laborious rebuilding of the hill. Jerry O'Leary's men had a fantastic system. They started with a layer of plastic, on to which the lorries and dumpers would tip their hardcore. This would be spread to a one-metre thickness and rolled to compress it to a hard, smooth consistency, and then the process was repeated *ad nauseam*. The driving and synchronization were a marvel. Every so often men with testing equipment would call a halt and sample the quality of the hardcore and its compression; an extremely low moisture content was required to guarantee no further slippages. In weeks the hillside was back and its tabletop prepared for the foundations of the Visitor Centre.

So the drains went in and dozens of machines transported the spoil from the waste tip into the bottom to build it up. Then suddenly, one day, only a small heap looking like a Christmas pudding was left on the skyline. Soon that too would be gone and the distinctive shape of the car park and the access routes to the Visitor Centre would become discernible. The large granite boulders that had been mixed up with the spoil were separated out into two huge piles. The ugly ones were crushed by a machine with a pneumatic drill at the end of its arm and used as fine-grade hardcore. The pretty boulders Dominic put to one side for use in the landscaping later.

While all this was going on our geological consultants, the John Grimes Partnership, were carrying out a thorough survey of the faces of the pit. Granite comes in four grades, ranging from Grade One – the hard stuff – to Four, which is soft and flaky. Obviously there had to be no possibility of material falling, sliding or eroding into the pit. The survey of more than a kilometre of cliff faces threw up massive variations, and for almost a year a team painstakingly worked its way around the pit driving rock bolts, steel screws up to fifteen metres long with large washers at their head, into the soft rock to take the pressure off the face. This would then be covered with what looked like heavy-duty chicken wire and sprayed with a bespoke concrete mix called gunnite that hugged the original shape and after weathering would take on the colour of the original rock. The team were to use more than 1,200 of these bolts. In other sheer areas the soft stuff was scraped off. In yet others, with a gentler rake, a glutinous preparation of grasses and a nutrient called hydroseed was sprayed over the surface with a large water cannon. A poisonous-looking patina the colour of verdigris would miracu-lously metamorphose in days into a fine green down, and in weeks, if conditions were right, it would become a thick and healthy grassland, its roots binding the fine sand and gravels, protecting us from the actions of the elements exactly as intended. If you had any fear of dentists this was not the place to be, for month after month the ceaseless drilling and the straining of engines under stress would be the soundscape of our lives.

By the early summer the muck-shift had changed from blunt instrument to rapier as the hard landscape began to take shape. Before long the outlines of the scimitar-shaped beds could be seen in relief and the arena moved from a rumour to a bowl of banked-up mud; the imagination could begin to dwell on thoughts of balmy summer evenings, picnics on the grass and magical performances. The lake that would one day frame shimmering reflections of our green cathedral might well be only a muddy pond with slicks of diesel, a few confused wildfowl and some undernourished rushes, but it didn't hurt to dream.

The Visitor Centre began life looking like a warehouse, all steel framing and rough concrete. Ken Fahey, who owned the concrete works three hundred yards up the lane from Eden, must have thought he'd died and gone to heaven, so much did we use over the construction period. The speed with which the work progressed was a real morale boost, which made all the years of planning feel like training for this moment. Now the job was being reduced to applied skills everyone felt more comfortable; with

every passing day we were spending money but the risks were getting smaller. Jerry O'Leary's team had, against all odds, broken the back of the muck-shift, and that made the constructor feel a little less anxious.

The building of the Visitor Centre wasn't expected to be a problem. We called it the banana split because it was divided into two parts: the public space comprising three large rooms on a curve overlooking the pit with a decked viewing platform cantilevered out into space in front of it; and a range of glass-fronted offices, storerooms and plant rooms which contained the services. There was a generous thoroughfare that separated the public space from offices; the Street, as we called it, would be lined with beautiful laminated wooden masts supporting a tented awning, all of which would be lit by recessed uplights.

The central public room would be an interpretation hall, and later our 'departure lounge' – the ticketing hall. It was deliberately dark, the only natural light

The Visitor
Centre: the
awning goes up
over the Street

coming from a line of small clerestory windows at ceiling height. We were determined that the first full sight of the pit should not be spoiled by a preview. On its
right was another large room where we would have a café and shop. At its far end
there was a glass wall with a door through into a conservatory area which would
be used for plant sales and exhibition. The room on the far left would have wow
factor 10. It was glazed from floor to ceiling on the curve, giving a magnificent
view of the biomes, and had an oak marquetry floor with a silk finish and an
earthen rear wall, a feature it shared with the café.

Of all the crafts exhibited at Eden perhaps the rammed earth walling of the
Visitor Centre caught the public imagination the most because of its rough
simplicity and beautiful terracotta hue. There was a shock value in seeing a
technology 10,000 years old juxtaposed with the boldly modern. We have become
so conservative in our approach to technology that we see the discovery of

something like the breeze block as an advance in quality rather than the response of an age obsessed with saving time. Rowland Keable, a Zimbabwean, master-minded the construction of the wall. His team erected facing pairs of shutters, scooping up local earth and filling the space between them, tamping it down with just the right amount of moisture for it to bond together, then allowing it to set in much the same fashion as in parts of Africa and the Middle East today. The Eden clay is a very particular colour, and we heard rumours, which we never sought to authenticate, that this was the pit from which the clay came that went into the making of the *Financial Times*, the pink 'un.

The wall was raised a metre or so at a time; any faster and we would risk insta-bility. When hardened off and finished with a fine layer of clay it looked magnificent. It would weather a little where exposed to the elements, but this was easily rectified by adding another dollop as and when required. McAlpine's were fascinated because not only was it erected relatively quickly but its insulation performance far exceeded that of modern materials. In summer it kept us cool, in winter it kept us warm. Grimshaw's had chosen this solution for both environ-

mental and aesthetic reasons. The use of natural materials, where possible, creates character, and even in a large space manages to reinforce the sense of individuality and humanity so often absent in modern buildings. Early on in our relationship with Grimshaw's we had voiced the reservation that many of their buildings, while gorgeously executed, lacked emotional warmth, and had discussed the Steiner approach to design – sympathy with the landscape, natural shapes, materials and light. To our delight, this was their response. Visitors would be greeted by the long sweeping curve of the earthen walls shaded by sails rigged on spars of fine timber.

Meanwhile, in the pit, genius was at work. The foundations for the conservatories were under way. I have described how the architects hit on the solution to constructing in an ever-changing landscape. Their problem was topographical. The engineers faced a far greater challenge. To my knowledge no one has ever tried to build inside a clay pit before. The obvious difficulties of drainage and stability have already been explored. The biggest problem, though, lies in the nature of clay itself. Imagine, if you will, millions of tons of material being lifted from your shoulders. If you are made of squidgy material you will breathe a huge sigh of relief, stretch and heave out a bit, becoming a giant sponge. That is what clay does. In its expansive mood it creates gaps, often deep underground, that fill with water, but you wouldn't know they were there unless you looked for them. The engineers had to trace the line their foundations would take and drill down at regular intervals to establish what was underneath. This involved two separate risks. The first was that the clay might be so mushy that you couldn't fix your foundations at all. The second was that you might fix your foundations and then, when their weight bore down, the sponge would slowly release its water and the foundations would sink, bringing everything else down with them. Bear in mind that the movement tolerance for the structure above is around twenty-five millimetres – that's in nearly a kilometre – and you get some idea of the challenge facing the team.

What follows, with apologies to any professionals reading this book, is an attempt to explain what they did. First of all they took their deep core samples to assess the likelihood of the events described above actually happening. Drilling is expensive, and the area they needed to sample so great that it was like looking for a needle in a haystack. Once they'd assured themselves that they had found

The Visitor
Centre:
the rammed
earth wall

nothing lethal they dug out the line of the foundations in the main body of the pit until they hit the hard granite of the cliff face. Into this hole they poured thousands of tons of granite waste to create a solid embankment shaped in section like an upside-down V. Through this material they inserted a grid of porous vertical drains penetrating up to thirty metres deep into the ground below. As the weight of the embankment bore down on the clay, water would bubble into these drains and rise to the surface. The embankment material was also pretty wet, and had horizontal drains inserted through it to dry it out as quickly as possible.

On top of this, in box section, were built the reinforced concrete foundations, the ring beam, on to which the superstructure would later be fixed. Then large hollow steel rods called ground anchors were inserted through both foundation and embankment, their ends fitted with spring-loaded fixing spikes (like the barbs on a fish-hook) to secure them to the bottom of the structure. Grouting material was then forced under high pressure down the tubes to solidify the embankment. The ground anchors were then tightened ever harder, embedding the foundations in the embankment and squeezing out the water below. It's hard to believe that such massive civil engineering has to be so delicately judged, but the foundations in the pit and those that were to be cut into the hard granite of the cliff face all had to work to the same tolerance.

What struck you about the foundations was that no stretch was ever more than about ten metres long before it leaped up or down or charged off at an unlikely angle up the cliff face, where it would be cut in steps into the hard granite. From the lip of the crater the foundation run looked like the Great Wall of China seen from the air, and as we watched men the size of ants working forty metres up a cliff face we wondered if anyone had ever attempted anything this complex before. We doubted it.

The most impressive feat our engineers achieved was that when the superstructure went up and so put its weight on the foundations, it exerted almost the same downward thrust as the rock anchors had been doing. The eventual movement across a foundation run more than a kilometre long was to be around ten millimetres. Brunel would have doffed his stovepipe hat to them for this incredible feat of engineering.

Not many have the privilege of working with so many talented people from so many different disciplines all at once. I found it humbling and incredibly reassuring to be with people who wanted to stretch every sinew, who wanted to be good, and most of all were good not just because they wanted to make some money but because they wanted to use their talent to serve a greater good. That was what really turned them on.

chapter 13

dancing with the professor of shape

The moment we saw the design for the domes we loved them. They felt right in their combination of high technology and mimicry of natural forms. Tests on the material for the roof, the ETFE foil, had proved encouraging; speed testing against breakdown from ultraviolet gave a life of twenty years minimum. On the horizon were a range of foils that could breathe and would have even better light-penetration qualities. What we needed was a building that was future-proof, capable of being upgraded as and when technology moved on; indeed, the hexagons were designed with a fixing system that could be adapted to other materials.

Now, however, we were faced with two problems. The first was that there were only two companies in the world which had experience of manufacturing and fixing the material, and both of them were small, lacking personal indemnity insurance to anything like the degree our funders would demand. The second was that we wanted to buy British steel, but the fabrication skills were just not available in this country. In fact there appeared to be only one company capable of doing the intricate work that we needed: Mero, in Bavaria.

We would eventually buy British steel, but it had to go to four other countries to be processed before finally arriving back in the UK. Ronnie Murning flew to Bremen with other team members to look at a hexagon that was being knocked up for demonstration. The photograph was impressive – a tiny man standing next to a large piece of clingfilm fixed to some steel. They pumped in some compressed air and it went pop. Ronnie and co. swallowed hard but were assured that this was just a technical hitch. The problem with the foil-fixing company wouldn't go away; they were just too small.

Mero could see disaster looming, and their managing director, a keen plantsman who was very taken with the project, decided to buy the foil company and take it under his wing. There was a long period of toing and froing and

A vision of hexagons

agreeing prices for the steel in Deutschmarks not pounds (on which, incidentally, Gay did a very smart deal which saved us a fortune through exchange rate fluctuations). But eventually terms were agreed and this particular crisis was over – assuming Mero could deliver.

They then entered a design phase so complex I wouldn't dream of attempting to describe it, except to say that there would be many different sizes of hexagon, all with different-sized fittings; there would be a number of perpendicular cross-members where one dome abutted another; there would be specially designed venting hexagons, and a rather unusual construction headache. The geodesic dome is by its nature one of the strongest shapes there is, but like a corbelled roof or archway it has no strength until the last piece is in. Mero had a senior director going by the fabulous moniker of Professor of Shape. He was in charge of engineering design, and it was he who pointed out that the conservatory site would have to be scaffolded to give total support. The computer-generated models that Grimshaw's had created looked stunning and were backed by racy music, all very designer, but if that looked complex nothing prepared us for the scaffolding.

The scaffolding for the Humid Tropics Biome took four months to build, and would require more poles than any building in history. It was awesome. It looked like the best adventure playground ever – more than two hundred miles of scaffold, fifty-seven metres in height, and covering almost all of the sixteen thousand square metres of the main conservatory space, except right in the middle where there was a huge crane that towered above everything. Day after day, with immense concentration, the crane driver manoeuvred bundles of scaffold poles and boards around the site from his eagle's nest, and thereafter would hoist each of the 502 individual hexagons into place. When the scaffold was up the erection team were awarded a *Guinness Book of Records* title for the largest free-standing scaffold in the world.

There is something deeply satisfying in the sight of tooled steel. The stuff arrived by the ton on the dockside in Par, to be shuttled the short distance to Bodelva on large flatbed lorries and delivered to the specially cleared compounds in front of both the biomes. In each place a mini-Steptoe's yard, usually thick with mud and subject to constant interruption as vehicles came and went, would grow up with a manky pair of portable buildings for shelter and rest breaks. Everywhere you looked there were pallets piled high with goodies, like the ultimate Meccano set. There were gorgeous nuts, bolts and washers shiny fresh and so full of purpose, every groove of the

screw fixings smooth, cold and precise. There were different lengths and thicknesses of steel tubing piled neatly like logs, and an array of wooden boxes containing steel balls, each with a different number denoting which of the hexagons they belonged to. These balls fitted on to the end of the bolts which held each of the six lengths of steel in position and protected them from rusting, and also provided a smooth sheath to protect the foil roofing material from accidental tearing on contact when it was fixed in place.

The hexagons were assembled on the ground by the fixing team before being gently lifted by webbing, so as not to scratch the surface, and swung into place by the crane, which would hold station until the fixers had bolted it down and given the thumbs-up before unhitching it. The first hexes were fixed to the foundations until a necklace had been formed around the most westerly dome and abutted the first of the large arches, which were also assembled on site and welded into place in sections. There was great variation in the size of the hexes because the mathematics of the curve are complex, and because the foundations changed angle and height with perverse regularity. They also had to fit around the ground-level vents and the emergency access doors, not to mention the air flues, looking like giant exhaust pipes, that entered the biomes at regular intervals. These came from the air-handling units (AHUs) whose task it was to heat the air in the biomes or, conversely, to pump cooler air in to create airflows.

Day by day the pattern would creep higher, until eventually a new shape was being assembled in the mud of the compound: the water-lily vents fixed like a crown at the highest point of each dome, each petal capable of opening on its own or synchronized to work with the rest. The computer model made my brain ache. Who are these people, that they can make sense of this? As the first section was completed there was a flurry of activity as the scaffolders rushed in to take down their work and erect it elsewhere. Bit by bit our silvery skeleton took shape. The strange symmetry of its finely sculpted bone structure made its appearance change according to the vantage point or quality of light. The hexagonal internal bracing frame, which gave the technique the name hex-tri-hex, described a model of the organic carbon ring molecule and thus added to the sense of a higher nature being at work.

The excitement of seeing this work of art emerge with every passing day concealed the urgency of the behind-the-scenes nudging, as the programme slipped a little week by week. The theory was that the construction team would get faster as they gained experience. They did, but Cornish weather is notoriously variable, and the hazards of working high up with the wind at full throttle and rain lashing with a vengeance hampered progress. Every month in the board meeting Tim Carter would face us like a prophet of doom and explain that something had to be done. Mero were summoned and harangued, then pleaded with. Barry

Johnson pulled every trick in the book to persuade the company to put extra men on the job. But it is highly skilled work, and finding these men was not easy.

The reason for the nervousness was that McAlpine's had the real client from hell, one that would die if they didn't keep to programme. This was a strange pressure, because Barry knew that it wasn't special pleading or even a case of prudent penny-watching – it was life or death. If the biomes weren't finished in time there would be the most dreadful consequences. The plants being propagated at Watering Lane were going to grow out of their home. Already we had had to take the unusual step of digging holes in our nursery floor to lower them and stop them going through the roof. If push came to shove we could have coped with this, but the worst problem was that many of our plants were going to arrive from nurseries in Italy. They were so heavy that we couldn't afford to double-handle the largest specimens, so it had been decided that the container lorries should come direct to site. Philip had said all along that the planting had to begin at the end of August or early September so that the plants would have time to settle and show growth in the following early spring. The large specimens had an even harsher deadline than Philip's to contend with. The lorries would have to cross the North Sea before the end of September; any later and the plants would be at risk from the icy blasts. The other option, heated containers, was so prohibitively expensive that we couldn't begin to consider it.

I am getting ahead of myself here as I'm already describing the game of Russian roulette that was the year 2000. I need to fill in the gaps a little to make sense of what happened next. In February 1999 we finally secured the bank funding that would make the Millennium Commission's grant award go unconditional, thus releasing the money we would need to pay the contractors and our own team. Evelyn and Gay then set about securing the other sums we needed to reach this mythical point called 'Financial Close', a term I don't think anyone on the team

'The plants were going to grow out of their home...'

had ever come across until Martin Peck began referring to it. All it means is that enough money is available to meet all known expenditure. We finalized a loan from Cornwall County Council for £3 million. This was generous, though on the other hand their demand for a new road had cost *us* £3 million. Our friends at Pennon Group, the holding company of South West Water, loaned us £1 million on easy terms, and the final arrangement with English Partnerships saw their contribution rise to £3 million.

This bald statement of fact hides the pain of the weeks of paperwork that went into securing the money. It was a nightmare because every single agency was giving grant on different parts of the project under differing conditions, and you could draw down funds from them only up to a capped limit of 50 per cent, or sometimes less, of the costs you'd incurred. They also had different timescales for payment, which meant that you could theoretically have the money sewn up, but because this month's work only met the criteria of Agency X you couldn't draw down any money from Agency Y. Boring as it is to describe, it's hard not to admire the juggling skill of the finance team, who had a duty to pay the bills for work carried out but also had to pay the wages of our own team, by now some fifty in number.

At the end of May, Evelyn Thurlby felt that it was time to move on and return to her consultancy. Evelyn's greatest contribution, among many, to the project was to secure for the Trustees their dearest wish. You will recall their unease at having outside interests take equity stakes in the Trust's management company. Evelyn felt the same, and though for a long time it appeared inevitable, she constantly avoided the issue, while at the same time rendering the matched funding more certain. There came a point, never marked in any way, when the

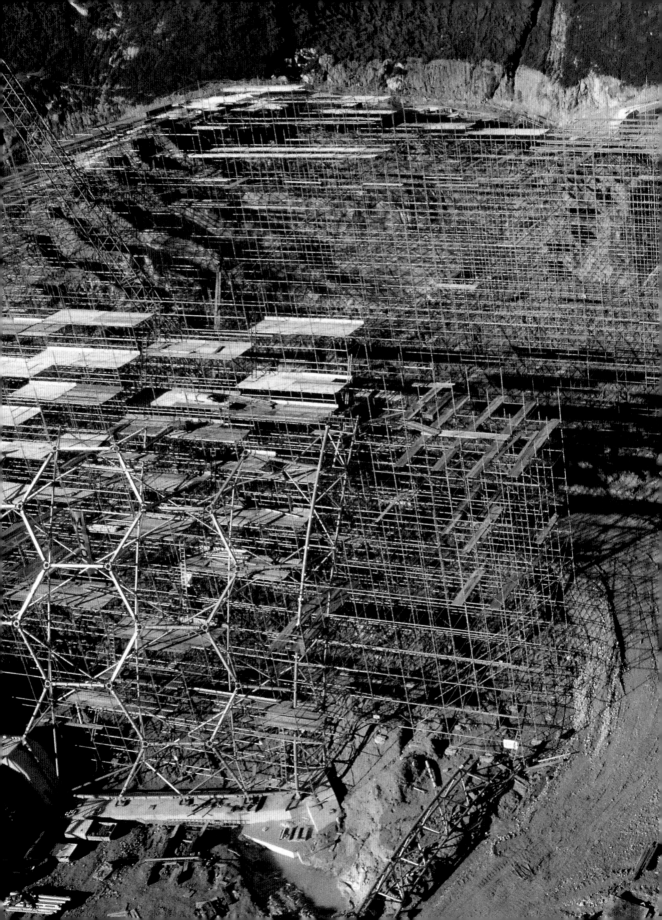

The Scaffold: 'Thank U Very Much'

banks relaxed in the face of the professional financial management the project was enjoying. Three things conspired to give Eden that most valuable commodity, independence: first, the European Commission voiced their grave misgivings at financing a project with private equity stakeholders; secondly, Evelyn convinced the bank that an operator was not only unnecessary but would in fact be a brake on Eden's potential profitability; and thirdly, McAlpine's agreed to loan money to the project without taking an equity stake. Great financial problems lay ahead, and we would need more money to deliver our dream, but Evelyn had steered us into a position where the Trust could take charge of its own destiny. This was a great achievement, and we will be forever grateful to her.

Deborah Clark and Paul Travers came to see me at home one evening. They said bluntly that if Evelyn was going there was only one person who could hold the project together in the interim – me. This was less to do with any talent I have and more to do with public perception that it was business as usual, thereby maintaining confidence at a time when things could have appeared sticky. Even if we started looking for someone else now, we would be well into the run-up to our first-phase opening before Evelyn's successor had his or her feet under the table. I remember feeling as if someone was walking on my grave. My wife Candy was horrified, and fled the room. She told me later that she felt as if our lives as we knew them were over; that to accept would entail a commitment that left no room for the personal, while to decline would be a betrayal of everything we'd all put into Eden over the last five years. I would need to discuss it with the other executives. We met in the Crown at St Ewe one weekend, and it was agreed that I should temporarily take over the reins. They would support this at the imminent board meeting. Another factor adding to the sense of flux was that earlier in the month Sir Alcon Copisarow had stepped down as Chairman of the company, to be replaced in the short term by Philip McMillan Browse.

The day of the board meeting was highly charged. The project had at long last reached a semblance of stability, and there was a genuine feeling that this was an important moment. McAlpine's were blunt. They admired Evelyn's work, and felt that I might be too much of a maverick in the job, dipping into what interested me but perhaps not prepared to apply myself to the grinding process of management necessary to keep a project of this size oiled. My thoughts exactly. In the absence of anyone else they were forced to agree that I was the only short-term solution. I discovered later that Colin Weekley had had a private chat with Gay Coley and asked her if she was staying, because frankly if she wasn't McAlpine's would want to take a very serious look at their involvement. She was, and would become from that moment on *de facto* deputy chief executive. We would actively search for a replacement for me and there would be a number of false dawns but,

Humid Tropics Biome: the landscape appears

given the happy progress of the project, after a while it ceased to be an issue.

Chief executive officer: three words all meaning more or less the same thing. Roughly the job entails being the chief accounting officer. In all matters financial and legal the buck stops with you, although you will have excellent team members who should make this part a formality. However, if you carry the title, you can no longer busk things; you have to read every document and understand it before signing it, whereas in a different position you might trust someone else to do it if the small print looked tricky. You are also the leader of the team, setting the tone of the organization, casual, collegiate and inclusive or formal, autocratic and hierarchical, or indeed a mixture of the two. If you're afraid of being disliked, you will be useless, because you will confuse your natural sympathy or friendship for people with judgement as to whether they are doing the job properly and pulling their weight. To be too judgemental and not supportive enough of human frailty creates a culture of fear that discourages people from daring to make mistakes in the quest for excellence. I am collegiate in that I believe good decisions are arrived at rather than dictated, and I believe in providing a safety net for those who dare to take risks. My sabre, while sharp, is rarely unsheathed.

Any one of the team could have earned significantly more elsewhere. Money was not their motivation. The Eden team was set up with success in mind, planning for a future in which we would have a big stage to play on. Over-qualified we may have been, but oddly it protected us from the trauma many organizations face when they grow rapidly, as people who thrive in a small team find themselves unable to cope with the changes growth brings. You can tell the quality of a good stereo when you crank up the volume, and so it was at Eden. As the challenge got stiffer, the more you saw people coming into their own.

The company had to grow up. We were dealing with large sums of money, and the media were starting to make the world sit up and turn its eyes on the hicks from the sticks in little old Cornwall. In a world where the cult of personality obscures the true understanding of the chemistry of success, it is hard for people to let go of the idea that an individual is responsible for everything. Eden is not the work of a person or a small cabal; its energy comes from a collective spirit free from the certainties of political ideology, celebrating the strength that comes from bringing together all the talents and giving ownership of the eventual direction it will take to the team. The captain's job is to remind people of past errors, gain a consensus on what success looks like, and then let them fly, making their own responses to the challenge. Mistakes will be made, but the sense of danger that comes with taking responsibility for delivering something beyond expectations is a heady brew which creates an unexpected dynamic.

It is ironic that when people are allowed to fly they start to desire the certainties that they would previously have fought against. That is why at Eden we have a combination of those with big-company experience, who understand the dynamics and processes of running an organization and the obligations that go with the responsibilities, and a maverick crew who have never worked for anyone else in their lives, who question every constraint and demand freedom of expression. The secret of success would appear to be to teach respect for process to the latter and encourage flexibility in the former, and create a happy family by meeting them all in the middle.

I was asked to address the AGM of a national newspaper group about the Eden Project and my approach to management. At the end of the speech, the chairman, to start questions off, asked me what I thought I could teach his company. Nothing, I said. The problem with large companies is that they demand a regularity in the pattern of employment, salary bands, working hours, attendance and so on that would exclude the very people capable of putting a bit of stick about or providing the lateral thinking that they crave.

Organizations which have those annoying slogan boards saying things like 'You don't have to be mad to work here, but it helps' are usually the dullest. Innovation is not about hiring an Einstein or creating a slogan. Everybody is capable of it, and

(opposite and overleaf) Sky monkeys in their natural habitat

the first sign that it is happening is when people work together, excited because they want to be there, focused on finding a solution to a challenge they all understand. At Eden we have all had the privilege of seeing what others are capable of, and coming to understand, albeit imperfectly, what could be achieved in this wedding of the talents. Of course we argue, of course we get petty, and of course we get as defensive as anybody else when we are criticized. But we question why we do things all the time, and this is in itself a liberation.

In 1999 we added our first non-executive directors to the board. After publicly advertising and going through a series of interviews we appointed Ken Hill, the group finance director of Pennon Group, Peter Hardaker, the chief executive of Cornwall Farmers, the biggest farmers' cooperative in the South West, Dr Alan Stanhope, principal of Cornwall College, and lastly Richard Sandbrook, the director of the International Institute for the Environment and Development (IIED) and the co-founder of Friends of the Earth UK. They represented finance, agriculture, education and the environment respectively. Philip viewed his chairmanship as a stopgap and asked the board to elect a replacement. Ken Hill was elected unanimously, and what a good choice this would turn out to be.

Anyone put in the position I was in should take my advice. Don't pretend to know what you don't, and beg your colleagues to compensate for your weaknesses immediately. I was quite capable of walking into a room with funders and getting them excited about the project. Taking it from there, wading through mountains of legal work, exploring innovative mechanisms that would satisfy such a disparate group and then finally delivering the project, was completely outside my experience.

Gay Coley would save my life. Although she'd been with the Project for nearly eighteen months our paths had rarely crossed for any length of time, and we hadn't worked as a duo. The next two years would be a Beirut basement job by comparison. We were a bit wary of each other, and one day she decided to break the ice by making me coffee. It was without doubt, excepting a misadventure with some yogurt at university, the worst I've ever tasted. It wasn't a fluke, either; there was a terrifying consistency to her culinary awfulness that she cheerfully admitted to, and we all soon exempted her from team coffee duties on health grounds.

Gay was made for Eden. While she oozed professionalism, backstage she was the complete team player – leading the Eden tap-dancing team, acting as a willing waitress at the staff party, always one of the first on to the dancefloor, and, most importantly, always making time to listen. She had trained to follow her mother into teaching, but was tempted from her Welsh roots by the lure of the City. Mammon's gain would also be Eden's, as she put her professional skills to work in pursuit of her passion for education for all.

'Clingfilm with attitude...'

Fiona Cattrell, who had been working for Evelyn, took over as Gay's PA. She would become the high priestess of the paperwork, keeping the Board and Trust papers rolling out, taking the minutes that took hours, bearing as much of the load as she could, working ridiculously long days while running a family and commuting from Helston, nearly forty miles away.

In turn the contribution of Martin Miles, who on my appointment I requested be seconded to us from McAlpine's, would be pivotal over the next six months as we raced towards the Phase One opening of the Project.

The programme we had signed up to would see the Visitor Centre and all the infrastructure outside the pit, such as roads and highways, handed over to us in April 2000. The biomes would be finished in August, and planting would begin in September in the Humid Tropics and November in the Warm Temperate and outdoor landscape. The outdoor landscape schedule was hugely dependent on the biomes remaining on programme, because huge chunks of it had been levelled and not hard landscaped to enable the steel to be stored on site.

Throughout the summer and autumn the sky monkeys could be seen painstakingly putting the hexagons in place. The Humid Tropics was being fast-tracked because at a pinch the Warm Temperate could be planted a little later. Barry Johnson and his team had no such luxury with the tropics.

Superstition is an odd thing; not wishing to tempt providence can create inertia. The Lost Gardens of Heligan had opened only a year into the restoration because of a mistake on *Gardeners' World*, which had filmed us and forgotten to mention that we weren't open to the public. So when coaches started to arrive in our works area we just gave up explaining and decided to open. The result was that we gained a huge number of friends who returned many times to see the work in progress and who took ownership of the project. This is probably the greatest single reason for its enduring success. The Eden team agreed that this 'preview' approach could be an excellent way to satisfy the interest in Eden that was being fuelled by heavy press coverage. But how to do it?

We had taken on an operations director, Ian Cunningham, who had run Sea Life Centres prior to setting up a successful aquarium operation of his own which he had recently sold on. He would focus on the practicalities of dealing with the visitors when they arrived. He immediately launched into a review of the catering and retail facilities and visitor flows. At a memorable staff awayday chaired by Richard Sandbrook in October 1999 the team was forced to focus exclusively on what we were going to do to be ready for opening the following spring. We came up with 'The Big Build' as the title for our first-year exhibition, a celebration of the construction of the project. David developed a leaflet with a fantastic picture of a sky monkey in relief against a blue sky perched perilously on the top of a biome of gleaming steel. We would open on 15 May, a Monday and my son Alex's twentieth birthday. He wasn't impressed.

The roads were completed and the road-builders took us at our word when we said we didn't want the roadside walling to be made out of small bits of stone. They built walls with boulders so large they could be shifted only by swing

The Creative Team: Ben Luxton, Peter Hampel, Sue Hill

shovels, but we'd never seen walls that imposing anywhere. They were covered in a skin of earth and seeded, and by opening they would look as if they had been there for years. As visitors crested the brow of the hill they would suddenly be presented with a vista of St Austell Bay in the distance, with the Visitor Centre and a tantalizing glimpse of the top of the Humid Tropics Biome closer at hand. Thousands of trees were being planted down the access road and throughout the car parks to provide the screening – and the dramatic effect – we wanted. Dominic Cole's bold plan was coming to life, and the terraced car parks and sculpted drains, rills and culverts already hinted at the distinctive patterning which would be the hallmark of the hard landscape inside the crater.

Within the Visitor Centre the café was being made ready. Ronnie Murning had designed the retail and café layout and furniture to create the effect of a relaxed refectory. We had decided to appoint Emma Cummings, Philip's PA, as retail manager on the grounds that she had exquisite taste in everything, and it would be much easier to teach her retail skills than to train someone else's taste. She went into a whirlwind of meeting reps, travelling to trade exhibitions and beginning the process of developing our own distinctive products using local suppliers.

Education, education, education: Pam Horton *(l)*, Jo Readman and Gill Hodgson *(not pictured)* have welcomed 70,000 school-children to Eden in our first season

Meanwhile Dave had commissioned our first publication, *Eden – The First Book*, which concentrated on our history, the construction, the plants in waiting and our plans for the future. Elsewhere, on the Street, probably the finest toilets in the world were being installed; heating systems, fire alarms, intercoms, telephones, lighting and all the paraphernalia of existence were being plumbed in. Now all we needed to do was to decide what we were going to exhibit.

For more than eighteen months Peter Hampel had been nurturing a range of interesting artists who would be commissioned to create works for our Interpretation Hall. Here we would give the public their first taste of our vision for an unusual language fusing science and the arts. He was to be helped in this by Sue Hill, a long-time friend of mine responsible for much of the highly distinctive promotional artwork for Cornwall's Kneehigh Theatre, and also one of its lead actresses. She introduced Peter to many of the international artists who had chosen to make Cornwall their home. Between them Sue and Peter, charged with telling a number of simple stories provided by Jo Readman as well as some that had evolved from suggestions made by the artists themselves, selected the first commissions. This would result in the concept of using the garden shed, the archetypal British retreat, as a metaphor for worlds within worlds.

Visitor Centre attractions: Tim Hunkin's drawings of Rubberworld and the Edeon Cinema

There are many ways of telling people that without plants there is no life on earth. Finding a way that is beguiling and amusing and memorable enough to make people reflect on the message is more tricky. Eschewing the traditional wall-mounted information boards, Jo Readman had suggested the idea of a breakfast scene from which one by one all the plant-based products would be removed. Sponsored by NESTA, the National Endowment Fund for Science, Technology and the Arts, it was politely referred to as 'Plant Takeaway', but before long everybody would be calling it Dead Cat. Paul Spooner, Will Jackson and Tim Hunkin, collectively known as Mongrel Media, are automata makers. Their creation is possibly the most talked-about work on the site. It comprises a kitchen scene where a family of two adults and a child are waiting for breakfast. A table and chairs, tablecloth, glasses of fruit juice and a bowl of fruit are in place. There is a fire, a hearth and a dog with a rolled-up newspaper on the floor. A fridge opens and closes to reveal the food. To the accompaniment of Elvis's 'Wooden Heart', all the plant-based materials are removed by way of a Heath Robinson series of wheels and pulleys. The family ends up naked and collapses, the lights dim, and the spotlight falls on the family cat. The milk drains from its bowl, followed by the cat keeling over and its eyes popping out on stalks. Dynamite.

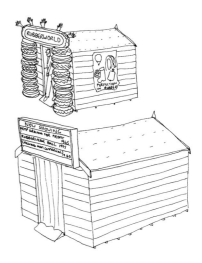

The big build: highs and lows

You enter the shed called Rubberworld through a gateway of tyres accompanied by a necklace of rubber gloves that inflate and deflate at regular intervals. Inside a wonderful array of rubber goods through the ages includes an army-issue condom of the 1950s which would leave most males feeling horribly inadequate and an exhibition case of rubber footwear that suddenly bursts into automated dance to the accompaniment of 10cc's 'Rubber Bullets'. Elsewhere a superbly engineered steel globe revolves while a giant finger points out the places being described to an audience listening on headphones to humorous animated tales of plants. On request, two animated snakes mounted on lampposts slide down from above to encourage you to behave badly towards the environment and tell you to stop listening to the do-gooders who just want to stop you having fun.

In the main gallery Jo was developing the Big Build exhibition and a series of beautiful canvas banners produced by Gendall Design. Tessa and Phil Gendall were responsible for the beautiful graphic design that gave the exhibition space – and our early literature – so much of its character. Each banner would be presented as an advertisement hoarding with an unusual twist, highlighting a plant-based story. Here a Bob Carlos Clarke model in rubberware, an electric guitar, an orang-utan and other powerful and provocative images were used to catch the attention. In the middle of the room on scaffolding towers Jo mounted huge photographs with accompanying words describing the construction challenge that could be seen outside the windows. There were samples of the foil to touch and some of the steel fixings for the roof were displayed. The original model was there, as was the wind-tunnel model and two works of art in maquette form. Tim Shaw's 'Bacchanalia' showed Dionysus in the form of a bull, surrounded by cavorting Hieronymus Bosch-inspired maenads engaged in various acts associated with drinking – not all of them wholesome, which would excite some controversy. The other was a model for Elaine Goodwin's mosaic floor proposed for the Warm Temperate Biome, a snake of golden olive oil meandering through a floor of white. On the rammed earth wall would be a collection of paintings by Anthony Frost in his trademark bold slabs of colour.

One of the crucial lessons we learned at Heligan was the importance of owning our history. We had allowed the BBC to film our early work and then found we couldn't get access to the film. We were determined not to make this mistake at Eden, so we collaborated with Gwynhelek, a local production company, to make a documentary series for National Geographic. Robin Kewell was the camerman who made it his personal mission to capture the birth of our fledgling institution, taking hundreds of hours of his own time to capture everything of moment. He became a fixture in all our lives, persuading the nervous, the cussed and the camera-shy to perform. He was everywhere, even out in Guyana with Jo and Robin.

As well as the documentaries, Robin's work led to an archive unparallelled in its thoroughness and a superb series of cameo pieces produced by Anna Meneer which were to be shown in the Visitor Centre. It is even more amazing to see the whole story of Eden, from mud to paradise, in three minutes. Oh, the wonders of technology – imagine if this had been available for Eden Mark 1!

Offsite Kary was recruiting the operations staff, and setting up workshops, lectures and special training in operational protocols. We were about to triple our workforce to around 150. Ian Cunningham, the ops director, was busy working out rosters, training the managers and coming to terms with the computer systems that would give him and Gay the data they would need. So that visitors could share in the excitement of the Big Build close up, he made an impassioned plea for land trains to take visitors on a circular route from the Visitor Centre down an access road to the side of the Humid Tropics Biome. We duly bought two, sucking our teeth hard because we couldn't really afford it.

The shop was kitted out, the catering team were in place. Suddenly, before we knew it, it was 14 May. The whole team gathered in the gallery for pep talks. I told them that we were an international project in Cornwall and that we had to set the highest possible standards in everything. I said that as a team we relied on one another to make decisions, and that if anyone found themselves in a position in which action was needed but no help was at hand they should do what they thought right. If it turned out wrong no one would blame them. If they did

(opposite)
Elaine Goodwin's beautiful mosaic path in the Warm Temperate Biome

'They would
remember
this day...'

nothing they'd be fired. As for our visitors, my Heligan experience had taught me that though there are some people who complain for a living, there would be others who had genuine grievances. It was vital to deal with them equally and restrain the temptation to throttle the professional moaners. I finished by speaking of our commitment to making a place where everyone could look forward to a long-term future, and of our desire to create a culture where we could enable people to train for the jobs that they wanted if they were capable of it. Eden wasn't going to be a low-paying exploitative leisure attraction.

Outside, the sky monkeys were still weaving their magic. The Humid Tropics Biome was complete in skeleton, and some of the pillows were fixed into place. The giant crane protruded through the middle of the highest dome, dwarfing it. We couldn't see how they were ever going to get it out of there without damaging anything. It was so big and the hexagons looked so delicate in comparison. I walked out with Paul on to the viewing platform outside the gallery, and we watched the work going on below. The muck-shift was nearly done, with the arena half completed, leaving only the hard landscaping of the works compounds and the final sculpting of the lake to finish.

We made a number of media calls that afternoon, waxing lyrical about the following day. We were ready, hot to trot. The *Western Morning News* would carry the story, and we featured on the six o'clock news on both local channels. While people were tucked up in bed the crew were making their final touches. Sue Hill was filling in all the slate information boards in the café in her exquisite handwriting. Being an actress, she was quite sure it would be all right on the night. Jo was putting the final touches to the gallery. Emma was still loading shelves and getting cross with the bar-coding system. Ronnie was minutely altering the displays to achieve the artistic effect he desired, so that just for one moment everything might be perfect, never mind that the first customer would wreck the symmetry he was taking hours to achieve. Gay was checking that all the tills worked as expected. Kary was patting noses and proffering sugar lumps to all, and Martin was patrolling the patch lending support wherever it was needed. We joked about the tape I'd made for the land train. He wondered how many times the drivers could bear to listen to it before going mad. No one would sleep much that night. We would all gather for the opening ceremony at eight the following morning.

Some weeks before, we had hatched a cunning plan for the Phase 1 opening ceremony with our friends at McAlpine's. Only about six people knew officially what was going to happen, and about a hundred unofficially. Jerry O'Leary was asked if he would do us the honour of coming down to the Visitor Centre to collect the celebrity from the gallery after the opening. Paul had done his usual stuff of preparing the room for the media, and it looked beautiful. There was a speech from Mike O'Connor, the chief executive of the Millennium Commission, which was followed by my reply, in which I was intended to introduce the celebrity. I began by saying that there was one man who had come to represent all that was best about the project and who, in the judgement of his peers, deserved a special accolade. Mr Jerry O'Leary, come here. He looked totally shocked, but his crew were egging him on and he walked up with a big grin on his face. Paul had meanwhile disappeared into the kitchen behind the stage. Jerry, I said, when you took on this job didn't you say you wanted to do it so that you had something to tell your grandchildren? He grinned. Yes, I did, and I shall, he said. Indeed, Jerry, well why don't you tell them yourself right now? Come on out…

Then out from the kitchen came his wife, his children and a phalanx of grand-children, all immaculately turned out for the occasion. The big man had tears running down his face and so had the rest of us. Barry Johnson and Keith Titman, who'd arranged for the family to come down to Eden in secret, were grinning fit to bust, and that was how it should be. Jerry and his family went out on to the platform in a hubbub of excitement to have their picture taken. They would remember this day, and that too was as it should be.

chapter 14

working the knight shift

Having what you thought you wanted in your hands can be a bit like the male black widow spider's drive to procreate. At the very moment when the post-coital cigarette seems in order, you get eaten by your mate. From mid-1999 to mid-2000 life was a bitch. I wouldn't say cash was tight but every morning Gay would have to satisfy herself that we could meet our liabilities. Promises are all very well, but they are no substitute for having the actual loot. There was another problem looming. Superstition prevents you planning for success in case a thunderbolt should strike you down for your presumption. Eden was going to be big, we could feel it in our water, and we wouldn't be able to cope on the site as currently planned.

A reappraisal of our needs showed that it would cost us a further £13 million to upgrade. We swallowed hard. There was no option but to find the money. Rule no. 1: never disappoint your visitors. Rule 2, see Rule 1.

Then there was the millennium. Funny, really. Eden is a millennium project, but the actual millennium as a point in time passed me by. When we were sent four tickets to the Dome opening, we put all the staff names in a hat and drew for it. My millennium was spent watching the television with a cup of tea. I had a bottle of champagne, but circumstances conspired against wild abandon. We had invited my great-aunt Cecily down to Cornwall for Christmas. She was born in 1906 and was very frail on her pins, but she made light of her long journey down from Cheshire by train. She was bright-eyed right up to the point where we opened the Christmas presents, and then she fell asleep. She slept through Boxing Day like a dormouse and she would stay in bed for the next two months. Candy tried to look after her, but it was soon obvious that we needed help; it's a job for a professional when someone is that old, and very soon some wonderful carers were visiting regularly. The determination of these home-helpers to cater for Cecily's best interests and offer her some sort of quality of life was humbling, and provided me with a much-needed reminder of what really matters. On Millennium Eve I woke Cecily at midnight as she had asked. I had the champagne in my hand, but she wanted a cup of tea and some porridge.

Cecily is an amazing and inspirational woman. She was the headmistress of Sale Grammar School for Girls in Cheshire. She never married, and had strong religious beliefs, which I don't share, but she never let that get in the way. When I was younger and going through a ranting phase she would give me a patient look as if to say, I can wait. When it came time for her to retire she startled the family by announcing that she had privately learned to read, write and speak Thai and that she was going to Thailand to work in a home, set up by an old friend of hers, for the children of prostitutes.

She slept on earthen floors and ate nothing but rice for a couple of years, and then realized that she perhaps wasn't physically up to the life. She was on an index-linked state pension but led a life of extreme frugality, and she decided to put her money to work. She hatched a deal with some of the teenage children at the home whereby she agreed to sponsor them to come to Britain for training in anything from secretarial skills and English teaching to nursing, on condition that, when qualified, they would return and devote an equal number of years to working in the home. Over the next fifteen years dozens of them were to stay with her, effectively welding themselves into her extended family. None disappointed her. She would often talk politics with me; she was a *Guardian* reader with a sympathy for the Liberal Democrats, although I was never sure whether this was a political statement or merely support for the underdog, which she would take to alarming lengths.

When I was sixteen she had decided to take me to Arisaig on the west coast of Scotland. We had time to kill in Glasgow waiting for the Fort William train and I suggested going to see a football match, Celtic versus Morton. To my astonishment she agreed; on getting into the ground at Parkhead I realized to my horror that we were in the standing end among the Celtic supporters. When Morton scored first and thirty thousand silent people looked round to see who the person shouting Bravo, well played was, I thought I had made a very big mistake indeed.

I would go to visit her at her tiny cottage in Kelsall, with its minute rooms and uncomfortable furniture and bookcases full of books she meant to read when she retired but had somehow never got round to yet. Her high collars, straight back and clear blue eyes would unnerve me slightly. She wasn't interested in small talk, fashionable issues or posturing, and reserved her deepest loathing for the moral relativism that passed as grown-up debate. She wasn't a puritan, and went to great pains to stress that although she was religious there was precious little she hadn't come across in her job. Your private life was your own. But if something was wrong with the big things – health, poverty and education – she felt it must be dealt with. We get used to dismissing opinions like this as naive, saying that we can't solve the world's problems and we must be pragmatic – but in the quiet of a little sitting-room, beside a coal fire, confronted by someone who has led her life in this belief and who has acted upon it, you realize that your sophisticated fake worldliness is nothing more than a barrier against having to ask hard questions about who you are, what you really believe in and what it would take for you to do something about it.

Her memory was prodigious: she could remember the First World War, aeroplanes coming into fashion, the growth of radio and then television. While she took most of the technological advances for granted and made use of them with breathtaking incompetence, to the extent that the family viewed the introduction of a microwave into her kitchen armoury with great trepidation, some, it turned out, had passed her by completely. Having spent two months pretty much asleep, I think she was amazed that she wasn't dead. We wondered whether she might have been holding on for the millennium, and now that it had passed uneventfully she had decided that her time hadn't yet come. In March Candy persuaded her to come downstairs for the first time in 2000, to watch Tony Blair coming to Eden on the television news. She was delighted, but when Candy played the video back later in the day, Cecily was startled to see that the Prime Minister had already made a return visit!

Cecily's most lasting influence on me is her unshakeable belief that it is individuals who change the world through their example, not politicians, and when you see what a small group of people did with a children's home in Thailand, who can doubt that it is so.

March was to be quite a month. We drove Cecily home to Cheshire, and as we packed her birdlike frame into the front seat of the Volvo and wrapped her in blankets I didn't think we'd ever see her here in Cornwall again. I felt so sad that she would never see the project I loved and so badly wanted her to approve of. I like to think she would have admired many of the people who'd come together to make it happen. She'd have saluted Philip's faith in the young, she'd have chuckled at the irreverence of our approach to academia and reverence for the power of education, but above all she'd have nodded her head at our certainty that the great majority of people want to do the right thing, whatever that is; and that is why every day we should be optimistic.

The Eden Trust was about to go through a great change. The sad death of Sir Ralph Riley was followed by the resignation of Sir Alan Donald, who would also be much missed. Then Sir Alcon indicated that his health made travelling to Cornwall very tiring and that he would like to stand down if someone could be found to take on the mantle. I had met Sir Ronnie Hampel in 1998 through his son Peter, our creative director. Ronnie, as he prefers to be known, having no time for formality, was then the chairman of ICI, a company he'd worked at for most of his life. He made some very helpful comments on Eden and gave me his number, saying that if I ever wanted to talk anything over I just had to lift up the phone. This was possibly not one of the best decisions he ever made, but it's one for which I will be eternally grateful.

The handover: Sir Ronnie Hampel *(l)* and Sir Alcon Copisarow

I spoke with Ronnie often, and after a while I asked whether there was any chance he would consider becoming a Trustee. After checking with Chris Smith that reverse nepotism would not be frowned on (I think with tongue firmly in cheek!), he finally accepted an invitation from the Trustees and was elected their chairman in January 2000. He immediately set about expanding the Trust in his own inimitable style. He wasn't interested in the Great and the Good who would just show up occasionally; he set his heart on bringing together a group of people whom he could depend on, who had something to give and were prepared to give it. So within a few months we had an expanded body of active Trustees with wide interests, who would open their address books, give us the benefit of their experience and generally demonstrate their commitment at every turn. As we entered the next phase we were going to need the advice and support of both Ronnie and Ken Hill, the chairman of the board, who made themselves available well beyond the call of duty. Both men are successful no-nonsense operators who have no compunction in pointing us in the right direction if they think we are making mistakes. Having mentors of this quality is a privilege.

Back to Rule 1 and the new money we needed to raise. We couldn't afford the interest payments if we upped the loan from the NatWest. Our only realistic option, without going cap in hand to public funders, was to embark on a complex deal whereby we effectively leased our site and liberated some money by having someone else pick up the immediate tab. This would involve having a lead bank, in our case the Royal Bank of Scotland, and a security bank to underwrite the construction costs, which would be DKB (Dresdner Kleinwort Benson). The process had stalled, so in the autumn of 1999 Gay put a bit of stick about and got the lawyers and finance people talking to each other.

At the risk of boring the reader I must try to explain the complexity of our problem. To recap: Eden had a range of public and private funders, namely the Millennium Commission, Cornwall County Council, the Borough of Restormel, Europe (via GOSW) and English Partnerships from the public side, and NatWest, Pennon Group and the McAlpine joint venture from the private. The rest of our money, a very small percentage, came from sponsorship and donations. Naturally, for security, all these parties sought to secure a charge on the asset (Eden). They had argued for hours about security back in 1998 until it was pointed out that a derelict hole in the ground is worth not very much, so why didn't we all move on? Now, a year later, it was different; the pit was half developed and was worth something. A fortune's worth of legal time had already gone into the horse-trading to establish a pecking order between the funders in case the project went belly up. After months the principle had been established that the private investors should have first bite of the cherry, on the grounds that they wouldn't release their money if they didn't. It hardly seemed worth worrying about, because if Eden failed the best bets for alternative uses for the site seemed to be either the tallest tomato greenhouse in the world or a half-built Center Parcs.

Ken Hill

All parties recognized the wisdom of investing more money to upgrade what was on offer. While the Royal Bank of Scotland's leasing arm (RBL) was interested, they demanded documentation and certainty way beyond what we were able to offer in the short term. All our funders had their own legal teams, and now they had to agree a new pecking order to take account of the two new banks that had

moved on to the patch, while Ernst and Young ran new sets of figures for us on a daily basis according to the ebb and flow of the financial potential in the RBL deal. We had spent quite a lot of everybody's money by then, except for NatWest's, simply because it would have been stupid of us to start paying interest on a commercial loan until the last possible moment. The lawyers and the financial advisers had been trying to sort it out on their own. There was a lot of posturing and misunderstanding, and the wheels were threatening to come off. Gay and I decamped to London to see whether we could get confidence back into the proceedings. A simple pee break with these people costs a fortune – I once lost my temper and reminded them that the collective cost of one of their little sandwich breaks would be equivalent to the annual salary of one of our gardeners. We would make fifteen separate visits to London to hammer heads together, read the latest amendments, suggest our own, cajole, threaten and plead for compromise.

During the first three months of 2000 Gay and I had rooms at the October Gallery, an ethnic art space belonging to our friends from Ecotechnics, who had been involved in building Biosphere 2 in Arizona. This was an oasis of calm, with its own courtyard dripping with plants and rooms that were reached by means of an external fire escape. You would never have believed you were in the middle of central London. Chili and Jessie, the mainstays there, were a reminder that there was another world far away from smoke-filled rooms and Gieves and Hawkes suits. They introduced us to some of the artists who exhibited there, who would, through Sue Hill and Peter Hampel, come to be commissioned by Eden.

The City is a dreadful place after 8 p.m. There's no life, you can't get a taxi and even the pubs seem to close early. These meetings would go on and on, and afterwards Gay and I would find ourselves in some late-night restaurant eating tired pizzas, reading mountains of guff and too weary even to bother with drinking.

John Brett of NatWest was fantastic. The parties actually boiled down to three: the public sector as a collective, NatWest and RBL. NatWest held a lot of the cards and John would encourage Andy Robertson, the RBL man, to make concessions in return for one by him. (Further complexity was added to the situation when in the middle of negotiations the Royal Bank of Scotland took over NatWest!) Gay would work out what moves we could make and when we should dig our heels in, constantly chivvying the E&Y team to greater efforts. My job was to make encouraging noises and tell occasional jokes to keep the mood right. I once halted a meeting to bring out a beautiful series of photographs of Eden in construction, and give them the lowdown on the project. I told them why it was important that we did this thing, and that no one would thank us for being small-minded now. Until then I'm not sure they had all grasped quite how big the project was, and there was a perceptible change of attitude in the room.

Eventually we thought we had it down to one last problem – a massive one,

I grant you, but singular. When the public sector awards you a grant the small print says that in the event of default it can claw back the money. RBL and NatWest saw this as unacceptable because it meant that no matter what charge they had on the asset (us) the government could, if it chose, bring the whole thing down like a pack of cards without any reference to the bank. We became belligerent ourselves and asked the MC and the Government Office for the South West to help. The result was a declaration that it was unlawful for government ministers to fetter themselves by waiving any rights whatsoever. Fettering effectively means limiting the freedom of a successor to act as he sees fit.

The deal was off. There was rage and disbelief, and also on the part of GOSW a dawning realization that we had stumbled on a real problem. While it may have been important to us, it would have a potentially devastating impact on future private/public partnerships. Richard Bailey, the new boss of GOSW, undertook to get his hands dirty, and miraculously over the next week managed to persuade Chris Smith, Minister for Culture, Media and Sport (the boss of the MC) and John Prescott, Secretary of State for the Environment, Transport and the Regions (the ultimate boss of GOSW), to exchange letters with a wording that satisfied the banks.

We camped in London for the best part of a week, making sure the legal documentation was signed by all parties, for there were many. Back at Watering Lane Kary and Martin were chasing and harrying people, arranging couriers and doorstepping, just to ensure that there would be no excuses. Our lawyers' offices in Moorgate became our London HQ. Toby Stroh was leading our legal team, and he looked as if he'd just come back from the Gulag. The paperwork was mountainous; every change had to be cross-referenced and run past all the protagonists. But we were nearly there.

Bang.

Isn't it O'Riley's Law that contends Sod was an optimist? Everyone had taken Dresdner Kleinwort Benson for granted. Not in our wildest dreams had we expected them to have a completely different take on things, for after all they would be fairly passive players, guaranteeing our payments to RBL. We met them and they were massively underwhelmed by our special pleading. We had our entire team, as well as the MC and Ernst and Young, running around like cats with fireworks strapped to their tails vainly hunting for a means of giving them confidence that we were viable. How do you demonstrate your future viability to guys who question whether the sun will come up tomorrow? The MC team worked with us until gone midnight looking for an elegant solution, but there was none.

There was only one way out: an audit by E&Y and a letter from them in effect guaranteeing our viability. Jonathan Johns of E&Y went berserk, pulling every favour within his organization that he'd ever been owed. An E&Y team would fly down to Cornwall from all over the country the following day.

Doing the business, part 2: Gay Coley flanked by John Brett of NatWest, Andy Robertson of RBL and fifty-seven contracts

The intensity of the next five days was unbelievable. We arrived back at base and Eden's finance team (George Musgrave, Liz Titcombe and Ellen Gordon) were in hyperdrive. Just about every document and piece of paper that had anything to do with money was set out ready for looking at. Gay was also going to have to justify all the assumptions of the business plan in a formal interview. The E&Y team under Steve Gratton were operating with a glass wall between them and the other members of our long-term E&Y team, which meant that they were un-influenceable. After five days we got the letter we required and headed back to London after virtually no sleep. Steve would send Gay and me a bottle of champagne six months later, after the successful opening of Phase 1, with a card which simply said, Congratulations – Thank Christ!

On 9 March 2001 we assembled at Druces and Attlee, our lawyers, and collated the remaining paperwork into the early hours of the morning. At teatime we confirmed to RBL that we'd be ready. It was touch and go, because a number of documents were still in transit and Andy Robertson would have to catch the last flight out of Edinburgh. He'd already had one abortive trip and he was grumpy. 10 March dawned, and a small army of lawyers and their assistants was packing cases to be put in taxis for the short journey down to the offices of Norton Rose, the RBL lawyers, where everyone was gathering. From the amount of paperwork you'd have thought it was an international peace agreement we'd been negoti-ating; the gangs of lawyers were exchanging papers for checking, talking in a low murmur, exiting for conferences, highlighting last-minute glitches: This one is a photocopied signature, will we accept it? Oh, for Christ's sake don't do this to me! It was late afternoon and dark outside, we'd been there all day, and the nice biscuits were finished. I'd started smoking cigars despite the signs; at these prices they'd have to put up with it.

Suddenly we were there, and dumbstruck. We started signing and exchanging contracts as if they were Christmas presents. An hour's worth of signatures later a photographer who'd been waiting for this moment all afternoon came in and organized a group shot. After one with us in suits I insisted we needed one with jackets and ties off. Gay and the bankers posed, pens raised, surrounded by thirty-two different contracts with copies for each of the participants. Champagne arrived, we went demob happy and drank far too fast, phoned HQ, home, Ken Hill, Ronnie Hampel. The legal bills would amount to nearly £1.2 million but we had pioneered a course that Gay would later share with many other projects, so it would prove worthwhile in the long run. We were all flying from the relief and elation. After all the haggling, the room now contained just one team. The people who had been on the opposite side for so long were congratulating us. They knew how much it meant to us, and over the last three weeks they'd become genuinely interested and excited. We told them to get down to Cornwall.

Toby invited us to supper at some Chinese restaurant he wanted to try. He remarked that the most extraordinary thing about it all was that we'd persuaded such a wide group of people, many of whom would have found it easier to walk away, to stay at the table and find a reason for saying yes. We sat there barely talking, just saying to ourselves, We're fully funded, like a mantra. Yes indeed, so we were. I started to feel a creeping gloom coming on. Everyone else thought we had been funded for ages.

An obsession is fundamentally different from a common-or-garden desire or need. A desire, however magnificent, can be fulfilled, and a need can be met. Obsession is a darker, more complex beast. The line between the object itself and the pursuit is blurred by the power of the quest. Success – the ecstatic, champagne-in-the-veins, God's in his heaven, my chest's so tight I can hardly breathe, I want to dance, whoop and punch the air moment of triumph, where you're bursting to find the words to explain how you feel but none of them quite hits the spot – soon gives way to something else. Being a successful alchemist must be a nightmare. What do you do for an encore?

Later, waiting for the train at Paddington, I looked at Gay. She hadn't slept properly for days but she was laughing, celebrating the now, not worrying about the future, and it was infectious. I packed my obsessions in a trunk and deposited them at left luggage, and then we screeched at the tops of our voices, frightening the pigeons and drawing disapproving looks from the cleaners.

chapter 15

guerillas in the mist

That first exhibition year was massively exciting.
The team welded together exactly as we hoped,
and the public came in huge numbers. Between
15 May 2000 and 7 January 2001 we had half a
million visitors, twice what we expected. Some
would stand on the platform outside the Visitor
Centre and stare, and some would become
emotional. But very few felt nothing. We had so
many strong characters in the team that it was
impossible to rid yourself of the impression that
you'd accidentally stumbled into a soap opera.
The Land Train drivers delighted their guests with
comic routines and exaggerated safety procedures;
donning helmets and high-visibility jackets for
what was in truth a gentle tractor drive
down to the biomes brought out the
Village People in everybody!

Some of the catering team served up their delicious food with an arch campness that brought a style all of its own to the business of feeding the five hundred thousand. Even the makeshift ticket office made of sandbags had a Dad's Army feel to it.

Carolyn Trevivian, my PA, started the Eden Friends organization, fondly imagining she could do it part-time. She was hoping for five hundred members in the first year and got them in the first fortnight. It was obvious to both of us that she had a tiger by the tail and would have to manage the Friends full-time. By the end of the year we had over 10,000 Friends, our ambassadors and keepers of the keys, for whom Carolyn produces a quarterly magazine and puts on a whole range of lectures, events and short courses, all of which seem to be oversubscribed – a remarkable achievement.

Like Kary before her, Carolyn's last task was to interview her successor, who then had to interview me. The wonderful Ellie Pyatt had been PA to two senior executives at Imerys (the former English China Clays), so she knew all about big holes in the ground. She immediately sat me down and, in a pincer movement with Fiona Cattrell, Gay's PA and soon-to-be Company Secretary, let me know how she expected to be treated. She had to know where I was at all times, and I wasn't to make any appointments without her say-so, or there'd be trouble. She protects me like a she-wolf, and is another in the long line of women who are far too good for me. I make the best of it while I can.

The year had two social high spots. The first was Eden's role as the South West's focus for the BBC's Children in Need appeal, which attracted thousands to share the evening with us. The staff marathon tap-dancing team was a thing of great

'...women who are far too good for me...': Ellie Pyatt, TS, Carolyn Trevivian

beauty, though some of its members should never have been allowed anywhere near a tutu.

Then there was the Eden Christmas party, which began in the most bizarre way possible. I was about a mile from the site when I saw a man and an Irish wolfhound running towards me. They raced past completely oblivious, as if the devil himself was at their heels. A little further on I came upon a car upside down in the middle of the road, with its headlights blazing, and a man in full seventeenth-century courtier's rig. It was Tim Carter, the first witness to the accident from which man and wolfhound had apparently scarpered. The next on the scene was Jo Readman in a state of undress, trying to put on a punk fairy costume. It was only later that I realized what was wrong with Tim's get-up, impressive though it was; the party was supposed to be seventies fancy-dress.

It was only after we opened the 'Big Build' exhibition to the public that we began to think, as a team, about the plants – by this I mean the whole team and not those already in the field. It is a measure of our trust in the horticulturists that we had never thought to worry about their role. They were starting a new foundation, building a nursery, putting in place a sophisticated database to enable them to deal with all the other botanic gardens around the world; introducing pest and disease controls and a quarantining system that would have to take account of a range of nasties beyond the experience of any of them; advising world-class engineers on climate-control systems and fighting their corner when they thought the advice was wrong; setting up an academic network to corroborate the stories they wanted to tell and a research team that could find the plants they needed; going to the major countries they wished to represent to create the partnerships that would give their work credibility, and then arranging for the delivery of the plants, with all the customs and transport difficulties involved. But on top of all that they had to bring their plants into a newly created world with no soil, and manufacture it themselves from scratch. Now that would verge on a miracle.

One of the great lessons of horticulture is to treasure your soil. From the seventeenth to the nineteenth century French head gardeners were so attached to their soil that they would bring it with them in wagons from wherever they had previously been working, and take it away again when they left. Finding sufficient high-quality topsoil was always going to be a problem, and the transport costs would have been prohibitively expensive even without taking into account the environmental issue of using so much haulage. Tony Kendle was a soil expert, and he put together a team of colleagues from Reading University and Eden in partnership with Hanson's, the bricks-to-waste conglomerate who had composting expertise. Imerys lent us a large former clay pit near Bodelva called Penhedra to act as our soil-manufacturing base. It sounds deceptively simple: using large amounts of china clay spoil, old ball-clay waste (used for lining lakes and ponds)

Andrew
Ormerod *(l)*,
Peter Whitbread-
Abrutat *(r)*

and an assortment of composts created from bark, mushrooms, chicken manure and domestic waste all mixed together in varying degrees of concentration, they created Eden's growing medium in seven major recipes. This would not actually be soil, but a compost. Its richness, grain and water-retentiveness would be modified according to the taste of the huge range of plants it would have to service.

Back at Watering Lane the soils were tried out in experimental containers and the plants closely monitored to see how they acclimatized. Once the recipes had passed muster the major work began. By the middle of 2000, trucks started appearing at Bodelva, and the white hillsides and plateaus began to turn grey, then the rich dark colour of loam. The depth of soil would vary greatly. Rainforests have notoriously poor soil, their nutrient constantly washed away by

the rainfall, or sucked up into the trees. Rainforest trees, with few exceptions, don't have the deep anchoring taproots associated with our climate, and a remarkable 85 per cent of their root systems are concentrated in the top eighteen inches of earth. This explains why when large-scale clearance is started on the outer fringe of a forest the trees inside will often topple over under their own weight, having previously been supported and sheltered by their neighbours. The deepest soil would be reserved for some of the domesticated areas, but even here a metre would be considered deep. The deepest soil of all within the Humid Tropics Biome was reserved for our largest tree, the kapok, which weighed in at just over three tons and was lifted by crane into a hole a metre and a half deep. The kapok, regarded as the magic tree in the South American tropics, held great significance for us; it is only under one of these beautiful trees that the shamans, or magic men, will work their spells, and it was important that it thrived.

The Warm Temperate Biome needed poorer soils. The Mediterranean-type areas of the world, such as parts of southern Africa, California and Australia, are the richest in flora, but ironically the plants thrive on stress. Too much nutrient or water can kill them off. The soil would be deeper here to accommodate some of the mature productive trees such as olives, but even then it was rarely more than a metre deep. In the Outdoor Landscape, the average depths would be slightly greater to allow our deep-rooting trees and shrubs greater purchase, but because the clay pan under the soil would be soft enough to allow root penetration it was felt that even here we didn't need to be excessive.

Before the soil arrived, brigades of swing shovels and dumper trucks were sculpting the biomes' internal landscape to Dominic's design. Philip's brief for the biomes was that something like 45 per cent of the surface area should be flat or thereabouts, 30 per cent with a camber of less than 45 degrees, and the rest would be the cliff faces and steep ground that only climbing plants could colonize. Shaping such a landscape was a mighty task in such inhospitable terrain, and was complicated by the fact that the foil we were using on the roof was highly susceptible to damage and staining from petrol fumes. The hire company were required to convert all their vehicles to a zero-emission filter system. (Interestingly enough, having done so they found that there was a large and hitherto unsuspected market for their services.) Over a mile of footpaths of varying degrees of severity formed a network round the biomes to enable both the fit and the disabled to get around them. For months the swing shovels had been sculpting the flat areas, gouging out the watercourses and then laying the soil. Underneath the soil a web of hosing and service ducts would ensure that every plant could be reached by water and heating. As the soil went down the abseiling team went into action again, pinioning huge carpets of coir matting over soil that would otherwise have slipped down the steep hillsides where plants would grow. The idea was that the roots of the plants should grow through the coir so that in a year or two they would have established themselves sufficiently to prevent the earth from slipping, while at the same time the matting would have rotted away.

The team leaders charged with delivering this monumental planting project were Ian Martin, the nursery manager working back at Watering Lane; Tom Keay, curator of the Warm Temperate Biome and the Outside Landscape; Helen Rosevear, our in-house landscape coordinator; Robin Lock, our Humid Tropics curator; Peter Whitbread-Abrutat, our scientific officer, charged with the technical aspects of pest and disease control, database management and the other tricky sciency bits; Andrew Ormerod, who carried out much of the specialist sourcing research on the plants; and Jo Readman, who in her capacity as head of education worked closely with Helen in sorting out how the plants could best be shown off not only horticulturally but also thematically for educational purposes. Jo would be largely responsible for writing the official guidebook to Eden.

During the summer of 2000 there had been a fever of activity at Watering Lane as all the glasshouses filled to bursting – literally. Trucks were arriving daily from the continent with more plants for the exhibitions. One of the old glasshouses was full of Warm Temperate verging on Arid zone materials. Ian had set up long propagation tunnels inside to bring on his precious seeds, while elsewhere in the house he was trying to bulk up some of the rare productive plants. It may seem obvious, but if you want to demonstrate, for instance, a type of millet grown in the Andes, you have a problem. It is rare and unavailable in seed catalogues. If someone

The onsite
horticultural team

brings you seed you will then have to bulk it up over a number of seasons to give you the quantity necessary to provide a good representation of what it might look like in the field, or to show school groups what the distinctive tortillas from the region taste like. There were tiny wild tomatoes from Mexico that had once been viewed as the aphrodisiac *par excellence* in the salons of Europe, where they were called 'love apples'; spiky agaves of the type that produce the drug mescalin of Carlos Casteneda fame; yet others from which tequila is distilled, and a host of other strange plants, each with their own story. Selecting which tales to tell would be a daunting task until we realized that we didn't have to do them all at once. Part of the pleasure at Eden will be to create ever-changing exhibitions and narratives, so that there is always something new to delight the senses.

Next door to this glasshouse was another. When you opened its doors you were hit in the face by a warm loamy fug that took you straight into the rainforest of your imagination. Here in row after row were the plants that made up the understorey of the rainforest, the ferns and the big-leaved light-guzzlers that had adapted to living in semi-darkness by developing extraordinarily effective powers of photosynthesis. Many of them had dark backs to their leaves that act in much the same way as black paint behind a mirror, reflecting light back through the leaf to create a double hit. Only now are the multinational companies exploring the energy potential of this sophisticated natural technology. In this house too were the orchids in serried ranks hanging in baskets from the roof spars or on wooden benches, the giant stag's horn ferns and the climbers; morning glory and bougainvillea and a cast of thousands all ready for the big day. I think the plant that most fascinated me was vanilla, the most valuable orchid in the world; the products from it were so familiar, yet I had no knowledge of

Humid Tropics
Biome: Paul
Spooner and
Will Jackson's
Cornucopia Arch

their source. The vanilla pods hang off it like runner beans. Remarkably, humans discovered by picking and drying them that the fermentation of decay creates the treasured flavour we are all so familiar with.

Outside in a range of poly-tunnels of different sizes all the Temperate plants were being assembled: a squadron of tree ferns, a gaggle of datura and legions of magnolias, camellias, rhododendrons and gunnera, the giant Amazon rhubarb often seen in Cornish valley gardens. There were palms beyond counting and thousands of plants that you recognized but couldn't remember the name of, or that's my excuse anyway.

Then on the levelled bank overlooking the original nursery were the two giant glasshouses that had been built through that dreadful winter of 1998/99. Set apart from them at the far side of the open field were two further plasticky-looking structures which were the quarantine houses. The rules of entry were very strict – I was certainly never allowed in. The giant glasshouses mirrored the biomes – with one being kept at the temperature and humidity for the rainforest, while the other was set for Mediterranean climes. The rainforest house was chock-a-block: rows of bananas, kapok, papaya, palms of all descriptions, pineapples, exotic flowering climbers, all packed in like sardines.

We were having real problems with the balsa, which grew six metres in a season and had to be cut; then it did it again. Everywhere you looked you could see the glint of the white sachets which contained the bugs used by the pest and disease team for biological controls. I fantasized about being able to amplify the sound in there to such a level that you could hear all the insects devouring one another in a crunching bloodthirsty theatre hidden from us all. Although nicotine was sprayed from time to time to curb the worst infestations of nasties, the team was very sensitive about the use of chemicals because of the delicate balances that needed to be maintained.

The Warm Temperate side was an explosion of colour and an assault on the senses; oleander, bougainvillea, citrus of every description, sunflowers, vines, the biggest collection of peppers you've ever seen, all vied for attention. One of these was the famous Mexican duelling pepper, made legendary by the sheriff of a Mexican town fed up with the mortality rate of his citizenry from ill-considered duels. He enacted a law to force people to settle their differences by eating from a bowl of these peppers. The first one to reach for a beer was the loser. To this day some dentists in Honduras rub the pepper on their patients' gums, completely numbing the affected area.

Also in this house we had a large collection of mature oranges and olives brought over from Sicily. It was discovered that they were infested with nematodes, little eely worms that are found on all olives – but they are not found in Britain, therefore we had to try to get rid of them. Poor Peter Whitbread-Abrutat was given the job of decanting hundreds of trees, pressure-washing their roots to clear off the soil, and then smothering them in a preparation before repotting them. Was it necessary? God knows, and that's the truth. All botanic gardens have nematodes, and no one has researched them very deeply. The risk for us was that the pressure-washing would blast off the tiny root hairs of the trees, making it difficult for them to establish themselves when they were replanted. In the event Peter managed it with considerable loss of temper but little loss of life, and the subsequent survival rate was high.

'Truck after truck reversed up to the opening...'

Imagine tens of thousands of plants arriving from many different sources, ranging from collected seed to individual gifts from people whose prized plant has outgrown their domestic greenhouse, to lorryloads from nurseries and generous scientific institutions. Someone has to log every one, give it an individual number, enter its provenance as exactly as possible and cross-reference it with the literature, as well as issuing instructions about its growing habits and personal preferences. On top of this, a label must be produced with the coded information on it as well as its Latin name, so that the staff working in the greenhouses will know its history. Peter Whitbread-Abrutat was in charge, but the bulk of this heroic work was done by Louise Frost, Alistair Griffiths and Martin Fellows. In this detail we were laying the foundations of our ambition to become a serious scientific resource.

Alarums and excursions aside, by the early autumn of 2000 you could cut the air of expectation with a knife. The public were piling into our Big Build exhibition in numbers that far outstripped our hopes, and they were loving it. Our staff were loving it, and the media were being very supportive. The Green Team were ready for their turn to strut their stuff.

In the late summer a huge crowd had gathered to witness the extraction of the giant crane from inside the Humid Tropics Biome. Unbelievably an even larger crane arrived – it had taken several days to get to us – and lifted it out in bits as dozens of men with spanners swarmed over it. In days it was gone and the roof was filled in.

Bugbusters!

There was one more crisis for Barry Johnson to weather. Even when he isn't worried he looks it, so when I say he looked worried, it was worried with attitude. One of the engineers had spotted some minute cracks in the steel of one of the main arches in the Humid Tropics Biome. They were so small you could barely see them with the naked eye, but there was the possibility that the whole structure was afflicted. This was the stuff of nightmares. Barry summoned Mero, the manufacturers, who in turn laid on a team of x-ray boffins. They spent a long time testing the steel, and eventually gave it a clean bill of health apart from seven tiny cracks which were cut out and new steel welded into place.

Barry then gritted his teeth and set up a really hairy test which involved filling giant bags with 150 tons of water and suspending them on ropes from the arch, a stress equivalent to the maximum possible from snow build-up. There were actually two tests: did the arch behave as it should under the pressure, and did it spring back to its original position? The answer on both counts was yes, to our immense relief. The tests took weeks to complete, by which time Barry was

Robin Lock in his element

wrecked. I don't think he slept properly in all that time, and although the financial implications weighed heavily, far worse was the thought that he might be prevented from bringing his beloved project in on time as he had promised.

The main panel at the front of the Humid Tropics had been left open save for plastic sheeting to keep out the weather, and through this crawled a new crane. Robin and his team had foreseen the amount of work that would have to be done lugging heavy trees into place, in the heat, over hundreds of yards of rough ground. Robin and Tim Carter had worked out that a crane placed in exactly the right spot could reach all the locations planned for the big trees. Getting these in position was of course the first major task. Helen Rosevear and Robin needed to make sure that the trees were in the right place from the aesthetic point of view. The biggest trees were all waiting at the greenhouses of René van de Arend back in Holland. The moment the green light was given his twelve pantechnicons would be on the move, and our team had to be ready. The practice run was memorable. Robin wanted to make sure that the system would work and decided to experiment with a large palm we already owned. The crane worked very well, and the team found that they had developed a successful technique for slotting the palm in place. Once in, though, it looked ridiculous; a thirty-foot palm shrank to a tiny twig. We were all rather shocked, fearing that the overall effect of the planting would look bathetic in a building of such scale. We needn't have worried.

Go! It was my birthday, 25 September. Truck after truck reversed up to the opening, where its precious cargo was suspended on webbing from the crane hook and swung to its appointed place. One by one the trees settled into their new home. Imperceptibly at first the biome acquired a patina of green, until after two weeks the giant conservatory was beginning to feel tropical in every sense of the word. The team were working unbelievably long hours in hot conditions, losing weight and dehydrating, but they kept going. They had screamed when I said we would open come hell or high water on 17 March 2001. We won't be ready, they insisted, the plants will still be dormant, they won't look their best, and the Outside Landscape will be naked, spring won't have sprung…

Did I mention that the weather in the winter of 1999/2000 was even worse than the previous year's, which had been the worst in recorded history? The ground was

waterlogged and the new soil was sodden and
in places slipping from erosion. Tom was
frantic. Give me until Easter, he begged. No. I
knew that to allow delay would result in more
time lost. Just like a stage show, if you don't accept
it can't be done it will be. In private, of course, you
know that if probably the best team in the world
come to you on their knees saying it can't be done then
you listen, but until that moment we had to stay firm.

I wasn't actually at Eden on my birthday. I was in Totnes with Candy, watching
my friend Pete Goss relaunch his revolutionary Team Philips catamaran outside
the Baltic Wharf. I had last seen Pete the previous November, when he and I had
attended the Lord Mayor's People of the Millennium Banquet at the Mansion
House as the representatives of the South West. We'd both been rather embar-
rassed and tongue-tied in the presence of so many household names. What on
earth do you say to Geoff Hurst or Bobby Charlton that doesn't sound school-
boyish? We did say hello to Matthew Pinsent, because he's Candy's second cousin.

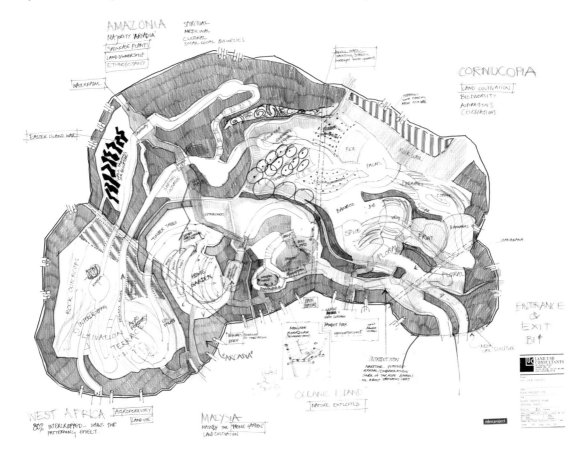

Anyway Candy and I had been invited as official guests for the Team Philips launch, but there was something about the crowds of well-wishers lining the opposite bank that drew us there instead. Thousands of people milled around in festival mood, cheering every appearance of activity, until finally the cranes started to lower their precious charge into the swirling waters of the River Dart. They all loved Pete and his team – no stupid hype, just a simple brave endeavour. Everywhere it was the same: you heard people talking about him as if he was a lifelong friend. They hoped he wouldn't take any risks because of their expectations; they just wanted him to do his best and come home safe. It was an extraordinary thing, and so different from the usual cynical hope that someone will get his come-uppance for daring to put his head above the parapet. How we wished that it would end in the success it deserved to be; how disappointed for him and his team we would all be when things didn't turn out that way in the teeth of a mid-Atlantic hurricane, and how relieved we were that they were all safe. I admired him for his ability to deal with success and failure with equal dignity and humility.

Remarkably, in the pub the night before the launch, Candy and I had watched Matthew Pinsent celebrating his fourth Olympic rowing gold in Sydney. What a weekend!

Back in the Humid Tropics, Robin Lock, the curator, was leading from the front. In typical Dutch style he was blunt with everyone and demanded what he needed without fear. Everything that could go wrong did. First of all the constructors were supposed to be out by the time planting began. They weren't, through no fault of their own, but imagine how difficult it is to carry out a planting régime when you have vehicles going up and down the paths and rock faces are still being sprayed with concrete above you. The dust left strange chalky watermarks on all the plants and the soil was going a weird colour. The roof was on, but the access points into the biome were unsealed save for hastily fixed plastic sheets that kept the worst of the weather out but didn't keep the temperature in. The temperature drops in the low-lying tropical island areas were extreme, and most of the palms suffered badly. The environmental controls would not be fully operational until mid-January 2001.

November was a great morale-boosting month. The temperature dropped to 11 degrees centigrade and humidity to 27 per cent for many consecutive nights, and rose only to 15 degrees in the day. The plastic sheets were shredding and it felt anything but tropical. Still, things could be worse – and lo they got worse. The pump for the waterfall exploded and the misting system, choked by dust, went on the blink. It would take three weeks to repair, and meanwhile everything had to be watered by hand. There was the odd landslide caused by over-enthusiastic irrigation, but on the plus side the temporary

bridges remained for so long that by the time the real ones arrived, beautifully fabricated in steel, we decided that the temporary railway-sleeper look was more appropriate anyway. We put the new bridges in store for when we raised the money for another biome.

Robin was everywhere. His love of the tropics was plain to see, and soon a style began to emerge unlike anything you would see in a botanic garden. Robin had spent the last seven years on tropical forestry projects, working with plants and people in agriforestry, ethnobotany and social forestry integrated with agriculture and education. His stamping grounds were the Philippines, Malawi, Sabah and Botswana, where he had been the forestry officer in the Okavango Delta. The themes he had inherited from Philip and Peter were: the Wild Places, where the essence of the rainforest in the areas where we had established partnerships would be displayed, and where people would get a sense of what it might be like to be in a rainforest; Shamba, a loosely interpreted Swahili word which we used in-house to reflect people's adaptation to the wild and its domestication for local consumption; and Cornucopia, later referred to as Crops and Cultivation, where the commercial productive plants were displayed.

The Warm Temperate Biome

Robin set out to tell a number of stories in his kingdom. He had two cardinal rules. Each of the communities he wished to represent would have to be visited by members of the team; he had no time for armchair expertise. He also believed that the most appropriate way of getting the information required was through using local students working to a brief he had written. The Seychelles were chosen for telling stories about biodiversity and conservation; Malaysia, for its home-garden culture where issues of nutrition and cash cropping could be explored; Cameroon, for the interpretation of agriforestry and the impact of erosion and land use on the marginal steep slopes; and Guyana, representing tropical South America for the study of non-timber forest products and shifting cultivation systems, known pejoratively as slash and burn – actually an efficient system if managed sensibly.

The first port of call was Guyana. This came through an introduction from Sir Ghillean Prance to Dr Mark Johnston at the University of the West of England. Mark was working with a Commonwealth/World Bank project in Guyana called Iwokrama. Robin went out there for ten days with Jo Readman. He commissioned some local students to write a report on the agricultural systems in use there and then tracked down all the plants from already domesticated sources in Europe,

The Warm Temperate Biome: Tim Shaw's Dionysus surveys his domain

beginning with RBG Kew and Brest Botanics who had links with French Guyana. A truckload arrived from the University of Wageningen in the Netherlands and still more came from the University of Kassel in Hesse, North Germany, where they have a fine conservatory of productive plants including cola, stevia and the big-leaved *Thaumatococcus danielli*, probably the sweetest thing in the world.

This was followed by the creation of a Malaysian home garden, of which Robin and one of the gardeners, Mark Biddle, had long experience. This connection with Malaysia was made through Wye College. Mark would lead the building of the Malaysian Bamboo House, with its corrugated-iron roof and its living spaces lovingly recreated right down to the crockery, cutlery and beaten-up moped parked up against the wall. Before long, if you closed your eyes, you could imagine yourself there – the veranda a riot of floral beauty and heady scent, dripping with hibiscus, bougainvillea and orchids, while a few metres away would be the quick vegetable garden where chickens would have rooted. *Basalla* (spinach), coriander,

bitter gourd, okra, amaranthus, sweet potato and beans would be planted in rows in a tropical version of our own kitchen garden. Beside the house you would see a crop of khat, the cocaine-like leaf chewed as an appetite suppressant, its effects released by lime juice and strongly favoured by the hard-working water-buffalo drivers of the region. Beyond the vegetable garden would be the larger crops, cassava, peppers, bananas and papaya, and then out on the fringe of the secondary forest you would find the tall palm-like betel nut, chewed throughout the area and famed for its deep-staining black juice. Taro, always located some distance from the home because of its attraction for mosquitoes (fast becoming a problem at Eden) would be grown alongside the paddyfields. Next would come the secondary forest proper, with its mangosteen, durian, rambutan, jackfruit and breadfruit as well as rattan, that fearsomely sharp but highly useful climber. Deeper still would be the virgin forests, dominated by the Meranti species of *Dipterocarps*, the hardwoods used all over the world. Interestingly, in Sabah 80 per cent of the virgin forest is *Dipterocarps* of the same species, whereas in Africa you would find only one useful hardwood tree per hectare. This concentration in South East Asia represents perhaps the greatest threat to the region's ecological balance – the guarantee of easily logged high-standard hardwoods.

The plants we use are not particularly rare, that is not the point; we are trying to create a sense of the human interface with the natural world and by and large it is common plants that provide the everyday feeling we require. All our Malaysian plants were sourced from European institutions such as Wageningen, Bonn and Kew, or through the famed Dutch nursery of René van de Arend, who has strong connections with nurseries in Malaysia and South America. By all accounts René's nursery is awesome – hectares of glass housing trees of great size and variety bred to add grandeur to corporate atria. It is salutary to note that the failure rate in most atria is around 60 per cent, while at Eden it has so far been less than 1 per cent. Robin was very pragmatic in his selection. He knew that we could probably have afforded bigger plants, but his view was that it was ethically and horticulturally wrong to leave them vulnerable by transplanting them into our more rustic compost, after their immersion in rich potting compost throughout the years it had taken them to grow to maturity. Young trees would be more adaptable. Eden wants to be around for a long time; far better to eschew the quick wow factor for the satisfaction of good long-term husbandry. Indeed the large trees that have fared worst in their new home have been our two most expensive ones. Our small trees grow much faster than the mature ones in the ideal growing conditions we offer them. However, Robin also had a nice line in buying up waifs and strays from nurseries – he views it as a personal triumph to take plants at death's door and bring them back to rude health.

The link with the Seychelles began with Tony Kendle's suggestion of twinning with a project he was working on in St Helena. This was obviously not nearly tropical enough. We could have chosen the Pacific islands, but their flora is very similar to that of Malaysia. The Caribbean has much in common with tropical South America. However, the Indian Ocean is interesting because of the high degree of endemism (plants unique to an area) combined with the impact of invasive species brought in by the spice traders. Andrew Ormerod was fascinated by the fabulous coco-de-mer, for example, famed for its huge double coconut seed-pod and verging on extinction. A link with Raymond Brioche, a student from the islands, and with the daughter of the President of the Seychelles, currently living in Britain, set up the relationship, and Tom, Helen and Peter Thoday had the task of flying out there to establish the formal ties with the government's environment service. It's a tough job, but somebody's got to do it.

The African rainforest zone includes Gabon, Equatorial Guinea, Congo and Cameroon. Robin chose Cameroon because he had long been fascinated by the

Efe, a tribe of Pygmies from that country, and his contact there was with Form Ecology, a consultancy who had previously offered him a job. He had declined, but a good friend had accepted, giving him a way in. He flew out with Ian Martin and spent ten days touring the area and collecting seed (permitted here under the Rio Convention on Biodiversity), which Ian propagated back at Watering Lane.

Crops and Cultivation in the Humid Tropics is full of the crops that have shaped our lives: rubber, cocoa, pineapples, sugar cane, a wide range of useful palms, chicle for chewing gum, coffee, cola, bananas of twenty-six varieties, a whole range of spices, dye plants and exotic fruits, timber and bamboo and so on, each with a story to tell. Our challenge is to bring them to life in a way that excites the interest without taking away any sense of their being part of the same natural world that we come from.

Pests and diseases are part of life in all botanic gardens, and controlling them is one of the great experiments. At Eden we use only the mildest chemicals for spot treatment, and a mild soap extract for direct applications on leaves, because we don't want to destabilize our biological control or put the public at risk from pesticides getting into the air in such a humid climate. At the time of writing we have just introduced twenty white-eyes from South East Asia into the Humid Tropics Biome. The favourite food of these tiny birds is mealy bug, whitefly and aphids, which they consume with a gusto to warm the cockles of a gardener's heart.

The Warm Temperate Biome: Heather Jansch's Cork Pigs

Minute nesting boxes of woven sisal have been fixed to strategic trees to encourage them to breed. Next came the ten breeding pairs of geckos (whose main diet is cockroach, aphids, whitefly, flies and mosquitoes), four bullfrogs, six breeding pairs of green ariole lizards and some tree frogs to keep the tree canopy clean. A small beginning, but we are anxious to look after the creatures properly and at the same time not create a theme park atmosphere. These are not actors but professional creatures brought in to do a job of work! We also use biological leaf enhancers – a sort of steroid for plants that stimulates growth – fungi that kill caterpillars, and slow-release nematodes that emerge from their little white sacks over a fifty-two-day period and set off in search of pests.

That covers the living things. Plunging from high up on the cliff face, our waterfall careers down the hillside, terminating in the tropical island pool at the bottom. Its theatre is matched by the comfort of the cooling breeze it gives off as you pass in front of it at the highest point in the biome, where the heat is at its most oppressive; anyone who needs convincing that hot air rises should come here. No wonder people linger. The water has been a constant source of worry to us. Agar, a bacterial residue, turns the pool scummy. Tests indicated that despite the fact that we had ultraviolet screens and filters we couldn't completely rid ourselves of it except by changing the water regularly, which is ridiculous for a sealed system. The computer-based environmental control mechanism is crucial to the health of our little world. The size of the Humid Tropics Biome posed a great challenge, because computer models can't take account of the effects of the ever-growing flora – but so far it has worked very well. We try to keep humidity at a constant 80 per cent. The humidifying sprayers scattered about the biome leave a trail of wispy mist that captures perfectly the atmosphere of the rainforest. The biggest problem is the heat. In summer when the vents open to allow hot air out the humidity immediately dissipates to reach equilibrium with the outside, so some days the humidity is 50 per cent inside and out and we can do nothing about it except overcompensate when it gets cooler at night. The suggestion is that the problems will recede as the tree canopy gets higher. Research from Gabon indicates that the humidity at the top of the canopy can be less than 30 per cent, while five metres below the humidity has risen to 90 per cent.

George
Fairhurst's
Hemp Fence

Maybe in the next few years the humidity loss and heat gain will become less of a problem, except for people climbing the trees.

The construction guys would eventually finish, the paths would be complete, the rock-faces solid, the safety lights installed and the fire standards met. There would be bizarre teething problems. The intercom that warns of a fire went hyperactive, and we couldn't shut it up; the plant-handling area was obviously designed by a city kid since there wasn't a single tap; and the chemical store was usefully built inside the fire-alarm box underneath a pedestrian walkway. But hey, as my drummer friend Louis la Rose used to say with a wicked grin, if you're going to make a mistake do it loud.

In the Warm Temperate Biome Tom and his right-hand man Glenn Leishman were facing altogether different problems. Tom's task was to ensure that the plants were stressed enough to adapt as they should in nature, but not so stressed that they died. He also had to contend with the fact that most people would find what appeared to be the more familiar flora of his zone less remarkable than the wow factor of the Humid Tropics. Dominic and Helen had given this a lot of thought. A piece of music that is always restless and passionate soon palls, as there is no ebb and flow, no light and shade. Dominic's approach was to consider the biome as a work of art. Just as in the Humid Tropics, there would be both wild and cultivated areas, but the scale of the biome allowed at least the northern end of it to be designed almost like a patio to die for. At the southern end the landscape would be relatively wild. The Mediterranean region itself has long laboured under the clichéd title of the Cradle of Civilization, and it is true that almost all of it consists of poor, unforgiving soils nurtured almost to death – the mark of intensive agriculture. But the sense of a nature so dominated by man that the landscapes have become inextricably linked with fashions in cookery or interior design offered Dominic the chance to play with perceptions of what is real and what is fake, leaving a question mark hanging in the air.

It is here perhaps that the interweaving of art or artifice with the displays is at its most powerful. The vine exhibit, with its reference to slightly unsettling Dionysian revelry, alludes to the darker, more powerful forces at work both in our own psyches and in the natural world. The cork exhibit is another case in point. What appears to be a representation of the cork forests of eastern Portugal and south-western Spain is accompanied by Heather Jansch's superb sculptures of wild pigs foraging among the acorns. The explanation, that the cork forests are under threat due to the move towards plastic corks in the wine industry, points up two things. The first is that the individual consumer has the ability to effect change by discriminating in favour of brands which use real corks. The second point is rather darker – what kind of world have we created where the casual choice of a bottle of wine can put an entire habitat at risk?

(overleaf)
11 August 2001:
rock 'n' roll
comes to Eden

My father lives in the South of France just outside the town of Grasse, the perfume capital of the world, and on first impression the contents of our biome would not look out of place there. Rows of mature olives stand in terraces contained within dusty stone walling; vines work their way up the hillside, along with almonds, citrus, figs and a stand of proud cypresses. The smell of herbs hangs heavy in the air. A vegetable garden with many varieties of tomatoes and squashes faces a range of maizes, millets and tobacco all squeezed up close, reinforcing the sense that land is scarce. While everyone may be aware that rainforest straddles the equatorial zone of the globe, most people probably haven't thought about the other zones in the same way. To see plants from southern Africa, California and the Mediterranean side by side, and in Crops and Cultivation literally intermingled, leaves an indelible impression of a great family gathering.

The Wild Places of the biome – the Californian Chaparral, the Namaqual and Karoo deserts and the Fijnbos from southern Africa, and the Maquis and Garrigue of Europe – are each displayed in stage sets to give the tiniest flavour of how they might look. The mechanisms employed by the plants to survive some of the most unforgiving climates in the world – from fire-climax ecology, where the plants are dependent on brush fires to create the conditions for propagation, to extreme-

water economy, for those which may have to wait months or even years for any rain – are fascinating.

Dionysus is symbolic of the whole biome. He began life as the god of horticulture and husbandry, discovered a taste for vines and hence wine, and then became the god of excess, for want of a better title – an enviable career path, I'd say. We have become so immersed in Mediterranean cooking, and the sense of health and abundance associated with it, that to say, as some do, that the biome will be nice when it's all greened up is to miss the point. Were we to shower water and nutrients all over everything, of course it would look like it does in the adverts, but the real Mediterranean isn't like that, except where artificial stimuli are added to the natural environment. It is the massive irrigation projects that enable us to have flawless tomatoes, peppers and aubergines in our supermarkets. Go to southern Spain and see the thousands of acres of crappy hydroponic poly-tunnels scarring hillside after hillside, their disused plastic blowing in the wind, and enjoy the chemical additives permeating every watercourse. Go to California and marvel at the millions of acres of citrus and vines and ask where the water comes from. The most environmentally literate population in the world is proud that its irrigation systems are now changing over to solar-powered pumps. Well, good, but the

water table is falling so fiercely that large tracts of the state are suffering from excess soil salinity, and many fear catastrophe. Eden must always be probing and questioning received wisdoms.

We move onwards and upwards into the last of our landscapes, our own Temperate one. What are we trying to achieve here? If you look down from the Visitor Centre, straight below you is the Eden Arena, the eye of our creative cyclone, if you'll forgive the pretension. Spinning out from the centre is a patchwork of familiar plants transformed into entirely unfamiliar shapes. Crops are usually planted square or at least in regular patterns; here they are not. On the outer ring, clockwise from the north-west, is the Wild Cornwall exhibit of moor and heathland with its typical plants and stone hedging, then along to the Steppe and the Prairie exhibits, the Prairie boasting an array of charred tree-stumps in illustration of the myth that these are natural places. All are man-made, cleared of trees for the grazing of animals, yet we would fight to the death today to preserve these natural eco-systems. A parallel would be Battersea Power Station; you wouldn't have a snowball's chance in hell of getting permission to build it today. Try to knock it down, though, and you will have people up in arms at the desecration of a master-piece of industrial architecture. The splendid joke is that some of the same people would probably be against both propositions. As the cyclone circles to the south the whole upper hillside and slope leading into the bottom of the pit is a representa-tion of Wild Chile, the temperate rainforest. In years to come this will be a spectacular cloud forest, starting admittedly from humble beginnings.

Then in the second cycle starting from the same place is a rich mixture of cropping tales: barley and hops in Beer and Brewing, the Origins of Agriculture, the Tea Plantation, Apples and Mythology, Sunflower and Lavender, all inter-spersed with works of art, carved hop poles, a giant bumblebee, a Heath Robinson cauldron at the Plants for Fuel exhibit, and a flat earth globe bearing sunflowers that follow the sun with the help of a cranking handle. A hillside of hemp attracts

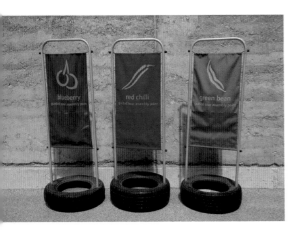

the sixties children and their streetwise offspring to the gently serrated leaf so much the symbol of peaceful revolution. This display is a revolution, but one that would need ten acres to give you a hit stronger than a brandy. The revolution is the story of hemp, introduced by a masterpiece of rope art that will one day end in the question: Why is hemp not the most plentiful fabric crop in the world? It is stronger and harder-wearing than cotton. One might also ask which industry has a vested interest (no pun intended) in seeing hemp demonized. Why is it banned anyway? Drugs will always pose problems of interpretation because of the static that comes with the very mention of their names. I'm totally against drugs of all description, of course; give me my brandy and cigars and I'm happy, ho hum.

The Green Team who began this journey back in the mists of 1995 are a different breed today, stronger, battle-hardened and worldly-wise. Having taken everything the elements and circumstance could throw at them, they went into a final push of Stakhanovite proportions. On 16 March we had our press day and hundreds of people from all over the world came to see inside our Eden for the first time. It was a hectic day and our guests were awed, but while we were grateful for their attention there was another restlessness among us, an impatience for some time to ourselves. When finally they'd departed with their miles of cables and tons of cameras we breathed a huge collective sigh of relief. Paul Travers and Deborah Clark and their teams had had their finest hour and done Eden proud. The Eden crew decamped into the staff room, where we drank sparkling wine and even a little champagne, and made a few speeches of encouragement and celebration. A Chinese takeaway was ordered in such quantities that the guy at the other end demanded a slow repetition in stunned disbelief. It came, we ate, and then in groups slowly drifted back into the biomes. I walked with Gay up to the highest point alongside the waterfall, to meet up with Peter Whitbread-Abrutat. The lights glowed, tracing the pathways into the distance below, and as the misters wove their ghostly spell we sucked on our beers in quiet reflection. Peter cocked his head and said in his soft Yorkshire burr, Aren't you proud? You must be. The question hung in the air, unanswered. Because *I* bloody am, he said.

The Operations Management Team *(clockwise from top left)*: John Lees, Dominic de Vere Green, George Elworthy, Neal Barnes, Pauline Mullan, James Barry

the big black box of dreams

At our press preview we dealt with the standard
questions about cost, ambition, visitor numbers
and so on, but we were also asked about the team;
many of the journalists had commented that
there was something different about the way we
worked together. They wanted to know whether I
had noticed that Eden functioned almost like a
musical composition. Of course I had, I thought,
but I was too tired to explain how Tchaikovsky
came into it, and anyway I didn't want to sound
pretentious. So let me attempt to explain now.

One of my earliest memories is of a huge black box, with three legs and two lids. It was dark and shiny and reeked of age, and it was obviously very precious because you couldn't open it. On top of it were framed photographs of people I did not know. That day one of the lids was open, and I was immediately drawn to it.

Imagine being three years old and finding a grand piano with the lid open. First you bang a few notes and they delight you with their shrill resonance or deep bass throb; you discover the sheer sensuality of fingers stroking ivory keys, though at first the ebony ones seem a little frightening. Hours are spent in aimless but pleasurable doodling. The next day something draws you back and you do it all over again…and again, and again…and that, if you're lucky, is your Mozart. After a while, if you're an ordinary mortal, you feel frustrated that your fingers are so small and the keyboard is so big. You get cross because you know there's something magic inside but you can't find your way in.

But still you return, and one day as you climb up on the piano stool you slip, and to stop yourself falling in a heap and banging your head you reach out for the piano keys at the precise moment that your feet land on the loud pedal hidden in the deep gloom below you. Suddenly the genie is out of his bottle. Here is a wondrous sound. After the impact of the big bang the notes seem to go on for ever, winding in and out of each other, merging and separating to create new blocks of sound like a mighty wind blowing through infinite corridors.

In the following days I was to drive my grandmother mad. Because I couldn't reach the keys and pedals simultaneously without falling over backwards, I learned that if I slammed my arms full length on to the keys and held them down I could achieve a similar effect. Initially I dreamed of bombers, not that I am sure I knew what a bomber was. Then I played the ocean. My strange addiction to the piano had begun. I was spoiled from the beginning by my imagination because, while most students dutifully embraced the classics via learning-by-numbers books, I never had much interest in playing the shapes and patterns of other people's melodies. I suspected that the beast inside the black box would be disappointed if, having learned its secrets, I gave up the opportunity for exploration.

I realize now what others presumably realized then, that I overplayed the creativity angle to cover up for my poor technique and inability to concentrate on formal practice. Something which I had understood intuitively as a little boy would be fully revealed to me only much later in life, when I was commissioned to compose a piece of music based on a classical tune. I had to look at the score of Tchaikovsky's Piano Concerto in B Flat Minor, Op. 59, the opening bars of which rank among the best-known in music. Such a simple melody, such a big sound; twenty-six different instruments at once, if memory serves. I will never forget thinking, as I recorded the twenty-fifth, that I had made the most monstrous mistake. It sounded like a huge noise. And then the twenty-sixth part went down and I was transfixed. Out of cacophony came this wonderful wall of sound which made the hair stand up on the back of my neck. For the first time in my life I understood, at least in part, the essence of genius. Harmony is chaos controlled.

If a journalist has the temerity to ask you to sum up Eden in a sentence, it's all very well getting impatient because it's far too complex for that. How about a few paragraphs, then?

We set out to build a place unlike any other, one that would capture the imagination of all who came upon it. Its landscape and buildings were to bear the hallmarks of a civilization at one with nature, strangely familiar yet somehow foreign – a place where the future would hold promise and restless discontent would become, for a while, a distant memory. This may appear childlike, but are we not all children who must occasionally act grown up in order to earn a living? The art, it seemed to us, was to create something that could provide everyone with as little or as much information and stimulation as they felt ready for. But the challenge would be to remove the barriers that prevent people from being ready to learn. There would be something for everyone: simply soaking up the Living Theatre as a spectacle on the one hand, something far more interactive on the other.

When I moved to Cornwall I discovered that Kneehigh, Cornwall's leading theatre company, had their rehearsal base just over the hill from my home. I soon got to know them socially. My first experience of them in performance was at the Minack Theatre, the famous open-air amphitheatre in the far west, in front of a full house of mainly local people who were clearly transported by what they saw. The show was *Tregeagle*, a Cornish reworking of the Faust story. The heady brew of strange music, brilliantly inventive stage props and fine acting hooked me completely. A deliciously familiar and sinister story seemed to connect all the more strongly because its images of transformation involved everyday objects. An actor in a bishop's mitre bent over at the waist, and his hat became a fish swimming in the ocean. After the show everyone was bubbling with excitement and talking about what they'd seen to anyone who would listen. I realized how powerful this type of performance could be, not only in terms of the entertainment, but also in its unlocking of the reserve that exists between people. I would go to see many of Kneehigh's shows, and eventually accepted

Sue Hill in her own write

an invitation to sit on their board. I became friends with Sue Hill, who not only acted with the company but was also responsible for much of their promotional artwork, which drew on influences ranging from Eastern to Celtic by way of her own singular imagination.

Sue has been a great influence on me. A cultural magpie collecting jewels from everywhere, she has an enthusiasm, presence and sheer lust for life that make her unique. I commissioned her and Pete, her brother, to create two works at Heligan, the Giant's Head and the Mudmaid, both made simply of earth. Pictures of them have featured in countless magazines, because they capture something wild that speaks to our childish imaginations. When Eden was in development we would often talk of the power of such images. We would discuss what responses we hoped to provoke. We wanted to make people look at the familiar with new eyes; we wanted them to talk to each other, to question, and we wanted them to leave us changed in some way.

Humid Tropics Biome: the art of Francisco Montes Shuma and Yolanda Pandura Baneo

As Eden began to take shape Sue came in to write the signs; her bold, classical-looking script perfectly captured the spirit of the place. She was also working with Peter Hampel, introducing him to artists and helping him to formulate briefs for commissioning. We knew that traditional scientific interpretation using touch screens and the like was by and large a turn-off, and that passive displays of information on boards wouldn't hold the attention. But we set our hearts on merging art with science and technology in order to get our message across in as friendly a way as possible.

Eden is about plants and people, and visitors will want to know what they are seeing. We are not a botanic garden, with thousands of little plant labels like tombstones all over the place; we are about putting plants into context. We want people to enjoy the atmosphere and sense of place first of all, wherever they are in Eden. I have described the regions of the world we exhibit and some of the themes. We name some individual plants on plant labels, giving basic information

about what each one is and what it does. The next grade up is a plant story which offers more of an explanation and maybe an anecdote or two, then there are the big stories which may concern something generic like the description of the Malaysian home garden or a major product such as coffee. For some of our visitors, to understand that rainforests have people living in them, that their livelihoods link with ours, that we use their resources every day and are possibly alive because of them, is a revelation. These messages are woven into the fabric of the project, not the signs. In due course we will tackle even bigger issues like biodiversity loss, waste, plants and the future of plants and health. We don't want to bludgeon people into submission with ridiculous amounts of information, nor do we want to tell all the stories at once.

A lot of thought has gone into the angle we take. A whole range of crops, such as chocolate, cotton or sugar cane, might have similar stories to tell on the subject of slavery, so only one will tell that story while the others will concentrate on other aspects. These stories are augmented on occasion by artefacts: the tools or products associated with the plants. The boundary between art and artifice is pretty moot, and we don't get precious about it. George Fairhurst's beautifully designed woven hemp ropes or David Kemp's tropical cargo boat defy easy definition.

Some things, such as the relationship between the shamans of Peru and the plants that they use, can best be communicated by art. We invited Francisco Montes Shuma and his partner Yolanda Panduro Baneo, with assistance from the British Council's Visiting Arts fund and the October Gallery, to come and paint on our cliff faces in the Humid Tropics Biome. Visitors were stunned by their startling imagery, and no one could see it without gaining a deep respect for their intimate understanding of the role of plants in our relationship with the earth.

The tension at the heart of Eden comes from daring to give artists a voice, yet harnessing their work to our agenda. One of the things I love about Kneehigh Theatre is that whole communities come out to see their shows. Audiences respond because they're not precious, and the cast often weave local characters into the storytelling for colour and humour. There is, however, something deeper going on with Kneehigh that we wanted to capture at Eden. We live in an age where so-called community values are often no more than romantic hogwash. The village or town gets together for a carnival or charity function a couple of times a year; people feel good about it, but soon forget. When I went round my village with a petition some years ago, I was horrified to find how many people played no part in the community at all. In an age when 'individuality' is so cherished, community values are probably of greater importance than ever.

What interested me was how we could create a climate of community at Eden. At Heligan we have more staff than any other private garden, and they are encouraged to spend a large part of their day talking to visitors. We also have about half a dozen guides who take tours around the garden. We wanted the same at Eden, only bigger, and Sue, Jo Readman and Kary Lescure made a very good case for specialist performance training. Led by our guide leader, Ruth Trevenna, our trainees worked on their technique with the Kneehigh team. We ended up with about twenty guides, explainers and storytellers, each with slightly different functions but with a common aim: to make Eden come to life. Our visitors appreciate this personal contact, and we could use a hundred of these wonderful people.

There is something deeper still about my reaction to the Kneehigh experience that I desperately want to capture at Eden. To explain it I must take a sideways leap.

Over the last few years we have seen significant advances in the study of genetics, to the extent that the Human Genome Project has mapped all the genes in the human body. The billions of pounds per annum now being spent on patenting potential medical applications of this knowledge is producing developments in six months that would previously have taken ten years. The functions of many of the genes are now well understood. What is not understood is what makes the genes switch themselves on or off to create traits that we associate with

individuality. A good analogy would be the Portuguese man-of-war, each of whose tentacles is an individual creature but whose whole being is something other than the sum of its parts. What is the organism that controls it? The organism that makes us human, as opposed to just the sum of our mechanisms, has something of this jellyfish about it. We protect our individuality with great passion, and individual liberty is cherished above all else in our society. Many have died in the name of liberty and individuality, and more will do so, yet I have come to the conclusion that our obsession with the individual at the expense of the communal is diminishing us. When you see great theatre, hear wonderful music or simply enjoy a wonderful joky evening in a crowd, there is an electricity in the air which for a moment bonds a community. The mistake is to assume that this feeling diminishes the individual.

TS attempts to explain the spirit of the samba jellyfish

Before we opened, Kary Lescure sent the entire staff to a local school for theatrical training as part of the bonding exercise. Kneehigh were there as trainers, and the idea was that the weekend would culminate in a mass samba in the hall. On the Sunday afternoon when we all gathered to play you could feel the fizz in your arteries: hundreds of people playing samba, dancing, singing, revelling in the sheer exhilaration of being part of such a monstrous sound. No solitary individual could ever experience that.

Capturing the spirit of the samba jellyfish, if you can imagine such a beast, is one of the things Eden is about. (I just wish old Tchaikovsky was still around to write the musical.)

The journey has just begun. What we have is an architectural icon and a symbol of regeneration and community. We have a superb educational resource that is entertaining and, we hope, inspirational; one that uses the language of Everyman

(previous page) Reece Ingram's Hop Poles

to open a window on the natural world and the part we play in it. To describe Eden as the world's first rock 'n' roll institution is a piece of fun, intended more than anything else to underline our commitment to using contemporary language and media techniques to get our message across to the widest possible audience. Underneath the fun, though, there is an attitude at work. The baggage of preconceived ideas about how things should be done has all but atrophied many of the older institutions, burdening them with a specialist, departmental culture. We will fight tooth and nail to ensure that, while Eden has all the expertise we require, there will never be any academic empire-building here.

The next dream is to bring the worlds of business and ideals together, so that each may profit from the other. This is not to say that there are no ideals in business, simply that they tend to come a poor second to the interests of shareholders, particularly when most of the shareholders in large companies are themselves large institutions with their own shareholders.

Over the past two years I have met many bosses of major corporations. I like to ask them a question: if you wanted to effect massive changes in the behaviour of your company, so as to reflect more accurately the sentiments and concerns of the public, how would you do it? First they tell me how frustrating it is to be perceived not to share these concerns, then they launch a thinly veiled attack on their own corporate structures. I have been completely taken aback at the impotence these big hitters feel in the face of their shareholders.

It is striking how many of these executives are children of the sixties, preserving a fundamentally idealistic outlook despite appearances to the contrary. They want to make a contribution to a better future, not just in their own companies but on a broader canvas. Many previously isolated pressure groups also want to see new 'partnerships for solutions' develop. Eden aims to play a part in this debate, bringing together people to shape policies that will deliver achievable strategies for change – if you like, as a Foundation for Possible Futures. It is important not to be over-ambitious when thinking about what we might do, of course; the old saw about not running until you can walk has stood the test of experience. Nevertheless we live in exciting times, facing some terrifying futures. It does not seem too much to hope that Eden can become what Davos was originally intended to be before it became a *Hello!* opportunity for the financial community.

You can love doing business and you can have ideals; the two are not mutually exclusive. However, living in a world where common land, the ideas and even the building blocks of life are owned by commerce will diminish us. The Industrial Revolution, with its patenting of ideas for commercial exploitation, saw the privatization of knowledge. Relationships which had previously been defined in terms of reciprocal responsibilities within a community were redefined in terms of hard cash. The advancement of science is important, but many scientists lost the moral high ground long ago, when their funding became dependent on private enterprise. We are not talking Boyle, Lyell or Newton here; they didn't have share options. Turning everything into a consumable product with added value dripping off it, where fortunes are spent branding items so that they appear to meet our emotional needs, is all part of the process of defining humans in terms of what they consume. We should not allow the world to be turned into a trough for us to bury our noses in. If Eden aspires to become at one level a mission control for an environmental United Nations, as well as a purveyor of fabulous horticulture and the steward of a wonderful destination for public entertainment, the fuel that drives it must come from an understanding of the distinction between quality of life and standard of living.

Many human interests are touched by issues raised at Eden. Take the creation of soil: the search for solutions to biodiversity loss, erosion, pollution and land degradation is our concern. Water – its supply and its quality – is an essential issue in our new world as it is everywhere else. The same goes for climate, for obvious reasons. If nothing else, Eden should demonstrate the interconnectedness of the plant kingdom with all these elements in the creation of the conditions for life, and by implication raise awareness that if any of these elements is damaged there will be an impact elsewhere on the life-support system. It follows that Eden should address the major human factors that affect these conditions. Eden isn't about the environment; that's like saying life is about air. It is concerned, in partnership with others, with exploring development in the fullest sense of the word: the sustainable development of human potential and the achievement of the optimum quality of life for all, across economic, social and cultural boundaries.

Eden's evolution has depended, and will continue to depend, on encouraging people of many disciplines, backgrounds and political persuasions to work together towards a common goal. But to describe Eden as being fired simply by the desire to get people to work together is a little bit 'Kumbaya M'Lord' and cocoa round the campfire. There has to be a vision that drives the desire. Attractive as alternative lifestyles and holistic approaches to life may appear to the individual or the small community of like-minded souls, a future must be built which addresses the major issues that affect the bulk of the world's population.

So much of what appears in the press about the developing world appears irrelevant to the people who live there. If you are freezing you will inevitably cut down the world's rarest trees for firewood. You will burn unwashed coal, creating a smog so thick it damages your health, because the cold hurts more. If you are starving you will eat the seeds you should save for next year, or you will clear part of a rainforest. You will drink poisoned water if the alternative is to go without and die. The evidence is, ironically, that people living under this sort of pressure are more aware of their 'environment' and the need to conserve and nurture it than anyone else. They don't need lectures on what they are doing wrong; they simply don't have the time or the money to invest in better alternatives. At a less dramatic level, if you live in a rural community with no bus service, you will use a car. So many of the black-and-white alternatives presented by those in no immediate danger of death by starvation or cold or dirty water are embarrassing in their blindness to reality, and patronizing in their notion of charity. They seek to impose solutions, authority and a particular perspective, rather than demonstrating solidarity, a partnership of equals committed to the struggle together. People need livelihoods.

There are thousands of organizations and individuals concerned with these issues around the world who are doing their best in trying conditions to make a contribution to improving people's lives. It is worth remembering that the rich OECD countries invest some $55 billion a year in official development

Richard Sandbrook: the big picture is never just black or white

aid, and the voluntary sector adds a few billion more. Richard Sandbrook has been a big influence on me in this regard; he has decided to step outside the development arena to take a look back in, to establish how practical steps can be taken to effect change. The actions of those who would bring down global capitalism, while travelling to make their protest in the aircraft, motor cars and trains spawned by it, make him smile wryly. It is certainly difficult to know how to react to recent events in Genoa and Gothenburg. The violence is dismaying, but it should be remembered that we have all benefited from the rebelliousness of people who bring the unacceptable to public notice. So many political and environmental causes are first espoused by people whose passion and commitment we find unsettling if we're looking for excuses not to act or hoping simply to assuage our guilt by coughing up £5 a month to save the whale. It is the contributions made since the 1960s by brave activists like Rachel Carson, with *Silent Spring*, and the many campaigners since, that have brought the environment to the prominent place in the global agenda it occupies today.

If you are an activist on the streets of Genoa you will believe that there is someone who has power over you. The extraordinary thing is that captains of industry, the very people most of us think of as 'they', seem to believe the same thing. The use of the word 'they' is telling: 'they' will have to do something about it; it's 'their' fault. But there *is* no 'they'. Our future is being dictated – or worse, stolen – not by 'them' but by our own inertia.

Globalization and the multinationals are sold as the enemies of the people, and are certainly part of the problem. But they are easy targets; to assume that multinationals are of themselves bad things is too simple, in my view. Indeed I would argue that it is only in collaboration with them that global 'sustainable development' (leaving aside whether the term itself is an oxymoron) can be delivered within a time frame that will make a real difference. Their capital, infrastructure and webs of connection make them necessary partners in the new future, if only a modus operandi can be worked out.

The big politics of development and the environment have been hijacked by spin doctors and propagandists to compensate for lack of action on the ground. The Rio Conference of 1992 delivered little that was binding on anyone. The climate and biodiversity conventions were agreed beforehand, and the event's most famous outcome, Agenda 21 – the 800-page blueprint for pursuing sustainable development into the twenty-first century – shares with the Maastricht Treaty the dubious honour of being one of the most-cited, least-read documents ever written. They came, they partied, they signed the protocols, but somehow they forgot to leave a cheque. There were some great slogans, though. Sustainable development was defined as 'meeting the needs of the present without compromising the ability of future generations to meet their own needs', a phrase in fact dusted down from the 1987 Brundtland Report on global poverty and the environment, *Our Common Future*. It would be hard to find a slogan that appealed equally to any political hue, but they did it. Another slogan, 'Act Local, Think Global', was intended to reassure individuals and small communities that they could make a real difference. Is it too wicked to see this as a marvellous exit strategy for those charged with acting globally?

Rio, Montreal, Kyoto, Bonn, The Hague – famous cities reduced to the buzzwords of summitry. The tragedy is that statesmanship seems to be going the way of the dodo. Perhaps it never existed; perhaps the absence of media attention in former times allowed the illusion to persist, whereas now the relentless focus on human weakness reveals us all to have feet of clay. It is

an irony that our information age seems to conspire against genuine communication as we all drown in a sea of statistics, 'facts' and 'informed opinion'. The time seems right for an organization or communication system which enjoys the trust of a wide range of respected partners – and an even wider audience – to disseminate options and ideas collated under widely agreed methods. A network, in effect, that brings together differing opinions and establishes a common ground, with a view to establishing what is fact and what is special pleading. The trade-off of this free exchange of perspectives would be an understanding of economic activity more sophisticated than the usual theory of a giant conspiracy orchestrated by 'them'.

At one level what Eden could be about is radicalizing the Establishment, working with it to arrive at solutions that it couldn't have arrived at on its own because of lack of time, organizational atrophy, vested interests or the absence of lateral thinking. But this is not possible in a vacuum; in order to effect change, all the parties involved in an issue need to have their seat at the table. This is precisely why Eden, if it is to play this role, should be as apolitical as possible.

One of my heroes is Muhammad Yunus, the Bangladeshi economist from Chittagong University who founded the Grameen Bank. In his autobiography, *Banker to the Poor*, he describes a chance encounter with a woman who made bamboo stools, a meeting which was to change his life. She had to borrow the equivalent of 15p to purchase the raw materials for each stool, but after paying the loan shark at rates of 10 per cent per week she made only 1p profit. If she had access to better loan facilities, Yunus realized she would be able to raise herself above subsistence level. He began by making personal loans of £17 to forty-two basket weavers. Not only did this help them survive, it created the spark of hope that would enable them to pull themselves out of poverty.

He began to explore the issue of micro-credit, which is simply the lending of small sums of money. He was told by all the banks, including the World Bank, that it was unsupportable because of the high administration costs and the high default rates to be expected among the poor. They'd looked at it, they said; it was a non-starter. Undeterred, he hit on the idea of lending to groups of borrowers, so that a successful monthly repayment by one would trigger a loan for another and so on. It thus became a communal responsibility to ensure that individual members repaid on time. In 1983 the Grameen Bank was founded, giving micro-loans on principles of trust and solidarity. Today there are 1,100 branches of the bank with 12,500 staff serving 2.1 million borrowers in 37,000 villages. Of the borrowers

94 per cent are women; over 98 per cent of the loans are repaid. Now the World Bank has itself acknowledged the success of this business approach to the alleviation of poverty. The quality I most admire about Yunus is his understanding of the power of hope. Micro-credit provides that.

At Eden we are committed to trying to walk the talk of sustainability as far as we can, but we are determined to avoid superficial 'greening' of the site. The current debate about waste in the UK verges on the infantile; the political aspirations for recycling and the measures taken to make it happen are completely at odds with each other. There are no tax incentives to recycle, nor indeed any penalties for not doing so. It is vital not to get bogged down in tokenism, such as high-visibility recycling projects where the separated material ends up in a landfill site because there is no market for it. In Cornwall, as elsewhere, we separate our glass into bottle banks. When it is collected it is mixed together again and taken to York, where most of it ends up in a landfill site because there is little market for mixed glass. There are many such examples; 75 per cent of what we put into the recycling arena meets the same ignominious end.

This is not the case in Germany. Why? Because the Germans have enacted laws, not relied on voluntary codes of practice that achieve nothing apart from making us feel good as we drop our bottles into the bin. Leadership is required. Legislation is essential, and this should be matched with a taxation system that profits good behaviour and environmentally friendly technology while penalizing profligacy. To propose that sustainable solutions lie with incineration as opposed to landfill is to miss the key point: incineration, far from discouraging waste, makes us feel better about it because it disappears in a puff of smoke; instead we need encouragement to use sustainable resources – and fewer of them. 'Waste not, want not' is a phrase common to most cultures, and we should not be surprised to find ourselves in a situation where it actually means something once more.

Anthony Eyton RA has been chronicling Eden from the start

The laws enacted in many northern European countries have led to a big drop in the use of excess packaging and non-biodegradable materials. Just as important is the psychological shift from seeing waste as a problem, with a cost attached, to a commercial opportunity for those who master the technologies of recycling. Forty per cent of all household waste is organic material, and therefore suitable for composting. This is a vast tonnage in a country like the UK. We at Eden are interested not only in the compost but also in the opportunities for using plant materials as substitutes in current manufacturing processes. With thousands of acres of derelict land in our neighbourhood, the idea of collaborating on an integrated waste-management system, where factories are built to take all the segregated waste materials along-side a landfill site that never fills, represents a huge opportunity to contribute to the development of a civilized future. Eden would be acting local, with an eye on influencing national and, if appropriate, global interests. If education in its widest sense is what Eden is all about, then becoming involved in the practical applica-tion of the lessons learned would be the logical next stage of its evolution. Eden would, in short, like to play a role as broker for possible futures, which will of course require both a knowledge of the past and an awareness of the constraints of the present.

A major plank of our strategy will be to host what can be called the Tithing College, a repository for thinking about possible futures. Here leaders in their respective fields would devote between three and five days a year to sharing their experience and listening to others in focused debates on major issues. The poten-tial of the recommendations from these forums would be tested rigorously, and if they had merit they would then become part of what the Tithing College promoted to the outside world. In short I want Eden to bring the ideas people, the liberators of dreams, face to face with a jury made up of those capable of delivering those ideas, locking them metaphorically in a dark room until they reach consensus.

It is not our intention that Eden should become a quasi-Masonic order of fellow travellers all believing the same thing. None of us has the monopoly on being right. We live in an age when we are expected to have views on everything, but we don't have the time for the background reading or the focused thought. What do we do? Most of us, I suspect, borrow opinions from those we trust, and question them only if personal experience suggests the opposite.

I have a fantasy that I entertain regularly. It started as a game, but has begun to take on a life of its own; I have shared it with people from all walks of life, from government ministers to my mates in the pub.

One night there is a bang in my orchard. My dog Wilbur and I go down to investigate – he goes first, because he's either braver or more stupid than I am. There, in the tangled mess of what was my finest old apple tree, is a spacecraft. Inside is a humanoid of my own age, and it is hurt. Just like in the movies I have the choice of calling the authorities or bravely trusting my hospitable instincts. I choose the latter and soon have it ensconced in my spare bedroom, where I pander to its bizarre dietary requirements (it seems to like beetroot and chocolate). It has a contraption like a stethoscope, one end of which it fastens to its chest and the other to mine.

Amazingly, we can now communicate. It tells me where it has come from and what life is like where it lives. I reciprocate as best I can – it is hard enough representing my country, let alone my species. I am struck by its confusion when I am unable to answer the simplest of questions, such as what makes us all happy and what are the values we all share. Then things get really tricky. My alien is completely nonplussed to find that I cannot tell it what my species does to ensure universal happiness, indeed that a concept of such fundamental importance as happiness cannot be described. That we can live in the knowledge that we are not happy and yet we don't do anything about it, it finds completely incomprehensible.

We talk of education, my alien and I. It is amazed by what I don't know, when I call myself knowledgeable. Feeling more and more uncomfortable, I realize that I am a jigsaw with half the bits missing; I achieve ridiculous levels of detail in certain, generally useless areas, with large gaps in between. It had never struck me before that remembering bits of English and European history, being moderately well read, knowing something about how we conduct ourselves in business and politics, enjoying the music of Beethoven and Led Zeppelin and being able to scuba-dive, drive a car, cook a basic meal and so on is not at all the same thing as understanding the world. Where are the foundations common to all?

My alien friend, much restored by the diet, repairs its craft. On the eve of its departure it gives me a present. It is a machine to create a pill that can be infinitely replicated but never changed. It is a pill of Knowing and Understanding. I am charged with selecting the ingredients, the knowledge or developed senses, free from cultural bias, that will make up this gift to the people of the world. My alien leaves, never to return, and I'm stuck with this machine and an extraordinary challenge: what should the ingredients be?

To my horror, I realize that I have skated over life; I myself possess hardly any of the knowledge or understanding that I am now coming to think of as crucial for all people to share. I realize – and I share this reaction with the others with whom I have discussed it – that I have never addressed the issue of what should be the purpose or substance of an education system. We have merely grazed on information, as a commodity, in the hope of acquiring the skills we need for life. I don't mean to be prescriptive; on the contrary, the debate opens education to the widest possible audience. It asks uncomfortable questions about the nature of happiness and the human condition. Is it more important to know the dates of Ethelred the Unready, do trigonometry, deconstruct Shakespeare's sonnets and be able to speak French than, for instance, to understand the frontiers of your mind and body?

The challenge I would like to set is this. If we were starting from scratch and we did have this fabulous machine, what ingredients would we put in it? If they are fundamentally different from what we now teach, should we review the system? I have come up with only three things so far, but they are huge. The first I have called 'balance', which is code for all that knowledge that allows people to understand that they live on a small, fragile planet in orbit round the sun, with its own moon, and then gives us an understanding of the seasons and the natural forces that shape the way we live, and that in turn enable us to respect our place in nature. The second, 'function', involves a real understanding of the mechanics and potential of all aspects of the human body and mind. The third, 'empathy', would be the ability to imagine yourself in other people's shoes and to sympathize with their position. This is where it all gets a bit woolly. Why is it that almost all young children can dance and sing and have a sense of rhythm, yet lose it in shyness and stiffness as they grow older? (Except in Latin America, it would seem, to judge by the Buena Vista Social Club!) How can we rediscover this joyous liberation? We should learn to think in an unconstrained way; quite how I haven't a clue. Neither am I close to understanding what heading the comfort of belonging goes under, but we all need that sense of community.

Another of my heroes, Primo Levi, writes brilliantly about the qualities shared by survivors of Auschwitz. Survival did not appear to depend on any particular physical characteristic. It dawned on him that the survivors all shared one thing, an unquenchable sense of hope. Even in the face of the most terrible circumstances the flame did not go out; it was the fire that gave them the will to live. How do you put hope in a pill, or even give hope? I am convinced that the alien in my orchard has something crucial to add when we explore our priorities for the future. To ask such questions, and to interpret the responses, lies right at the core of what Eden should be about. What we are talking about here, it occurs to me, is a twenty-first-century Tree of Knowledge – highly appropriate in the circumstances, since in our garden we are once more faced with a choice.

So what is Eden's agenda? Why am I writing about micro-credit, recycling and education at all? The answer is simple. Eden was built by many committed people. Many more have become our partners. The public – through the Millennium Commission – have invested in Eden. None of this happened in order to provide Cornwall with a theme park – it has some excellent ones already. We had to prove that we were capable of delivering a monumental construction project and demonstrate the financial acumen and operational professionalism to win the respect of some tough judges: the state, the City and the public. But Eden was built on a trust ticket, which we now have to honour. It was trusted to make a difference – to build on hope. Eden is fun, and it must stay fun. But it must be brave too; the world is confused by the threats it faces, and equally confused by the array of possible solutions. Perhaps Eden can help bridge some of the gaps. We have a duty to hope.

As I look out over our Eden in the setting sun, I see the buzzards once more wheeling upwards in the thermals, tracing shadows on the cliff face. I look round and absorb Dominic's majestic landscape; at the centre of his cyclone, the grass arena. An insistent rhythm carries in the breeze and a happy crowd lies transfixed, content just to be.

The words transcribed on the wall of Eden's entrance come to me:

Work like you don't need the money,
Love like you've never been hurt,
Dance like nobody's watching,
Sing like nobody's listening,
Live like it's heaven on earth.

I'm sitting where I sat when first I came here. As I puff on my cigar and watch the blue smoke drift away, I think back over the six years that have passed. So many good people, such special times and what a privilege to be alive and allowed to see it through. The sun dips lower and the roofs of the great conservatories turn to raspberries and cream and the texture of fine parachute silk. Yes, we've built our Eden, but the journey's just beginning. As I take one final look at the thousands who've come to share this beautiful place with us I know that we were right and it makes me smile. This was never a product, and one sentence can never do it justice. You see, Eden may be a destination, but you can only reach it with your heart.

acknowledgements

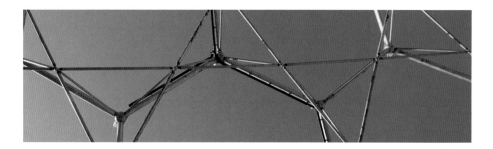

Eden is the creation of so many people that it is impossible to mention them all. Forgive me. This book is a personal account of a great shared adventure and is not intended as an official history. What I have sought to capture is the spirit that brought it into being as well as the attitude that we bring to the search for possible futures.

As I repeat like a mantra throughout the book, Eden is the result of a huge number of people saying yes when they had every excuse to say no; with each voice of support we grew stronger. The joy we feel is tempered by sadness at the passing of some good friends who were unable to complete the journey with us: Bill Rickatson, the former boss of Goonvean, who led us to Bodelva pit; James Wilson of the Green Team; Sir Ralph Riley, who widened Eden's scope to look at development issues; and Michael Montague, the Millennium Commissioner who first championed our cause. We miss you, but we won't forget.

I cannot say loudly enough how grateful we are to our friends at the Millennium Commission. Without their support, which went way beyond the call of duty, we would not exist. So thank you Doug Weston, Jerry Michel, Bill Alexander, Steve Boxall and Mike O'Connor for making it possible, and thank you too to the Commissioners who dared to take a gamble in the name of the spirit of the Millennium. Neither can I let this opportunity pass for thanking all our many friends at the Borough of Restormel, Cornwall County Council, English Partnerships, the Regional Development Commission, the Government Office for the South West, the Devon and Cornwall TEC, Pennon Group, NatWest, RBL, DKB, the Headley Trust, the Weston Foundation, the Trust House Trust and our good mates at Sir Robert and Alfred McAlpine.

What about the fantastic Design Team? Their main players are mentioned, but there were many more who made a massive contribution and continue to do so, because Eden will never be finished. My admiration for the constructor, the McAlpine Joint Venture, will be clear from the book. My only sadness is that I haven't the space to highlight the superb work of the many individuals and sub-contractors who made our Living Theatre just that – the muck-shift team, the Great Wall of China foundation boys, the record-breaking scaffolders, the mechanical engineers, the hex-tri-hex erectors and the fabulous sky monkeys – you will forever be part of the Eden mythology. Half a million people voted with their feet to come and see what you were up to, and they left full of admiration at what determination and talent can achieve. We're proud to have had the privilege of working with you.

(previous page)
The cedar tiles on the wall of the Visitor Centre

On to our Trustees and Non-Executive Directors, who have been the most generous mentors a team could hope to have. The Trust began with Sir Alcon Copisarow, Sir Alan Donald, Sir Richard Carew Pole and the late Sir Ralph Riley; at the time of writing, under the Chairmanship of Sir Ronnie Hampel, it comprises Richard Cunis, Simon Robertson, Bryher Scudamore, Anthony Salz, Guy Whalley and Sir Richard Carew Pole. Thank you for your friendship and wise counsel. Thank you too to the Chairman of our operational company, Ken Hill, who I know would join us in thanking Dr Alan Stanhope, Peter Hardaker and Richard Sandbrook. It is humbling and immensely comforting to have people of their quality, commitment and experience at our shoulders when the going gets tough, and that's exactly where they were when it mattered.

The Eden Home Team, the crew who do the business on a daily basis, numbers 470 full-time and 60 part-time members at the time of writing. Thank you for what you have done already, but more importantly thank you for what we are about to achieve. It is an honour to be part of the team.

I must thank others too: Roderick James, for suggesting the name the Tithing College and for his ideas on how it might work; my wife Candy and my children Alex, Laura and Sam for putting up with chaos, making suggestions, providing hours of hospitality to our friends who came to stay while working on the project and for their studied irreverence whenever I took myself too seriously; Mike Petty, my editor, who has the patience of Job and the diplomacy of a saint when I get precious and purple and who has had the unenviable job of knocking the book into shape in a ridiculously short time; Charlie Webster, who has yet again designed a beautiful book against the clock at the College Farm workhouse; Herbie Knott, Charles Francis, Simon Burt, Claire Travers, Steve Tanner and last but not least Richard Kalina (with the unflagging assistance of our own Jonathan Pearce) for their superb photographs; Katrina Whone, who has cajoled, encouraged and pampered the book into existence; Sheila Lee, picture researcher extraordinaire, and Deborah Adams, most meticulous of copy-editors; and Transworld colleagues Patrick Janson-Smith, Larry Finlay, Sally Gaminara and their team, who have taken Eden to their hearts and made the first bold steps towards a long partnership between us that is unique in publishing history.

My gratitude to Richard Sandbrook is enormous. His generosity in sharing his many years of experience in development and problem-solving has been a rich source of inspiration.

I need to give a big hug to the wonderful Ellie Pyatt, my PA, for being both my first line of defence and attack and making the world appear to be organized, and Fiona Cattrell for keeping me sane when I threatened to give way to hysteria. Big squeezes too to my friends and colleagues Dave Meneer, Philip McMillan Browse, Kary Lescure, Tony Kendle, Jo Readman and Tim Carter for reading, correcting, making suggestions and offering general advice on literacy – and lastly to Gay Coley who has shared the leadership of the project with me and without whom I would quite simply have drowned.

The final word must be for all of you who have come to Eden, or have followed our progress from afar, and share our vision of an optimistic future and a commitment to make it happen. We may have had the privilege of laying Eden's foundations, but the responsibility for shaping its future belongs to everyone.

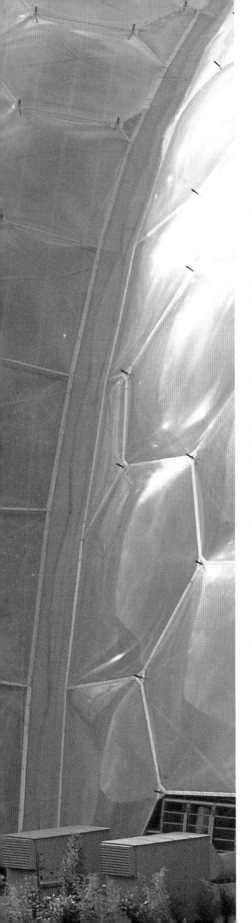

the photographs

Apex: 75 (Simon Burt), 144 (Simon Burt), 163 (Simon Burt), 192 (Simon Burt), 193 (Simon Burt), 244 (Simon Burt), 250 (James Whatling), 251 (Mark Passmore), 303 (Simon Burt); photo Bob Berry, courtesy Gendall Design: 242; courtesy Mark Bostock: 89; Bridgeman Art Library: 25 (bottom); British Library: 62; courtesy Tim Carter: 240 (bottom); Crown copyright: 225; © Michael Dyer & Associates: 96 (right), 108, 109; © Eden Project/Charles Francis: 65, 66-67, 86, 90, 106, 111, 125 (both), 134, 142, 143 (bottom), 161, 190, 191, 194, 196, 197, 198-9, 216, 232-3, 262 (bottom), 275 (top, both), 284-5, 288, 306, 307; © Charles Francis: 16, 46 (all), 73, 119, 120, 136, 200, 201, 204, 206-7, 209, 211, 224, 226-7, 228, 238, 240 (top); © Andrea Jones/ Garden Exposures: 18-19, 28-9: © Gendall Design: 113 (map by Luke McDonald); Nicholas Grimshaw & Partners Limited: 96 (left); Harpers & Queen/Boris Baggs: 146-7; © Derek Harris: 23; © Tim Hunkin: 239; courtesy Anthony Hunt: 82; © Hulton Getty: 25 (top centre); © Imagination: 186-7; Richard Kalina: 1, 2-3, 6-7, 12-13, 14, 27, 30, 35, 36-37, 38, 39, 42, 49, 50-51, 52, 55, 57, 58, 71, 76, 78, 83, 84, 98, 100-101, 103, 116-17, 122, 127, 128, 130, 131, 132-3, 135 (top), 137, 140, 143 (top), 150, 152-3 (both), 154, 155, 158, 159, 164-5, 172, 175 (bottom), 181, 202-3, 214-15, 218, 222-3, 236, 237, 246, 252-3, 258, 260, 262 (top right & left), 265, 266, 267 (both), 270, 272-3, 275 (bottom), 276-7, 278-9, 281, 282, 286-7, 289, 290 (both), 291 (both), 292, 296-7, 298-9, 300, 304-5, 314-15, 318-19, 320; Royal Botanic Gardens, Kew: 32; © Herbie Knott: 4-5, 10, 17, 80, 135 (bottom), 170, 205, 229, 235, 241, 268, 309, 313; © Mary Knowland: 44-45 ; © Land Use Consultants: 87 (top & bottom), 97, 148, 175 (top), 176, 183, 184, 271 (both); courtesy Rolf Munding: 95; National Portrait Gallery, London: 25 (top, l & r); courtesy RIBA: 188 (both); © John Sturrock/Network: 220, 221, 230, 269; Ken Dickinson/Photolibrary Wales: 40; courtesy Anne Rickatson: 56; © Dawn Runnals: 8; © Paul Spooner: 178-9; © Julian Stephens: 61; courtesy Mark Stocker: 33; © Steve Tanner: 92, 156, 160, 295; Claire Travers: 213; © Bernard White: 20.

The publishers have made every effort to contact the copyright owners of the illustrations reproduced in this book. In the few cases where they have been unsuccessful they invite copyright holders to contact them direct.

(final page) **Wild Cornwall: Paradox Boot by Peter Martin and Sarah Stewart-Smith**

TRANSWORLD PUBLISHERS
61–63 Uxbridge Road, London W5 5SA
a division of The Random House Group Ltd

RANDOM HOUSE AUSTRALIA (PTY) LTD
20 Alfred Street, Milsons Point, Sydney,
New South Wales 2061, Australia

RANDOM HOUSE NEW ZEALAND LTD
18 Poland Road, Glenfield, Auckland 10, New Zealand

RANDOM HOUSE SOUTH AFRICA (PTY) LTD
Endulini, 5a Jubilee Road, Parktown 2193, South Africa

Published 2001 by Bantam Press, a division of Transworld Publishers

Designed by Charlie Webster

Printed in Great Britain by Butler and Tanner Ltd, Frome

1 3 5 7 9 10 8 6 4 2

www.booksattransworld.co.uk

Eden Project information 01726 811911/www.edenproject.com

Eden Friends

For information on becoming a Friend of the Eden Project
write to Eden Friends, Bodelva, St Austell PL24 2SG,
phone 01726 811932, email ctrevivian@edenproject.com

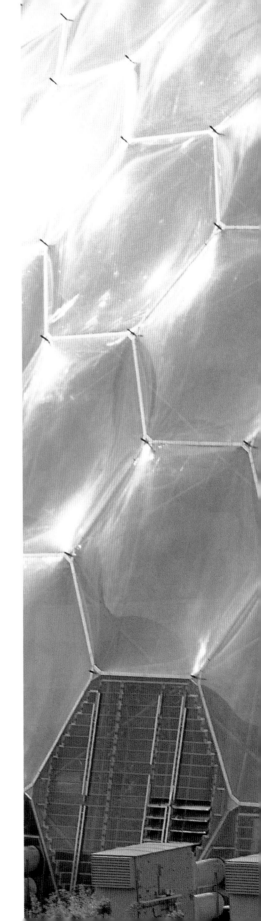